Social Work Approaches to Alcohol and Other Drug Problems: Case Studies and Teaching Tools

Senior Editor
Maryann Amodeo

Editors
Rosalie Schofield
Trudy Duffy
Kay Jones
Trudy Zimmerman
Melvin Delgado

Council on Social Work Education
Alexandria, VA

Library of Congress Cataloging-in-Publication Data

Social work approaches to alcohol and other drug problems: case studies and teaching tools / senior editor, Maryann Amodeo; editors, Rosalie Schofield . . . [et al.].
        p.   cm.
   Includes bibliographic references.
   ISBN 0-87293-053-X
   1. Social work with alcoholics—United States—Case studies. 2. Social work with narcotic addicts—United States—Case studies. 3. Social work with alcholics—Study and teaching (Graduate)—United States. 4. Social work with narcotic addicts—Study and teaching (Graduate)—United States. I. Amodeo, Maryann, 1945– . II. Schofield, Rosalie.
HV5279.S623   1997
362.29′ 18′ 0973—dc 21
                                   96-52842
                                      CIP

Manufactured in the United States of America

Table of Contents

Preface

This book is designed to help social workers learn methods for intervening with alcohol and other drug abuse (AODA). Social work faculty, students, experienced practitioners, alcohol and drug counselors, and other human service providers will benefit from the case studies, vignettes, and teaching tools included here.

In these cases, as in real life, AODA is interwoven with other individual and family difficulties and life events. Clients struggle not only with AODA but with grief and loss, marital conflict and domestic violence, social isolation, teenage pregnancy, major mental illness, incarceration, and economic disadvantage. Thus, the materials can be used to illustrate assessment and intervention methods with a variety of client problems.

The case studies and vignettes are written in such a way that the clients and their problems come to life in an immediate and compelling way. Reading these cases, social work students and professionals will find themselves in the shoes of the worker and will feel compelled to question the significance of the presenting problem, determine a diagnosis, think of alternative ways to engage the client, examine the transference and countertransference, and decide on a plan of action. They will find themselves judging the worker's approach and bringing into the open issues that were buried in the cases.

The impetus for developing a book of case studies came from requests from students, faculty, and practitioners over the years. Students wanted more clinical focus on AODA in the curriculum; faculty wanted case material that was sophisticated, easy to use in class, and did not require that they become addiction experts;

practitioners wanted to learn to use principles and theories in resolving real-life problems.

AODA has a long documented history as a social problem in the United States, but never has the issue provided such a widespread challenge to society as a whole and to the social work profession in particular. Although the social, economic, medical, and public health costs of alcohol and other drug abuse have been calculated for years, knowledge of these figures has done little to diminish the problem and cost estimates continue to rise dramatically. Lost productivity, excess mortality, health care costs, and property loss and crime, due to alcohol use and abuse alone, is projected to reach $150 billion in 1995 (Walsh, 1990). Current estimates suggest that the cost of alcohol and other drug abuse to the U.S. economy exceeds $238 billion annually (Lewis, 1994). Use of tobacco, alcohol, and other drugs was estimated to account for almost $8 billion in Medicaid expenditures in 1994 for substance abuse–related diseases (Fox & Merrill, 1995). In addition, more individuals have been imprisoned for drug offenses than for all violent crimes since 1989. Attempts to address poverty are also confounded by substance abuse. Workfare and job training programs remain inaccessible to large numbers of welfare recipients who are abusing and addicted (Califano, 1995).

This text is meant to raise awareness about the pervasiveness of AODA, illustrate the many settings where AODA appears, and demonstrate its pernicious effects on the client systems it touches. Several factors make AODA an urgent issue in social work education requiring specific attention in the graduate and undergraduate curriculum:

- Every social system in which social workers function is affected, including hospitals, mental health centers, schools, day care programs, courts, prisons, child welfare, and employment settings.

- It creates or is a major contributor to a host of other social problems such as unemployment, domestic violence, teenage pregnancy, suicide and homicide, and HIV and AIDS.

- When unidentified, clients can make little progress on other presenting problems because it undermines their ability to carry out a service plan.

- When unidentified in mental health settings, it confuses the diagnostic picture and leads to inappropriate treatment.

- When unidentified in child welfare settings, it can lead to incorrect assessments of the safety of children.

- When unidentified among pregnant women, it may lead to birth defects in the children.

- When unidentified and unaddressed in families, it is likely to lead to intergenerational transmission.

Not only should attention be paid to the late stages of alcohol and drug misuse, represented by alcoholism and drug addiction, but also to the earlier stages when problems are just developing. Use by high-risk groups such as pregnant women, youth, and the elderly; use by anyone who finds that repeated negative consequences ensue; and use by anyone who finds that alcohol and other drugs are becoming necessary for coping with daily life demands as much concern as does abuse or dependence.

The human suffering in these situations is difficult to capture quantitatively, yet this concern is especially compelling to social workers. This suffering occurs with the erosion of the most intimate human bonds, the frequent accompaniment of violence and physical abuse, the struggle to trust or hope again in human relationships, and the loss of self-esteem—not just for the person who abuses drugs and alcohol but for all those whose lives are touched.

Social workers are employed in many agencies today where the majority of clients have alcohol or other drug problems, that is, clients (a) have abused alcohol and other drugs, (b) live in families where the problem is currently an issue, or (c) are directly affected in other ways. One of the unique contributions social workers can make is to use the skills and methods currently offered in their training to heal the individuals and relationships fractured by AODA.

The Faculty Development Program for the Health Professions, funded in the late 1980s by the National Institute on Alcohol Abuse and Alcoholism, the National Institute on Drug Abuse, and the Center for Substance Abuse Prevention of the Alcohol, Drug Abuse and Mental Health Administration, was a multiyear effort focused on achieving institutional change through the development of faculty specialists in selected schools of social work, nursing, and medicine and departments of psychology across the country. Schools of social work that were awarded funds for this effort were Boston University, Case Western Reserve University, Rutgers University, the University of Connecticut, the University of Denver, the University of Maryland, and Virginia Commonwealth University. A major goal was to reduce institutional denial and highlight AODA as an urgent social problem requiring attention in the classroom and integration into the curriculum.

This text grew out of the Faculty Development Program's efforts to develop educational materials that could be widely disseminated to schools of social work. In 1993, the Boston University School of Social Work faculty sponsored a national competition for AODA cases for use in a social work casebook. Cash prizes were awarded for the best submissions.

The faculty then edited the cases and added discussion and teaching points for each case. The resulting text integrates micro and macro perspectives, facilitating the material's utilization across the curriculum. The cases selected represent a wide range of AODA clients and contexts and fall into four areas of social work practice—individuals, families, groups, and communities.

Collaboration among faculty, a goal of the national effort, characterized our work at the Boston University School of Social Work. The most pleasurable aspect of developing the text was the opportunity for those of us who edited the book to work with each other.

We thank all those who submitted cases for consideration. Their work helped us achieve our goal of making AODA teaching materials more available to social work educators, students, and practitioners.

References

Califano, J. A. (1995, Jan. 29). It's drugs, stupid. *New York Times Magazine*, 40-41.

Fox, K., & Merrill, J. C. (1995). Estimating the costs of substance abuse in the Medicaid hospital care program. *American Journal of Public Health, 85*, 48-54.

Lewis, D. C. (1994). *The need for substance abuse treatment: A research and public health perspective.* Unpublished manuscript.

Walsh, D. C. (1990). The shifting boundaries of alcohol policy. *Health Affairs, 9*, 47-62.

Acknowledgments

This work was completed through grant #5 T15SP07501 awarded by NIAAA/NIDA/CSAP for 1990–1995, to the School of Social Work, Boston University.

For their invaluable assistance in preparing this manuscript, the editors wish to thank Ms. Susan Gavini and Ms. Laurie Yates. Susan spent countless hours typing, revising, and reformatting cases which had been submitted in styles and formats as varied as the many individuals who had submitted them. Laurie made herself available to produce interim drafts as deadlines approached. We also thank Ms. Christine Josti, Ms. Aimee Scanlan, and Ms. Suzanne Hogan for dedicating themselves to producing the final version. For their generous contribution of energy and good humor, we thank them all.

Editors

Maryann Amodeo, MSW, PhD, Senior Editor, is Director of the Alcohol and Drug Institute for Policy, Training and Research at Boston University and Associate Professor at the Boston University School of Social Work, where she teaches clinical courses as well as electives on alcohol and other drug abuse. She developed the Postgraduate Certificate Program in Alcoholism and Drug Abuse for experienced social work professionals and directed two Faculty Development Programs for the School of Social Work. In 1989 she received the Massachusetts NASW award for the Greatest Contribution to Social Work Education for integrating alcohol and drug issues into the social work curriculum.

Melvin Delgado, MSW, PhD, is Professor of Social Work and Chair of the Macro Practice Department. His research focuses on the use of Latino natural support systems in substance abuse prevention. He is the co-director of Boston University's current Faculty Development Program.

Trudy K. Duffy, MSW, is an Associate Clinical Professor at the Boston University School of Social Work and a certified trainer/practitioner in psychodrama. Her specialties include group theory and method, expressive approaches, and substance abuse treatment. She has been a Faculty Fellow in Boston University's Faculty Development Program since 1990.

Kay Jones, MSW, is the Director of the Refugee and Immigrant Training Program at the Boston University School of Social Work, where she also teaches clinical and human behavior courses. She has many years of experience in international social work and specializes in diversity issues and cross-cultural practice.

Rosalie Faulkner Schofield, MSW, PhD, is the project director for the social work component of the New England Regional Addictions Training Center at Brown University. She teaches social policy at Boston University and has been a Faculty Fellow in Boston University's Faculty Development Program since 1990.

Trudy Zimmerman, MSW, is a Clinical Assistant Professor and Director of Field Education at the Boston University School of Social Work. Her practice and teaching experience has been in the fields of health, gerontology, and substance abuse. She has been a Faculty Fellow in Boston University's Faculty Development Program since 1990.

Contributors

Lisa Acosta, MSW, who submitted the "Gloria" case, graduated from the Boston University School of Social Work in 1995.

Jeffrey Albert, MSW, who submitted the "Carter" case, is a doctoral student in Social Work/Sociology at Boston University. He has co-authored a book on substance abuse treatment, *Clean Start: An Outpatient Program for Initiating Cocaine Recovery* (Guilford Press, 1992), and also designed a pilot pre-release and relapse prevention program for county and state correctional systems.

Lynne Assaf, MSW, who submitted the "Jose" case, graduated from the Boston University School of Social Work in 1996.

Alex Chasy, MSW, who submitted the "Ben" case, graduated from the Boston University School of Social Work in 1995.

Heidi Conner, MSW, who submitted the "W Family" case, is a clinical social worker at the Boston University Medical Center Hospital. She is currently developing outpatient services, including services for substance abusers and their families. She received her MSW from the Boston University School of Social Work in 1991.

Monica Fernandez, MSW, who submitted the "Clara" case and the "Estella" case, graduated from the Boston University School of Social Work in 1995.

Clay Graybeal, MSW, PhD, who submitted the "Tommy" case, is an Assistant Professor at the University of New England School of Social Work in Biddeford, Maine. He received his master's from Fordham University School of Social Work in 1981, and his doctorate from Rutgers University in 1990. His areas of practice and teaching include Substance Abuse, Brief Therapy, Family Therapy, Advanced Psychosocial Assessment, and Integrated Practice.

R. Kevin Grigsby, DSW, who submitted the "Intensive Family Preservation" case, is an Associate Professor and the Director of Social Psychiatry in the Department of Psychiatry and Health Behavior at the Medical College of Georgia and an Adjunct Associate Professor at the University of Georgia School of Social Work. He has served as a consultant on an extensive variety of mental health issues. Along with E. Susan Morton, he recently completed an edited collection, *Advancing Family Preservation Practice*, published by Sage.

Barrett L. Johnson, MSW, who submitted the "Bobby and Susan" case, received his MSW from the Boston University School of Social Work in 1994. He has worked in a wide range of settings with children and adults, including special education, addictions treatment, and inpatient and outpatient mental health treatment. He currently works with urban children and families.

Rhonda Kaplan, MSW, who submitted a sample response to the Planning and Program Development Assignment focusing on Latino youth, graduated from the Boston University School of Social Work in 1995.

Karen Kasameyer, MSW, who submitted the "Arthur" case, graduated from the Boston University School of Social Work in 1995.

Larissa Kravchuk, MSW, who submitted the "Jeff" case, graduated from the Boston University School of Social Work in 1995.

Ellie Lane, MSW, who submitted a sample response to the Planning and Program Development assignment focusing on Latino youth, graduated from the Boston University School of Social Work in 1995.

Peter Manoleas, MSW, who submitted the "Mr. Pines" case, is a lecturer and fieldwork consultant at the University of California at

Berkeley, School of Social Welfare. He has 25 years of experience in the fields of mental health and substance abuse as a clinician, administrator, and consultant.

John Northridge, MSW, who submitted the "Hot Case," worked as an alcoholism counselor for several years prior to obtaining his MSW at the Boston University School of Social Work in 1979. He has been the Director of Mental Health and Social Services at the South Boston Community Health Center in South Boston, Massachusetts for 12 years and maintains a limited treatment and consultation practice.

Saly Pin-Riebe, MSW, who submitted the "Mrs. Sann" case, works for the Massachusetts Department of Mental Health's Refugee Assistance Program. She is Co-Chair of the Southeast Asian Substance Abuse Treatment Working Group, and chairs the Refugee Health Advisory Committee.

Nancy Robb, MSW, who submitted the "Chum Family" case and the "Phoung and Thi" case, works in the Employee Assistance Program at Massachusetts General Hospital, and provides training and consultation related to Southeast Asians for the Boston University School of Social Work's Alcohol and Drug Institute.

Deborah Shay, MSW, who submitted the "Richard" case, graduated from the Boston University School of Social Work in 1994. She was a Fellow at Boston University's Danielsen Institute and an addictions counselor at Heritage Hospital in Somerville, Massachusetts. She currently works in a dual-diagnosis setting.

Aaron A. Smith, MSW, MPH, PhD, who submitted the "Time Out" case, is from the University of South Florida School of Social Work.

Leslie Stanley-Cox, MSW, who submitted the "Peter" case, graduated from the Boston University School of Social Work in 1993. She is currently employed as a social worker with the Center for Health and Human Services, Family Care Center, Fall River, Massachusetts, providing sexual abuse and substance abuse treatment to children and their families with the State's child welfare agency.

Paulo Torrens, who submitted the "Brazilian Immigrants" case, is a doctoral student and Brazilian psychologist.

Elizabeth M. Tracy, PhD, who submitted the "Ms. C." case, is Associate Professor of Social Work at the Mandel School of Applied Social Sciences, Case Western Reserve University. She is interested in social work models which support families and make use of and strengthen natural helping networks. She was a Faculty Fellow at Case Western Reserve University's School of Social Work.

Laurie Van Loon, MSW, who submitted the "Pilar and Eduardo" case and the "Ana" case, works at Metro West Mental Health Associates, serving mental health, substance abusing and dually diagnosed clients and families.

Consultants

The following individuals reviewed cases and made helpful suggestions for modification:

Deborah Applegate, MSW, private practice, Boston, MA.

Kaaren Strauch Brown, PhD, East Michigan University.

John Goldmeier, PhD, University of Maryland.

Andrew Hamid, PhD, University of Michigan.

C. David Hollister, PhD, University of Minnesota-Minneapolis.

Katherine Kranz, MSW, Salve Regina University.

Craig Mosher, MSW, University of Iowa.

Rita Rhodes, PhD, University of South Carolina.

Susan Weingar, MSW, Valparaiso University.

Introduction

Overview of Alcohol and Other Drug Abuse and Social Work Practice

In the social work profession today, and in other professions involved in the study of alcohol and other drug problems in our society, a range of opinions about methods for assessment and treatment is available. Indeed, there is a range of opinions about the causation of alcohol and other drug problems, the point at which alcohol and drug-related behaviors should be defined as problems, whether abstinence rather than controlled use should be the central treatment goal, the type of treatment that is most effective, and the point at which a person would be considered "in recovery." It is beyond the scope of this book to describe these various perspectives and persuade the reader of the wisdom of a particular point of view.

Instead, a set of assumptions about alcohol and other drug problems that have served as the theoretical underpinnings of this text are identified and discussed. Many of these assumptions overlap with ones contained in the policy statement regarding alcohol and other drugs approved by the NASW Delegate Assembly in 1987 and later revised. In general, these assumptions reflect the current thinking and clinical practice of mainstream alcoholism and drug abuse treatment agencies in the United States. They are also ones consistent with the values and ethics of the social work profession.

Multivariate Conditions

Alcoholism and drug dependence can be viewed as multivariate conditions resulting from a variety of factors including genetic, biological, familial, cultural, psychological, and social. They display themselves in multiple patterns of dysfunction requiring a range of interventions (Pattison & Kaufman, 1982; Schuckit, 1986).

Prior to the American Medical Association's formal decision in 1956 to classify alcoholism as a disease, it was seen as immoral behavior, and alcoholics were viewed as self-indulgent, narcissistic, weak willed, and morally inferior (Doweiko, 1993). The "disease model" has helped society view alcoholism and drug addiction in biological terms, which facilitates diagnosis and treatment. But the model has resulted in the "medicalization" of these conditions, making them the province of the medical field. Models more consistent with the social work perspective include the person-in-environment or biopsychosocial model (Wallace, 1989), and frameworks that emphasize not only deterioration and illness but also client strengths (Weick, 1985).

Primary Illnesses

Alcoholism and drug dependence are primary illnesses rather than symptoms of other disorders. Although heavy or habitual or dangerous use may begin in response to another disorder or personal problem, once alcoholism or drug dependence has developed, it has become a condition in and of itself and requires treatment as such. Alcoholism and drug dependency often present with other Axis I and Axis II mental disorders.

Definitions

Dependence is characterized by a pattern of repeated self-administration that usually results in tolerance, withdrawal, and compulsive drug-taking behavior. There is a persistent desire or unsuccessful effort to cut down or control use, and the pattern continues in spite of negative consequences. These symptoms are similar across the various substances, but for certain classes some symptoms are less salient (American Psychiatric Association, 1994, p. 176–181).

Abuse is characterized by a maladaptive pattern of substance use with recurrent and significant adverse consequences. There may be repeated failure to fulfill major role obligations, use in situations in which it is physically hazardous, and recurrent social and interpersonal problems (American Psychiatric Association, 1994, p. 182).

Drug Use Patterns

Alcohol is the most widely used drug in the United States. Individuals with alcohol problems are also likely to be using other drugs. Among those who primarily use drugs other than alcohol, a significant proportion also suffer from alcoholism (Helzer & Pryzbeck, 1988).

Routine Assessment

Routine assessment for alcohol and other drug problems should occur as part of every psychosocial history. Clients need help in examining their current use of alcohol and other drugs, as well as assessing their personal risk factors for developing a dependence on alcohol and other drugs. Risk factors include such considerations as parental and extended family attitudes about drinking and drug use, family history of alcoholism and drug dependence, age when drinking and drug use first resulted in negative consequences, experience of early trauma, and peer group involvement with alcohol and other drugs (Liftik, 1995).

Abstinence as a Treatment Goal

In general, abstinence rather than controlled use should be seen as the treatment goal for individuals who have developed dependence (Helzer et al., 1985; Pendry, Maltzman, & West, 1982). Although some individuals, especially young people, may be treated for misuse of alcohol and other drugs and return to moderate, non-problem use, practice experience supports the need for abstinence as a treatment goal for those who have developed alcoholism or drug dependence (Miller & Hester, 1995).

This issue is controversial, however (Schuckit, 1989). Research is underway that may someday identify individuals for whom a controlled-use treatment goal is more appropriate, but data from such research are not currently available.

Confrontation

Confrontation should be thought of as a goal of treatment rather than as a style of the worker. Miller and Rollnick (1991) use the term "awareness-raising confrontation." This is not a heavy-handed, coercive method but is consistent with Rogers's (1951) client-centered philosophy which recommends that the therapist create an atmosphere of safety allowing the client to examine the possibility of change.

Ambivalence

Initial ambivalence on the part of clients about seeking abstinence should not result in termination from treatment. Workers should expect ambivalence and should anticipate spending the initial phase of treatment helping clients see both the gains and losses to be incurred by abstinence (Miller & Rollnick, 1991).

The choice to change behavior (such as establishing abstinence as the treatment goal) rests with the client. The worker can employ a number of strategies to work through the client's denial (Amodeo, 1995a, 1995b) and resolve ambivalence (Brown, 1985; Miller & Rollnick, 1991). Interventions that attack the client's self-esteem and dignity are counterproductive and are not in keeping with the values of the social work profession.

Labeling

Expecting clients to accept the label of "alcoholic" or "drug addict" during the early phase of the helping relationship is ill advised. In spite of repeated problems with alcohol and other drugs, clients generally believe that their problems are not that serious. They are often alienated and lost to treatment as a result of abrupt labeling by the worker. Instead, workers should help clients see that drinking and drug use causes them to endure painful consequences, and that use of these substances, which once resulted in pleasure and brought relief, may now be consistently associated with pain (Brown, 1985).

Treatment

An adequate treatment system involves intervention methods along a continuum from acute to chronic care, including detoxification, inpatient and outpatient, long-term residential, and relapse prevention services.

When offering treatment options, workers should consider the gender, age, ethnicity, culture, and sexual orientation of the client. These factors will influence the client's ability to respond to "typical" or "mainstream" treatment methods, which were often designed for middle-aged, white, heterosexual males. Effective treatment methods for some clients may include use of an indigenous community healer rather than appointments with a psychiatrist, joining the neighborhood Pentecostal church rather than attending Alcoholics Anonymous, residing at the local Buddhist temple rather than going to a residential treatment facility, or going to a "sweat lodge" rather than a detoxification center. Delgado (1994) has taken this idea a step further in recommending that substance abuse treatment agencies collaborate with natural support systems in communities of color to ensure that the delivery of services is culturally specific.

Matching Clients to Treatments

While researchers and practitioners agree that no single treatment is effective for all clients, much disagreement exists between them about which modalities are most effective. The treatment approaches for which there is scientific evidence of benefit are generally not the ones used in U.S. alcoholism treatment programs (Miller & Hester, 1986). Ongoing broad-scale studies of client–treatment matching are expected to provide crucial data to increase positive treatment outcome. These studies are designed to identify the types of clients who do best with certain forms of treatment. An extensive range of client and therapist variables are being examined, as well as many outcome variables including drinking and drug use, social and psychological adjustment, and health and occupational functioning (Hester & Miller, 1995).

Client characteristics found to have "matching effects" include demographics, severity of drug problem, and personality or psychological variables. Tentative research conclusions are that (a) clients with more severe problems, such as chronic drug dependence accompanying psychopathology, and lack of social supports do better in intense treatments; and (b) clients with sociopathic traits do better with coping skills training than with treatments relying on relationship building.

Areas for further research include whether some clients do better in treatments that emphasize health and well-being rather than focus on drinking and drug use, whether some clients benefit from more choices, and which type of counselors work best with which type of clients (Allen & Kadden, 1995).

Group Treatment

Group therapy is particularly helpful for substance abusers and family members because it reduces the sense of isolation by grouping together people who have a common problem, stimulates hope when members see others getting better, changes distorted self-concepts by giving members the chance to get group feedback, and reminds members of their vulnerability to negative consequences if they continue to use or relapse. Treatment outcome data for substance abusers suggest that group psychotherapy is at least as effective as individual therapy (Vanicelli, 1995). A number of types of groups have been used in treating substance abusers including those based on educational, motivational, cognitive-behavioral, psychodynamic, and relapse prevention principles.

Twelve-Step Programs

There is evidence that 12-step programs such as Alcoholics Anonymous and Narcotics Anonymous are important resources for the treatment of alcohol and other drug problems. Although they should routinely be considered as treatment options, they are not the only means to recovery, and client participation should not be required as a condition for receiving other types of treatment.

High-Risk Groups

High-risk groups, often requiring specialized services, include pregnant and parenting women, individuals with HIV or AIDS, youth, the elderly, persons with dual diagnoses, and communities of color where access to services may be limited or traditional services may be inappropriate.

Family Members at Risk

Family members of alcoholics and drug-dependent individuals develop their own maladaptive patterns in order to survive. These include an increased risk for alcohol and other drug problems, chronic health disorders, depression and anxiety, and difficulties with intimacy. Treatment of family members, even when the alcoholic or addict is not in treatment, is an important goal.

Addiction impairs the family's ability to regulate its members' behavior, engage in problem solving, develop an identity, and leave behind a positive legacy (Steinglass et al., 1987). However, there is no single picture of an addicted family. A number of variables must be considered in assessing the health or dysfunction of a family system including the sobriety–intoxication cycle (Steinglass, 1980) and the family's ability to maintain rituals (Wolin & Bennett, 1984).

Studies of children of alcoholics who have shown particular resiliency identify characteristics that offset the impact of parental dysfunction: an active approach toward problem solving, a tendency to perceive experiences from a positive rather than negative point of view, the ability to gain the positive attention of others, and the use of faith to maintain a sense of meaning about life. Resiliency is fostered by a close relationship with at least one caregiver during the first year of life, opportunities to be helpful that do not involve being overwhelmed with responsibility, and the ability to find satisfaction through hobbies or talents (Coombs & Ziedonis, 1995).

Family Treatment

Family interventions should not be saved for substance abusers with serious marital and family problems secondary to, preceding, or coexisting with an alcohol problem. With therapy, couples and families with less serious problems can also be helped to support the client's abstinence and improve family relationships damaged by substance abuse–related dynamics (Usher, 1991). Healthcare standards for accrediting alcoholism treatment programs in the U.S. now require that the partner or other adult family members who live with the alcoholic be included in at least the assessment phase. Research indicates that a range of specific marital and family therapy interventions can be used effectively at different stages: to initiate change when the alcoholic is unwilling to seek help, to maintain sobriety and strengthen relationships after help-seeking has occurred, and to provide support in ongoing recovery (O'Farrell, 1993).

Relapse

In general, alcoholics and drug-dependent individuals are considered to be at high risk for relapse during the first year of abstinence. Specific relapse prevention methods have been identified to assist clients in early and ongoing recovery. Such methods include avoiding high-risk situations, developing a drug-free peer group, and identifying physical, emotional, and cognitive signs of impending relapse (Gorski & Miller, 1986; Marlatt & Gordon, 1985).

Relapses can serve as learning experiences for clients and can provide safeguards against future drinking and drug use. Since clients generally experience relapses as personal failures, and can become depressed about them, the worker can make a substantial impact by (a) educating clients about relapse; (b) exploring "trigger events"; (c) identifying the tools that were helpful in maintaining abstinence; and (d) emphasizing areas of learning and growth that took place during abstinent periods.

Recovery

Recovery is a developmental process occurring over time and involving certain biopsychosocial benchmarks. Once abstinence has been maintained for some months and the tasks of early recovery have been accomplished, psychotherapy can be helpful to clients in grieving the losses experienced during the addiction, repairing relationships, dealing with shame and self-hatred, addressing experiences of early trauma, and reestablishing a sense of purpose in life (Brown, 1985).

Prevention: Risk and Resiliency

A number of prevention approaches for youth at high risk have been advocated in recent years. Strategies include those targeting individuals, peers, families, schools, and communities. Each reflects different theories of etiology.

A common way of viewing prevention has been to consider risk and protective factors. Research in this area has included longitudinal studies, adoption studies, biomedical and genetic studies, and cross-sectional studies. In recent years more attention has been given to protective rather than risk factors and the concept of building resiliency to prevent drug use. The assumption is that if risk factors can be reduced and protective factors increased, the vulnerability to alcohol and other drug use in youth will be reduced.

Research has shown that the more risk factors youth have, the more likely they are to become drug users. Other research suggests that protective factors such as interpersonal skills, long-term goals, planning ability, and a close relationship with a positive role model reduce poor outcomes (Kumpfer et al., 1993).

Social Work Roles

In addition to clinical work, advocacy for client services, research on clinical efficacy, grassroots organizing to promote school-based and community-based primary prevention efforts, and protection of the civil rights of clients and their families are essential social work interventions with AODA-involved systems.

Useful Theoretical Frameworks

Many theoretical frameworks guiding social work practice, including cognitive-behavioral, psychodynamic, family systems, and person-in-environment, have been used to view AODA. Each perspective has made a valuable contribution to understanding the helping process and has a place in examining and intervening with AODA.

Working with Alcohol and Other Drug Issues in the Context of Diversity and Multiculturalism

Because we feel strongly about multicultural issues in the teaching of social work and in substance abuse, the following section is presented as a paradigm for discussing AODA-related macro and micro practice issues. Readers are encouraged to review this section before moving onto the specific cases. The material presented here can inform the cases and respond to some of the questions for class discussion.

Basic Premise

The explicit focus on cultural issues in this casebook reflects the underlying premise that the diversity in our society is a source of great richness, strength, and potential. Working with and within diversity offers opportunities for self-discovery and growth, new personal connections, increased resources, innovative programs, and expanded vision. However, it also creates the possibility of poor communication, misunderstanding, conflict, ineffective and/or inadequate services, and discrimination. As educators and trainers seek to prepare practitioners to work on AODA issues in this increasingly diverse and multicultural world, three educational objectives appear essential:

- Practitioners will need to develop a greater understanding and awareness of how culture (as well as ethnicity and race) shapes individuals and families, their life experiences, perceptions, and interactions; and specifically how the above are related to AODA issues. They will also need to better recognize the impact of oppression on individuals, family systems, communities, and society, and understand that drinking and drug use may in part be a response to oppression.

- Practitioners will need to develop an appreciation for the strengths and resources found in diversity, and learn how to identify and utilize these in their practice.

- Practitioners will need to learn the integrated set of attitudes, knowledge, and skills that lead to cultural competency, and understand that there is a subset specifically related to AODA competency.

Key Concepts and Terms

In preparing practitioners to work cross-culturally on AODA issues, it is essential that they understand certain key concepts and terms.

Culture

Culture may be defined as "the sum total of ways of living developed by a group of human beings to meet biological and psycho-social needs . . . traditions that are linked together to form an integrated whole" (Pinderhughes, 1989, p. 6). Key ingredients in culture include shared values, beliefs, customs, world views, and ways of thinking and behaving.

Culture serves many functions for both the individual and the society: It defines what is good, right, natural, and real. It helps to make wide areas of life predictable by offering an abstract "map" or "guidebook." It organizes people, activities, and institutions, thus preserving society and ensuring group survival. In addition, culture serves as both a lens and a filter. It is the lens through which one sees, experiences, understands, and gives meaning to life events. It is simultaneously the filter which selectively screens information in or out, leading to a particular perspective and vision. If one is unaware of one's culture, of one's own lens and filter, it is easy to stereotype others who are different, to believe there is only one way to see, understand, and do.

Ethnicity and Race

Ethnicity may be defined as "connectedness based on commonalities such as religion, nationality and region, where specific aspects of cultural patterns are shared and where transmission over time creates a common history" (Pinderhughes, 1989). Race technically refers only to biological differences, such as skin color and other physical characteristics of genetic origin.

Despite the significant differences in the above terms, "culture" is often used in the broadest sense, encompassing both ethnicity and race. This is how the term is frequently employed throughout the remainder of this casebook. (We do not mean to diminish the importance of race or to avoid a discussion of racism; developing cultural competency requires an understanding of both. Nonetheless, this is not the primary focus of this casebook.)

It may be useful to ask practitioners to think of examples where culture, race, and ethnicity do or do not overlap. For example: African Americans and Africans (same race, different culture and ethnicity); White Jews in the U.S. and in Latin America (same race, same "ethnicity," different culture), and WASPs (White Anglo-Saxon Protestants) and Irish Americans in the same city (same race, same culture, different ethnicity).

Finally, practitioners should be encouraged to think if and to what degree the culture, ethnicity, and race of any given client is relevant at any given moment. At what points in engagement, assessment, relationship building, intervention, and accessing resources are these salient factors? When, where, and why are they not?

As practitioners further develop their cross-cultural skills, additional terms and concepts may be useful. *Ethnocentrism* refers to understanding and explaining everything in terms of one's own culture. The ethnocentric individual believes his/her own culture to be superior and assumes it is the standard against which one measures all other groups. *Cultural blindness* refers to the individual who believes all humans are basically the same, and therefore ignores cultural differences. For example, a culturally blind practitioner would assume that the meaning and patterns of use of alcohol are the same in every culture, thereby concluding that a Southeast Asian woman who drinks wine every day immediately after childbirth is obviously abusing alcohol. (In actuality, this is seen as an important time-honored medicinal treatment.) In contrast, *cultural romanticism* or *reductionism* is the tendency to explain everything in terms of culture; thus, a practitioner might automatically dismiss a Southeast Asian woman's use of liquor as an indigenous custom following childbirth, without even assessing the possibility of alcohol abuse.

Finally, there is the danger of *cultural encapsulation*. The culturally encapsulated practitioner lives in a "cocoon," evading reality by depending entirely on internalized value assumptions. The culturally encapsulated individual is totally isolated and trapped in one way of thinking, unwilling or unable to adapt to the ever-changing sociocultural context. For example, the culturally encapsulated practitioner might assume that Western approaches to AODA treatment, which are predicated upon the disease concept and primarily focus on the individual, are universally accepted and effective (Petersen, 1988, pp. 102–104.)

Yet another key concept in cross-cultural practice is the continuum of *adaptation, assimilation, acculturation,* and *biculturalism.* The first three terms are often used interchangeably, but they carry subtle nuances. Adaptation simply means learning to function in the mainstream, dominant society. Assimilation implies the acceptance of the dominant group's cultural traits and values, while relinquishing one's own. Acculturation refers to the acceptance of the dominant group's cultural traits and values, but with recognition that acculturation can take place in varying degrees and in different areas (e.g., language, dress, food, intermarriage). Biculturalism suggests successful interaction with mainstream, dominant society, while simultaneously maintaining one's own ethnic identity (as with acculturation, this may develop in varying degrees).

The concept of *sociocultural dissonance* (Chau, 1989) refers to the stress and strain of cultural incongruence, when norms and expectations of majority and ethnic cultures clash. For example, consider the relative degree of cultural incongruence experienced by an educated Russian from Moscow, as compared with that experienced by a rice farmer from Cambodia. Finally, the term *cultural pluralism* reflects a commitment to support the rights of different ethnic/cultural/racial groups to maintain their uniqueness. It further embraces and promotes a mutual respect for cultural differences and recognizes the cultural strengths inherent in these differences.

When discussing the above concepts and terms, the educator/trainer may wish to ask practitioners to think of them from multiple perspectives: in terms of their own beliefs and experiences; in terms of public attitudes; in relationship to particular clients; as they may be reflected in agency/system policies; and as they relate specifically to AODA issues.

The Concept of Cultural Competency

One final concept of great importance is cultural competency. This is defined by Cross and colleagues (1989) as "a set of congruent behaviors, attitudes, and policies that come together in a system, agency, or amongst professionals and enable . . . (them) to work effectively in cross-cultural situations." As outlined by these authors, cultural competency can be achieved only when it is developed both by individual practitioners and the system as a whole (Cross et al., 1989).

To become culturally competent, the practitioner must first develop an awareness of his or her own culture, assumptions, and biases. Secondly, he or she needs specific knowledge regarding sociopolitical systems in the U.S. and their impact upon "minorities," particular ethnic/racial groups being served, and pertinent practice skills. Finally, the practitioner requires new skills, such as presenting oneself as a learner; articulating problems from the client's cultural perspective, and cross-cultural communication techniques. Thus, the culturally competent practitioner seeks to become culturally self-aware and to attain new cross-cultural skills in engagement, interviewing, assessment techniques, intervention strategies, and advocacy and empowerment efforts. As well, the culturally competent agency effectively acknowledges and incorporates respect for the importance of cultural differences at all levels—policy, administration, and clinical practice.

Dr. Davis Ja, Associate Professor of Psychology, California School of Professional Psychology at Alameda/Berkeley, and recognized expert in the area of substance abuse treatment for Asians, also discusses cultural competency (1993). He describes its essence as being able to use cultural values and beliefs both as a context for treatment, and as resources for treatment. He further identifies two specific areas of competence: Affective competence is the ability to empathize with the culturally different client. Role competence is the ability to carry out, within the client's cultural framework, roles which are necessary to perform the helping function.

To highlight AODA issues in the context of diversity and multiculturalism, we encourage instructors to consider the following questions along with all the instructional material used:

- How does AODA present itself here, and to what extent might that be influenced by the client's cultural background?

- What were the barriers to services, and to what extent might those barriers have been influenced by the client's cultural background? (For example, services offered in an unfamiliar format; client's fear of stigma; cultural norms support excessive drinking and do not define it as a problem.)

- What facilitated the client's openness and ability to receive help? To what extent might that have been influenced by the client's cultural background? (For example, interventions that utilize natural support networks or include extended family.)

- What alternative intervention approaches could be used here? To what extent is the worker demonstrating "culture-bound" intervention approaches based on his/her culture or demographics?

- What made the intervention difficult for the worker?

- What would *your* agency have done at different points in handling this case? What would their rationale have been? Would this have led to an improvement in the outcome?

- Who in the community would have been potential collaborators in this case?

- What aspects of culture contribute to hiding or resistance? (For example, fear of difference; shame and stigma.)

Cultural Competency When Working with AODA

A practitioner working cross-culturally on AODA issues must recognize the specific beliefs, behaviors, and norms within that culture and the client's community that pertain to substance use and abuse. Just as culture shapes responses to illness and treatment, it also influences behaviors such as drinking and drug use, and the culture's response to individuals who develop problems with drinking and drug use: "An ethnic or racial group's shared norms, beliefs, and expectations regarding alcohol and its effects shape the group members' drinking habits, the ways in which the members behave while drinking, and their perceptions of personal and collective responsibility for the outcomes of drinking" (Orlandi, 1992, p. 4). Culture can contribute to the development of alcoholism by reinforcing the benefits of escaping from reality, or, in contrast, discourage drinking and alcoholism by educating people about the dangers of excessive use (Stivers, 1976). Societies may be relatively tolerant of it or act quickly to limit it.

The AOD Cultural Framework (Amodeo & Jones, in press) can be particularly useful in helping practitioners develop cultural competency. This framework outlines key factors to be considered when examining AODA problems, interventions, and services in non-mainstream populations (particularly within refugee and immigrant groups). It identifies two primary dimensions: culture-specific AODA dynamics and individual-specific dynamics.

Culture-specific AODA dynamics incorporate and reflect both the culture's belief system in general (e.g., values and behavioral norms, traditions, communication patterns, family structure) and the culture's specific responses to AODA (e.g., norms regarding use, abuse, or help-seeking). Individual-specific dynamics reflect the unique characteristics and experiences of individuals that shape their cultural identity and responses to AODA. Three key components are (a) subgroup membership (e.g., ethnicity, class, age, gender, rural or urban, religion); (b) the context of migration (e.g., circumstances of departure, trauma experience, or legal status); and (c) the degree of acculturation (e.g., "traditional," bicultural, acculturated, or assimilated).

Careful examination of each of the above dynamics, and the interaction between them, can be integrated into the assessment and treatment process as the practitioner considers such issues as: clients' attitudes and behavior related to using alcohol; attitudes and behavior related to using other drugs; attitudes and behavior related to the state of intoxication or being "high"; point at which the illness or related behavior would be defined as a problem; persons/institutions from whom clients or concerned family members might seek help; and the type of help expected, accepted, and potentially effective.

The AOD Cultural Framework can facilitate the integration of a cross-cultural perspective in teaching specialized courses on alcoholism and drug dependence, or in training/courses on primary prevention of health problems with AODA as an example. This framework can also be used in clinical settings to treat clients with AODA-related problems, serving as a guide for bridging cultural differences between clinician and client. By using the framework, practitioners can explore the client's unique experience with AODA, and in the process also become more aware of how their own culture has affected their views of alcohol and other drugs.

Organization of the Text

This volume has three types of teaching materials: case studies, vignettes, and teaching tools. The case studies are detailed descriptions of problems faced by clients or client systems, often over a period of time. These more extensive descriptions include a statement of the presenting problem, the worker's assessment of the situation, a description of alternatives, and information about the interventions chosen. The worker's observations and reactions are often detailed as well. Questions for class discussion, and teaching points which emphasize important concepts or principles, are included at the end of the case study, as well as references to facilitate further exploration of topics. Case studies can be used to illustrate

- methods for conducting assessments on any one of multiple levels (individual, group, family, organization, community), while paying attention to "indirect indicators" of alcohol and other drug problems;
- intervention techniques such as the worker's struggle to establish alliances with various parts of the client system, balance support and confrontation, and promote self-determination and group empowerment;
- the need for modifying assessment and intervention techniques dependent upon variables such as homelessness, multiple disabilities, and HIV status;
- issues common to the field of alcohol/drug abuse, such as progression of the chemical dependency, pervasiveness of denial within the system, relapse and relapse prevention, and the timing of and techniques for confrontation.

Instructors could use the case studies in several ways, such as giving a written take-home assignment in which students analyze the case and answer discussion questions; asking students to read the case and come prepared to critique it, working in small groups to outline alternative interventions; having students read through the case in class along with the instructor, stopping at various points to discuss worker and client motivations, and worker alternatives; using the case as the basis for a role-play in which the worker's interactions with the client system would be examined.

The vignettes are brief case excerpts or summaries providing "snapshots" of cases at a single point in time. These include a statement of the problem, questions for class discussion, and teaching points which emphasize important concepts or principles to be understood by students working with clients affected by AODA. Instructors can use these case vignettes to show

- the role of the worker in a range of practice settings, including the worker as advocate, manager, community organizer, referral agent, family therapist, or individual clinician;
- worker barriers (attitudes, values, ethics), worker expectations, and the impact of these on the intervention process;
- community referral resources and the organization of helping networks;
- the need for adapting assessment and intervention techniques dependent upon diverse characteristics of client systems, including race, ethnicity, educational level, language skills, acculturation level, socioeconomic level, gender, age, and geography.

In general, use of a case vignette will require 10 to 60 minutes of classroom time. The vignette can be read aloud to the class to illustrate a specific issue (10 minutes required) or handed out to students with instructions for work in small groups (60 minutes required).

A variety of teaching tools are also included in the text. Some can be used in foundation courses, while others are more appropriate for use in specialized AODA courses or agency-based in-service training programs. Introductory material is provided describing each of these teaching tools and the educational and practice settings where each could be most useful. Included are

- classroom exercises focusing on issues such as attitudes, assessment skills, and understanding of community resources;

- student assignments focusing on application of learning related to individual diagnosis, organizational dynamics, and community needs assessments; and

- reference material.

References

Allen, J. P., & Kadden, R. M. (1995). Matching clients to alcohol treatments. In W. R. Miller & R. K. Hester (Eds.), *Handbook of alcoholism treatment approaches* (pp. 278-292). Boston: Allyn and Bacon.

American Psychiatric Association (1994). *Diagnostic and statistical manual of mental disorders* (4th ed.). Washington, DC: Author.

Amodeo, M. (1995a). The therapist's role in the drinking stage. In S. Brown (Ed.), *Treating alcoholism* (pp. 95-132). San Francisco: Jossey-Bass.

Amodeo, M. (1995b). The therapist's role in the transitional stage. In S. Brown (Ed.), *Treating alcoholism* (pp. 133-162). San Francisco: Jossey-Bass.

Amodeo, M., & Jones, L. K. (in press). Viewing alcohol and other drug use cross-culturally: A cultural framework for clinical practice. *Families in Society*.

Brown, S. (1985). *Treating the alcoholic: A developmental model of recovery*. New York: Wiley.

Chau, K. (1989). Sociocultural dissonance among ethnic minority populations. *Social Casework, 70*(4), 224-230.

Coombs, R. H., & Ziedonis, D. (Eds.). (1995). *Handbook on drug abuse prevention*. Boston: Allyn and Bacon.

Cross, T. L., Barzon, B. J., Dennis, K. W., & Issacs, M. R. (1989). *Toward a culturally competent system of care, children and adolescent service systems program technical assistance center*. Washington, DC: CASSP Technical Assistance Center, Georgetown University Child Development Center.

Delgado, M. (1994). Collaboration between Hispanic natural support systems and alcohol and drug agencies: A developmental perspective. *Journal of Multicultural Social Work, 3*, 11-37.

Doweiko, H. F. (1993). *Concepts of chemical dependency*. Pacific Grove, CA: Brooks/Cole.

Gorski, T., & Miller, H. (1986). *Staying sober: A guide for relapse prevention*. Independence, MO: Independence Press.

Helzer, J. E., & Pryzbeck, T. R. (1988). The co-occurrence of alcoholism with other psychiatric disorders in the general population and its impact on treatment. *Journal of Studies on Alcohol, 49*(3), 219-224.

Helzer, J. E., Robins, L. N., Taylor, J. R., Carey, K., Miller, R. H., Combs-Orme, T., & Farmer, A. (1985). The extent of long-term moderate drinking among alcoholics discharged from medical and psychiatric treatment facilities. *New England Journal of Medicine, 312*, 1678-1682.

Hester, R. K., & Miller, W. R. (1989). Behavioral self-control training. In R. K. Hester & W. R. Miller (Eds.), *Handbook of alcoholism treatment approaches* (pp. 148-159). New York: Pergamon.

Hester, R. K., & Miller, W. R. (1995). *Handbook of alcoholism treatment approaches: Effective alternatives*. Boston: Allyn and Bacon.

Ja, D. (1993, November). *Culturally-specific substance abuse treatment for Southeast Asians*. Presentation to Substance Abuse and Southeast Asians Conference, Boston University, Boston, MA.

Kumpfer, K. L., Shur, G. H., Ross, J. G., Bunnell, K. K., Librett, J. J., & Millward, A. R. (1993). What to measure: Theories of causation and risk factors. *Measurement in prevention* (pp. 7-20). CSAP Technical Report 8, U.S. Department of Health and Human Services.

Liftik, J. (1995). Assessment. In S. Brown (Ed.), *Treating alcoholism* (pp. 57-94). San Francisco: Jossey-Bass.

Marlatt, G. A., & Gordon, J. R. (1985). *Relapse prevention: Maintenance strategies in the treatment of addictive behaviors*. New York: Guilford.

Miller, W. R., & Hester, R. K. (1986). Matching problem drinkers with optimal treatments. In W. R. Miller & N. Heather (Eds.), *Treating addictive behaviors: Process of change* (pp. 174-204). New York: Plenum.

Miller, W. R., & Hester, R. K. (1995). Treatment for alcohol problems: Toward an informed eclecticism. In R. K. Hester & W. R. Miller (Eds.), *Handbook of alcoholism treatment approaches* (pp. 1-11). Boston: Allyn and Bacon.

Miller, W. R., & Rollnick, S. (1991). *Motivational interviewing: Preparing people to change addictive behavior*. New York: Guilford.

O'Farrell, T. J. (Ed.). (1993). *Treating alcohol problems: Marital and family interventions*. New York: Guilford.

Orlandi, M. A. (1992). The challenges of evaluating community-based prevention programs: A cross-cultural perspective. In M. A. Orlandi, R. Weston, & L. G. Epstein (Eds.), *Cultural competence for evaluators: A guide for alcohol and other drug abuse prevention practitioners working with racial/ethnic communities* (pp. 1-22). Office for Substance Abuse Prevention, U.S. Department of Health and Human Services.

Pattison, E. M., & Kaufman, E. (1982). The alcoholism syndrome: Definitions and models. In E. M. Pattison & E. Kaufman (Eds.), *Encyclopedic handbook of alcoholism* (pp. 3-26). New York: Gardner Press.

Pendry, M. L., Maltzman, I. M., & West, L. J. (1982). Controlled drinking by alcoholics? New findings and a reevaluation of a major affirmative study. *Science, 217*, 169-174.

Petersen, P. (1988). *A handbook for developing multicultural awareness*. Alexandria, VA: American Association for Counseling and Development.

Pinderhughes, E. (1989). *Understanding race, ethnicity, and power*. New York: Free Press.

Rogers, C. R. (1951). *Client-centered therapy: Its practice, implications and theory*. Boston: Houghton Mifflin.

Schuckit, M. (1986). Etiologic theories on alcoholism. In N. J. Estes & M. E. Heinemann (Eds.), *Alcoholism: development, consequences, and interventions* (pp. 15-30). St. Louis, MO: C.V. Mosby.

Schuckit, M. (1989). *Drug and alcohol abuse: A clinical guide to diagnosis and treatment* (3rd ed.). New York: Plenum.

Steinglass, P. (1980). A life history model of the alcoholic family. *Family Process, 19*, 211-225.

Steinglass, P., Bennett, L. A., Wolin, S. J., & Reiss, D. (1987). *The alcoholic family*. New York: Basic Books.

Stivers, R. (1976). Culture and alcoholism. In R. E. Tartar & A. A. Sugarmen (Eds.), *Alcoholism: Interdisciplinary approaches to an enduring problem* (pp. 573-602). Reading, MA: Addison-Wesley.

Usher, M. L. (1991). From identification to consolidation: A treatment model for couples and families complicated by alcoholism. *Family Dynamics of Addictions Quarterly, 1*(2), 45-58.

Vanicelli, M. (1995). Group psychotherapy with substance abusers and family members. In A. M. Washton (Ed.), *Psychotherapy and substance abuse* (pp. 337-356). New York: Guilford.

Wallace, J. (1989, June). A biopsychosocial model of alcoholism. *Social Casework*, 325-332.

Weick, A. (1985). Overturning the medical model. *Social Work, 30*, 310-315.

Wolin, S. J., & Bennett, L. A. (1984). Family rituals. *Family Process, 23*, 401-420.

Assessing Alcohol and Drug Use in Adults

Arthur: A Cocaine-Dependent Client's View of Alcohol

During abstinent periods, clients may substitute one drug for another that they've stopped using. The rationalization that develops tends to be subtle, complex, and difficult to assess. In the following case, a cocaine-dependent client has stopped using cocaine but has continued using alcohol. The worker is concerned that drinking might trigger a return to cocaine, but the client is unconvinced. Teaching points suggest ways to discuss this while avoiding a power struggle with the client, and ways to approach family members who indirectly facilitate the drug dependency.

Client: Arthur is a 24-year-old white male from the South End of the city.
Setting: Substance abuse clinic.
Presenting problem: He called an alcohol and drug hotline after repeatedly binging on cocaine. He reported that he was scared and needed help.

In our clinic's assessments, we ask clients to report on the history of their use of all drugs and alcohol, regardless of whether or not they consider these drugs to be a problem. Our policy as an agency is that clients must be clean from all drugs and alcohol for at least five days to receive services from the clinic. This policy is based in part on the belief that people who have an addiction to one substance are vulnerable to developing problems with other substances as well. Clients commonly substitute a new substance for the one they have recently given up. And when under the influence of the substitute drug, they tend to have lowered inhibitions and are more likely to relapse to the original substance to which they were addicted.

Arthur had been cocaine-free for three weeks and had been going through the clinic's intake process prior to being assigned to me. When he came to see me, Arthur was open about his cocaine addiction. He described a pattern of repeated use that included (a) an inability to predict how much cocaine he would use in a given evening, and (b) impaired control in that he would use at times he did not plan nor want to. He also described that his use of cocaine quickly progressed from being "fun" and making him feel wild and adventurous, to a situation where he would "sit in the corner all night" feeling depressed and empty after using. It was this change in the effect of the drug, combined with the amount of money he was spending, that led him to seek help. He also described trying to create strategies that would help him stop using cocaine. For example, he gave his entire paycheck to his mother and had her give him a small allowance each day to prevent him from buying cocaine.

Although Arthur willingly admitted to a cocaine addiction, he was more guarded in describing his drinking. He refused to consider that his continued alcohol use could be a problem. During the portion of the assessment that deals with the client's history of drug and alcohol use, clients are asked to report on the frequency and duration of their use, as well as when they used each of these substances last. They are also asked at what age they began using and who introduced them to using. Finally, they are asked to report on their use at its absolute peak, as well as reporting their average use over their lifetime.

My concerns began when Arthur reported that he had "a few beers" on the previous Saturday night (two days prior). When I asked if he could recall the exact amount, he said six or possibly as many as eight. This appeared to be minimization, as he first said a "few" when he actually had eight beers. It occurred to me that this could be a form of denial and an attempt to deceive himself about the extent of his problem. I recognized this as one symptom of an alcohol problem. We discussed the frequency with which events like this occurred. He reported that he had six to eight beers two or three times a month. We discussed his motivation for drinking this amount. He initially stated that it was "not a problem" and that he did not feel he had any reason to cut down. When discussing his friendships, he reported that he had no sober friends, drinking was a consistent part of his socializing with his friends, and he would not know what to do if he did not drink. He denied drinking to reduce stress or anxiety.

Arthur told me that the system he had established with his mother and his paycheck was his way of making sure his drinking and cocaine use were under control. I recognized this attempt to structure or limit his drinking as another symptom. When I asked if he had ever had a period of sobriety in his life, he said that he had quit for three weeks this past summer because he was "working out." This attempt at limiting himself only furthered my concerns. This seemed like a "period of abstinence" in order to convince himself that he did not have a problem.

I presented my concerns about his drinking at this early point in his recovery from a cocaine dependence. I told him that people who have trouble with one substance often have trouble with other substances.

I proceeded to ask about his past use of alcohol. He reported starting to drink at age 13 and described a pattern of consistent weekend use until going away to college at age 18. At this time in his life, his use became heavier. Thursday through Sunday nights, he would drink 25 to 30 beers a night. This indicated to me that he had developed a physical tolerance and addiction. He said this pattern persisted for a year until he dropped out of college. He returned home, and although his drinking subsided somewhat, he still drank heavily and consistently on weekends. During this period he began using cocaine; eventually his drinking lessened and his cocaine use increased. He reported having blackouts consistently when he was in college and drinking at his peak. With his current pattern of use, he did not experience blackouts. Arthur had been arrested three times, all alcohol related (one for possession of alcohol as a minor, and two for driving under the influence).

I believe I was nervous in confronting him and felt at a loss when he did not accept my "party line" statement about the evils of any drug use in early recovery. More importantly, I felt a sense of urgency, in that I believed he was placing himself at great risk for relapse. When I realized that my attempts were not working, my level of discomfort and anxiety increased.

Questions for Class Discussion

1. What are the strengths and weaknesses of this agency's policies? Please explain your answers.

2. How serious is the client's use of alcohol? Would you categorize it as moderate use, abuse, or dependence? (Please refer to DSM-IV in making a decision.)

. What should the worker's short-term goals be with the client? What type of contract should the worker negotiate with the client and why?

4. If those goals can be achieved, what should be the intermediate and long-term goals?

5. Is there a way the client's mother can be involved in his treatment? How would you go about discussing this with him and/or with her? Are there drawbacks to including her?

6. How typical is the worker's response? What does her response tell us about the typical worker–client dynamics in the first phase of treatment?

7. What are the risks for individuals attempting to change addictive patterns if they do not have a sober or abstinent social network? How could the worker approach this topic with the client, and what points should be made in bringing this problem to the client's attention?

Teaching Points

1. Strengths
   - Assessing use of all drugs gives the worker an opportunity to determine which of them may have caused problems, regardless of the client's level of insight or denial.
   - Such a policy also provides the worker with an opportunity to do education and prevention concerning the effects of some drugs in stimulating the use of other drugs and triggering relapse.
   - Given that this is an outpatient setting, the requirement that the client be drug free for a period of time before enrollment helps the agency select those clients with the greatest potential to be helped at that point in time.

Weaknesses
   - Requiring that clients be clean from all drugs and alcohol for at least five days to receive services may be too stringent for some settings. It eliminates the possibility of recruiting clients who are actively using substances and motivating them to enter a detoxification program.
   - Clients who are not totally abstinent may be prompted to withhold information about their current use in order to comply with service requirements.

2. Given his entire drinking history, he would be categorized as alcohol dependent. In view of his cocaine dependence, however, he could also be called polysubstance dependent.

3. Short-term goals
   - Helping the client develop a social network of clean and sober individuals;
   - Motivating the client to keep a log of any substance use, with particular attention to quantity and frequency of alcohol use;
   - Decreasing use of "confrontation" with the client and increasing the use of reflective listening and helping the client articulate his own treatment goals.

4. Possible intermediate and long-term goals
   - Increased education about the course of drug and alcohol dependence and triggers to relapse;
   - Helping the client utilize an ongoing support network such as Alcoholics Anonymous, Narcotics Anonymous, or Cocaine Anonymous;
   - Helping the client take responsibility for his own paycheck;
   - Supporting the client in achieving ongoing abstinence.

5. Since Arthur's mother participates in doling out money to him in an effort to help him limit his use, she is already involved

in his "treatment" (however ineffective this "treatment strategy" may be). The worker could remind Arthur of his mother's obvious desire to be helpful and suggest that his mother may benefit from some support and guidance in her efforts. The worker could express an interest in meeting his mother and offering this support, or could recommend another worker in the clinic. Whatever drawbacks there might be would probably be overshadowed by the benefits of including a family member who might otherwise sabotage treatment unwittingly.

6. The worker's responses seem quite typical of new workers in substance abuse treatment roles. She may feel responsible for keeping the client clean and sober, rather than seeing her role as helping the client assess his situation and make the decision he deems best. Workers often get into power struggles with clients, trying to force them to choose abstinence rather than eliciting the client's views of the benefits and penalties of continued use, and the client's feelings of discouragement, anxiety, and failure.

7. Without an abstinent social network, clients risk being isolated and lonely, albeit clean and sober, or they risk relapse. Without interaction with others in recovery, newly abstinent clients are likely to forget their vulnerability to certain high-risk situations, decide that a periodic occasion of drug use will not lead to problems, or convince themselves that they were never really drug-dependent in the first place.

Suggested Readings

Levin, J. D. (1995). *Introduction to alcoholism counseling: A bio-psycho-social approach*. Washington, DC: Taylor and Francis.

O'Farrell, T. J. (Ed.). (1993). *Treating alcohol problems: Marital and family intervention*. New York: Guilford.

Schwartz, S. (1992). An ecological approach to treatment of cocaine and crack abuse. In E. M. Freeman (Ed.), *The addiction process: Effective social work approaches*. New York: Longman.

Washton, A. (1989). *Cocaine addiction: Treatment, recovery, and relapse prevention*. New York: Norton.

Providing Services
to the Homebound Mrs. King

Family members are often important resources for helping clients. When the client is elderly and homebound, it is especially important for key family members to be kept informed of the client's progress and involved in service planning. In this case, family members block the worker's efforts to address an apparent drinking problem. Teaching points emphasize ways the worker can engage the family and special dynamics that may be present when the identified client is elderly.

Mrs. King lives in the in-law apartment attached to her son Bill's house. Bill is married with three small children. Both he and his wife, Ann, work full time and requested services from your agency. You have been seeing Mrs. King since her recent hospitalization for a serious hip injury. She is frail and spends most of her time in bed or in a comfortable chair in her bedroom.

Last week, a neighbor of Mrs. King called you—the social worker—to express her concern about Mrs. King's drinking. The neighbor said that she has tried to talk to Ann and Bill, but feels that they aren't taking her seriously. The neighbor is especially worried because Mrs. King is also taking painkillers for her hip injury. The neighbor reported that on several occasions when she tried to visit Mrs. King at home, nobody answered even though she knew Mrs. King was there. One time, she did visit Mrs. King, who was rambling and seemed incoherent in her speech.

You decide to call Ann and Bill to share the neighbor's concern and get their perspective on the situation. You mention that at your last visit, Mrs. King found a bruise on her arm that she didn't know she had. You also say that another neighbor told you that she heard Mrs. King was "hitting the bottle." Bill is evasive on the phone and politely communicates the message that they can take care of their mother and you should stay out of it.

Questions for Class Discussion

1. Why might Ann and Bill cover up Mrs. King's drinking? List several reasons.

2. In subsequent conversation with Ann and Bill, how could you explore these possibilities?

3. What could you do to deal with the family's denial of a drinking problem? How could you respond if the problem is one of elder abuse and if Ann or Bill is the perpetrator?

4. What are some common stressors related to aging and associated with risk for alcohol abuse?

Teaching Points

1. Reasons for covering up:
   - Shame that she is an alcoholic;
   - Reluctance to be drawn into providing more care for her, since they have three small children and both work full time;
   - Possible drinking problem on the part of Ann and/or Bill. Since Bill is Mrs. King's son, the possibility of intergenerational transmission of alcoholism is high;
   - Embarrassment that they have not identified the problem themselves. Perhaps this generates guilt in them if they have not been very involved with her;
   - Possible elder abuse accounting for Mrs. King's bruises.

2. The worker can ask questions to determine:
   - Frequency of contact between Ann and Bill's family and Mrs. King, and quality of the relationship;
   - Whether they ever suspected there might be a drinking problem;
   - Whether caring for Mrs. King and having her live in an apartment next door has been a strain on Ann and Bill;
   - How Ann and Bill would feel if it turned out that Mrs. King did have a drinking problem.
3. The worker should not try to convince Ann and Bill that the problem is alcoholism. They may need time to adjust to the idea that Mrs. King has some kind of a problem. Instead, the worker could suggest:
   - a physical exam by Mrs. King's physician to determine which factor(s) might be contributing to her problems,
   - an assessment by the worker to see how much and how often Mrs. King is drinking,
   - closer observation by Ann and Bill of Mrs. King's behavior, and
   - a family meeting to discuss results. Prevention of future problems can be stressed, as well as the worker's availability to provide assistance throughout the assessment and intervention process.

4. Four common psychosocial stressors related to aging and associated with high risk for alcohol abuse include:
   - retirement, with possible boredom, change of role status, and loss of income;
   - deaths occurring among relatives and friends, and an awareness of one's own mortality;
   - poor health and discomfort; and
   - loneliness, especially in older women (Brody, 1982).

Thus, the elderly may use alcohol to medicate physical pain, treat insomnia, deal with grief and loss, or treat depression or anxiety (Amodeo, 1989; Hoffman & Heinemann, 1986; Rathbone-McCuan & Trigaardt, 1979).

References

Amodeo, M. (1989). Treating the late life alcoholic: Guidelines. *Journal of Geriatric Psychiatry, 23*(2), 91-105.

Brody, J. A. (1982). Aging and alcohol abuse. *Journal of the American Geriatric Society, 30*, 123-126.

Hoffman, A. L., & Heinemann, M. E. (1986). Alcohol problems in elderly persons. In N. J. Estes & M. E. Heinemann, *Alcoholism: Development, consequences, and interventions*. St. Louis, MO: C.V. Mosby.

Rathbone-McCuan, E., & Trigaardt, J. (1979). The older alcoholic and the family. *Alcohol Health and Research World, 3*, 7-12.

An Intake in an Employee Assistance Program: A Quick Diagnosis

The following process recording of an intake session shows a worker arriving at a diagnosis and making a referral without doing a thorough assessment. Although the client complies with the recommendation, it is not clear why the client came and to what extent the client feels helped.

This case can be used as a role-play in class using four students to play the roles of worker, worker's alter-ego, client, and client's alter-ego. During the enactment, the instructor should encourage the alter-egos to state the unexpressed feelings of the characters as the scene unfolds. Stop the action periodically to ask the class how the worker should proceed. Encourage class members to provide guidance for the worker, and have them take turns in the worker's seat to demonstrate their approach.

W (worker): Hi. My name is W.

R (client): Hi. I'm R.

W: I was looking over your intake form and I noticed you're feeling stress around your work. Can you tell me a little more about the problem?

R: Yes. For the past seven to eight months I've been on the road every week. My wife is home alone and the traveling is creating stress for her and for me.

W: What do you do for work? How long have you been doing this work?

R: I'm an auditor at the finance department and have been traveling a lot lately. I'm working in Chicago and I find myself going out after work and drinking 4 or 5 beers. My wife tells me she doesn't want me traveling so much and also questions me about my drinking. I don't drink when I'm at home and I don't seem to miss it.

W: I see on the intake form that you checked off some concerns around your drinking. Do you feel you're having a problem with alcohol?

R: I'm drinking more. I've been going to the Blue Lizard every night after work when I'm in Chicago, and sometimes I drink more than I plan to. I ran into an old friend, George, who I've been spending a lot of time with, and I'm drinking more when I'm with him.

W: How long has this been happening?

R: Well, the past four or five months.

W: How was it different prior to the past four or five months?

R: Well, I've been travelling the past eight years, but this is a recent problem. I met George and I started going out with him after work when I had business in the Midwest. Now I'm going out every night when I'm away.

W: What did you do at night after work before you ran into George and renewed your friendship with him?

R: I went out with the other guys I worked with. We would go to dinner, have a drink or two, and I'd go back to my hotel room. But the only thing the guys would talk about was work. I was sick of talking about work. I've been going out with George because he's fun and he introduced me to other guys, so I've met new people. After a day of business, I dread the thought of going to my hotel room and looking at four walls.

W: It sounds like it may have been lonely for you. Maybe that's why you've been going out drinking with George.

R: I am lonely. I miss my wife. I'm travelling too much. We've only been married a few years. We were very close initially, but lately she's been more distant. I guess it's not so easy to warm up to someone who's been away all week and suddenly appears on Friday night. But for the next four weeks, I'm working in the office here in town. My boss suggested it would be a good idea to come here and talk to someone. Well, I had an incident that occurred in Chicago. George took me to a strip joint. The bill was high. My boss questioned me about it. It was on my Visa card, so my boss knew I had gone there. I shouldn't have put it on my Visa, but I did. I was drinking at the time so I wasn't careful about what I was doing.

W: Would it have been different if you weren't drinking?

R: I wouldn't have spent all that money and I definitely would have paid cash.

W: It sounds like this incident happened because of your drinking. Has anything else happened while you were drinking?

R: No, that's the worst of it.

W: I'm wondering what else you could do at night when you're working out of town. After work, I mean. To avoid going out drinking. Do you have any ideas?

R: No.

W: Well, maybe you could go to dinner a couple of nights a week with the other men from your office. Call it a night after 9 p.m. Maybe you could see a movie, take a long walk, go to a museum, or stay in your room some nights. If you're trying to stay away from drinking, it's a good idea to limit the number of associates who drink and the places where you can get into trouble. Let me ask you, what is your idea of an alcoholic?

R: A person who drinks in the morning and drinks every day and has two six-packs a day.

W: Like you, a lot of people think of an alcoholic as someone who is on skid row or can't hold a job. But an alcoholic is someone who is either having external trouble as a result of drinking, or internal feelings that are uncomfortable about drinking, or sometimes both. It also refers to someone who can't limit himself when he plans to have one drink. Have you ever said you were going to have just one or two drinks and then found yourself drinking more than that?

R: Yes, I've been thinking about my drinking a lot. I say I'm only going to have a few and then I drink more and I feel lousy about it. Then I go out the next night and do it again. But it seems I only do it with George, when I'm on business trips. George has been great for me. He's very interested in my life and my future. He gives me advice about a lot of issues and is a real mentor to me. I feel like he's on my side.

W: I think it would be useful for you to try going to a few AA meetings. I know there's an AA meeting on Thursday nights at the Sacred Heart Church. I think you should get yourself there.

R: Well, if you're sure that's the problem. I told my boss I'd do whatever you recommended.

W: Would it be better if I asked you how I could help you and what you would like me to do?

R: Well, I'd like to come back here for counseling to try to get a handle on my problems. I'm still pretty confused about what's going on with me.

W: OK. We can set an appointment for you to see me next week. How many AA meetings would you like to attend before our next meeting? [I showed him the way to look up meetings and what kind of meetings to go to, e.g., Open Speaker Meetings vs. Discussion Meetings. I told him to pick up a meeting list at his first visit.]

R: I could go to two. Thursday and Saturday.

W: How will you feel about going?

R: A little nervous, but I can go.

W: Well, you could bring your wife if you wanted, or go alone, or you can call a central number. They can send someone to pick you up if you don't want to go alone. How does that sound?

R: Good. [He appeared willing to take suggestions but I wasn't sure if he was just agreeing with me to be a "good client."]

W: Well, I hope you get a chance to go and whether you do or don't, I'd still like to meet with you next week. You can tell me what the experience was like. From what you've said, it sounds like your wife is angry and has some resentment.

R: Yes. She is angry about the past four months and my drinking. I told her about meeting George again and the great times we've had. She enjoyed my stories initially. But now she seems to be withdrawing from me, like she's hurt. I think she's jealous of George or something. But I've been totally honest with her.

W: Well, it may take some time for her anger to go away. She may be supportive of AA or she may not be. There is also another program similar to AA for wives or family members of people who drink. If she is interested, let me know and I'll give you a list of meetings. Right now, concentrate on yourself and deal with your problem. Allow her to feel the way she does.

W: O.K. So I'll see you next week at the same time.

R: Great. Thanks. [This man seemed to have no resistance to the idea of having a drinking problem. He appeared very open to my suggestions. I'm not sure if he was eager to address the problem or was just placating me.]

Questions for Class Discussion

1. What are the weaknesses of the interview and why?

2. Find the place or places where the worker could have taken the interview in a different direction. List alternative interventions the worker could have made and the benefits of each.

3. What signs or symptoms of alcoholism do you see in this process recording?

Teaching Points

1. While drinking certainly plays some role here, it is not clear that drinking (or alcoholism) is the central issue. This is a case of premature, and perhaps incorrect, diagnosis. Other possible problem definitions include:

   • marital conflict for which drinking has become the identified issue or "lightning rod";

   • R's relationship with George, in which R has difficulty asserting himself;

   • R's lack of coping skills to deal with boredom and loneliness;

   • R's wanting a job reassignment so he doesn't have to travel anymore but being unable to make this request of his boss; or

   • R may even be setting the stage to say that traveling has negative effects on his work and home life and he should be reassigned.

When negative consequences occur from drinking or drug use, workers should hesitate to diagnose based on isolated incidents, but should look for persistent patterns. Diagnosis should come after a general assessment of family life, occupational and social functioning, health status, psychological status including self-image and self-esteem, and additional areas such as finances, contact with the legal system, and sexual functioning.

2. In several places, the worker could have asked R to describe more about
   - his relationship with his wife, including changes over the four years of marriage;
   - job satisfaction and ways this may have changed in recent months;
   - the significance of his relationship with George: does he have other friends like George? what is special or unusual about the relationship with George?

To have a clearer sense of the presenting problem, and to get the client thinking more about the nature of his situation and possible solutions, the worker could ask R about the following: If drinking could magically be removed from R's life, does R believe that this would clear up his problems? If travelling could magically be removed from R's life, does R believe that this would clear up his problems? If marital tension could be removed, would this clear up his problems?

3. Possible signs of alcoholism:
   - drinking more than previously;
   - when away on business, drinking every evening;
   - at times, drinking more than intended;
   - a pattern of four or five months' duration;
   - an incident of poor judgment—charging social expenses to a business charge card.

Indications against an alcoholism diagnosis:
   - does not drink when not away on business, and does not seem to miss it;
   - drinks only with George;
   - there seems to be only one isolated incident of poor judgment.

Suggested Readings

Hepworth, D. H., & Larsen, J. A. (1993). Multidimensional assessment. In D. H. Hepworth & J. Larsen, *Direct social work practice*. Pacific Grove, CA: Brooks/Cole.

Liftik, J. (1995). Assessment. In S. Brown (Ed.), *Treating alcoholism*. San Francisco: Jossey-Bass.

Metzger, L. (1988). *From denial to recovery*. San Francisco: Jossey-Bass.

Miller, W. R., & Rollnick, S. (1991). *Motivational interviewing: Preparing people to change addictive behavior*. New York: Guilford.

A Visit with the Elderly Mrs. Smith

Workers often wonder whether and how they should bring up the subject of drinking if clients have alcohol on their breath during appointments. Workers vacillate between thinking that the issue should be ignored because it is simply the client's way to relax, and worrying that it may indicate a serious problem. Even when additional signs of a drinking problem are present, such as in the case below, workers fear that bringing up the subject of drinking will anger the client and jeopardize the relationship. Attitudes about alcoholism in the elderly further complicate a case such as this one.

Mrs. Smith is a 78-year-old woman that you have known for the past four years. You've always looked forward to your visits with this kind, humorous woman. Over the past year, you have smelled alcohol on her breath during your visits. There seems to be a decline in her personal appearance and general hygiene. Taxis frequently pull up with deliveries, and the housecleaner reports that sometimes she finds empty wine bottles when she is cleaning up. However, she says that Mrs. Smith is never intoxicated. In addition, Mrs. Smith has been treated several times within the last year for injuries caused by falls which she has difficulty explaining. Today is your scheduled visit with Mrs. Smith. As you are driving there, you ponder what you should do.

Questions for Class Discussion

1. What worries you about Mrs. Smith's drinking?

2. What are the pros and cons of talking to her about this at this visit?

3. How would you bring up the subject?

4. How do you think Mrs. Smith would respond to your questions? If she denies a problem, what would you do? If she acknowledges a problem, what would you do?

Teaching Points

1. Indicators of a problem include alcohol on her breath on more than one occasion; decline in personal appearance and hygiene; taxi deliveries and empty bottles suggesting a high quantity of alcohol; unexplained injuries which probably result from balance and coordination problems when she has a lot to drink. The fact that she doesn't appear intoxicated may indicate
   - a high tolerance to alcohol (which involves risk for physical addiction);
   - an effort to remain sober on the days the housecleaner is scheduled to come; or
   - a level of consumption short of intoxication, but one that still might impair her balance and coordination.

2. Pros:
   - The situation seems to be quite urgent and possibly life threatening;
   - Perceptions are shared by the housecleaner and the social worker;
   - Additional indicators bolster their suspicions—taxi deliveries and several falls.

   Cons:
   - Mrs. Smith may become angry at being asked about her drinking. Thus, the worker may have to face a disruption in this relationship.
   - There is a small chance the worker will be wrong and will feel embarrassed, although the indicators of a problem seem overwhelming.

3. The worker could
   - review the positive relationship they've had over the past four years, and the worker's interest in seeing Mrs. Smith have the kind of satisfying life she desires;
   - describe her concern that Mrs. Smith may have developed a "problem with alcohol" (avoid labeling the client as alcoholic since the stigma alienates clients) without realizing it, and may now need help with it;'
   - list the factors that led to this conclusion so Mrs. Smith can see that there are concrete reasons for the worry.

4. Mrs. Smith may deny the problem initially, but the worker should continue to state concern for Mrs. Smith's well-being and express skepticism that these indicators could mean anything but a problem with alcohol.

5. Symptoms of alcoholism and problem drinking in the elderly are less related to quantity and frequency of alcohol consumption than in younger populations. Studies have shown that elderly alcoholics consume less alcohol per drinking occasion than younger alcoholics but are more likely to drink on a daily basis (Schuckit & Pastor, 1978). The average number of drinks per occasion often decreases (Harford & Mills, 1978).

6. The elderly alcoholic or alcohol abuser may need the same type of "continuum of care" that a younger person would require, including detoxification, residential services, outpatient treatment, participation in 12-step or alternative support groups, and family therapy. In addition, older persons generally need more medical services and attention to possible social isolation in recovery (Hinrichsen, 1984). Some recent programs for elderly alcoholics offer group and individual counseling within elder service programs, public housing, and senior citizen housing so as to reduce the stigma and convey to clients that they are valued senior citizens first, and recovering alcoholics second (Ruyle, 1987).

References

Harford, T. C., & Mills, G. S. (1978). Age-related trends in alcohol consumption. *Journal of Studies on Alcohol, 1*, 207-210.

Hinrichsen, J. J. (1984). Toward improving treatment services for alcoholics of advanced age. *Alcohol Health and Research World, 8*, 31-39.

Ruyle, J. (1987). Group therapy with older alcoholics: How it can happen and work. *Alcoholism Treatment Quarterly, 4*(4), 81-95.

Schuckit, M. A., & Pastor, P. A. (1978). The elderly as a unique population: Alcoholism. *Alcohol: Clinical and Experimental Research, 1*, 31-38.

Working with Children and Adolescents

Sidney: An Adolescent Girl in Recovery

Due to their developmental stage, young alcoholics and polydrug abusers are likely to enter treatment with particular social and psychological problems. This case suggests the possible connection between family relationships, trauma, and developmental challenges. It illustrates an adolescent's attempt to utilize several treatment resources while continuing to put herself at risk. It also provides the reader an opportunity to consider multiple intervention strategies.

Sidney is a petite, young-looking, 16-year-old high school sophomore who informally sought support from the Special Education Evaluation Service at the high school about five months ago. She is a gifted student both intellectually and musically. Her parents are divorced. She lives with her father, a psychologist; his wife, a school guidance counselor; and her older brother, a high school junior at a private school. Last fall, Sidney became clean and sober after two years of drug and alcohol abuse.

Since then she has sought help from the school addictions counselor, the juvenile probation officer in charge of her case, the Special Education Evaluation Service, a private psycho- therapist, a psychiatrist from the medical plan she uses, AA at least daily and three to four times a day when not in school, at least two AA sponsors, and an older recovering alcoholic on the school faculty.

Her father filed a CHINS petition (Children in Need of Services) two months ago. This was filed because Sidney went to AA meetings nightly, but would not return home until early the next morning. She also spent time at the meetings with men in their twen-ties and reports having been date-raped on at least one occasion. Her parents do not know this.

Sidney has no close girlfriends, nor does she desire to develop such friendships. She is in honors classes but is failing because she does not complete homework. She is excused from some classes to attend AA meetings. She also continues to associate with old boyfriends who are active drug users, and has difficulty terminating these relationships even with support from those adults providing her advice and guidance. She responds to any stress with severe anxiety and panic attacks, and has been unable and/or unwilling to find new friends and activities to build a safer, drug-free environment for herself. However, she has made strong connections with teens from out-of-town AA groups. She is able to enjoy typical activities with them on weekends.

She has been clean and sober for four months now, but is still unable to function well in school and feels fragile and tenuous in her sobriety. She is not able to engage in problem solving in difficult situations, and she prefers to attend AA meetings when faced with any and all uncomfortable feelings.

Questions for Class Discussion

1. List the problems with which Sidney is dealing. Consider criteria for prioritizing them.

2. What diagnosis or diagnoses do you think apply?

3. To what extent is Sidney actively engaged in her "recovery"? What evidence do you see that she is or is not pursuing recovery in an appropriate way?

4. What would be appropriate goals in family work if the family could be engaged?

Teaching Points

1. Problems:
   - lack of appropriate peer group, except for teens from out-of-town AA groups whom she sees on weekends;
   - severe anxiety and panic attacks;
   - poor school performance;
   - using AA meetings as an escape or avoidance of relationships;
   - a help-seeking pattern that could be both excessive and inadequate, since it involves more than a half-dozen adult "helpers" and may not be providing her with the continuity and depth of help she needs;
   - poor relationship with her father and stepmother, who seem unable to control or provide sufficient structure and guidance; they have turned to the courts for help;
   - an experience of date rape and the resulting trauma.
2. Diagnosis: She may suffer from an anxiety disorder or depression, among other possibilities.

3. Signs of pursuing recovery in an appropriate way:
   - help-seeking from professionals;
   - membership in a structured recovery program such as AA;
   - clean and sober for four months.

   Obstacles to her recovery:
   - lack of interest in friendships with girls;
   - continued relationships with drug users and difficulty terminating them;
   - staying out all night with adult men who may exploit her;
   - withholding information about the date rape from her parents.
4. Goals:
   - involving "both" families—the one with her father and stepmother and the one with her biological mother;
   - emphasizing safety issues in talking with the family;
   - focusing on Sidney's strengths in seeking help and maintaining abstinence;
   - suggesting to the family that her behavior may symbolize unresolved feelings related to the divorce and/or a request for more attention or structure from her parents.

Jeff: An 18-Year Old's Drinking and Marijuana Use

Adolescents often minimize their use of alcohol and other drugs, telling themselves and others that the use is occasional, experimental, and normal. In the case below, the worker takes a detailed alcohol and drug history, eliciting information that indicates the pattern is one of abuse and possible dependence rather than experimentation. The teaching points illustrate ways the worker can identify symptoms of alcohol and drug dependency, involve family members, ensure client safety, and help the client examine his need for drugs.

Client: Jeff, an 18-year-old high school senior, referred by his guidance counselor.

Worker: Social work intern.

Setting: A suburban high school.

Jeff was having difficulty keeping up in school, particularly in his math and science classes, though he is generally acknowledged to be a "bright kid." Jeff is the youngest of two siblings, having a sister seven years older, and comes from a white, upper middle class family. I learned from a conversation with his mother that Jeff's maternal grandfather was a "functioning alcoholic." His older sister also has a history of drug use, which worries his mother but has never prompted her to seek help for her daughter or herself. His mother's major concern during our initial phone conversation was about Jeff's grades.

Jeff admitted to having difficulty keeping up in his classes but rationalized his diminishing grades and effort with a non-caring attitude and by saying, "I do what I have to in order to get by." Without any prompting on my part, Jeff began to disclose a pattern of ongoing drug and alcohol use. He made no connection, however, between his drinking and taking drugs and his poor academic performance.

During the first meeting, I collected general information about school, friends, interests, and ambitions, as well as Jeff's use of drugs and alcohol. Jeff was smoking marijuana every day and drinking alcohol three to four times per week. He indicated that he "likes to party a lot" and does not feel that he has a problem with either smoking pot or drinking.

My second meeting with Jeff took place approximately five days later; this time we focused more on his use of drugs and alcohol. Jeff reported that he began drinking alcohol four years ago, at age 14. He primarily drinks beer and was introduced to drinking by the father of one of his friends. The father is an alcoholic.

Since he started drinking, Jeff has shown a marked increase in amount and level of tolerance. At first, he only drank on the weekends, but within the past year he began drinking one or two times during the week, as well. He drinks to become buzzed and enjoys the feelings of happiness and silliness that he associates with drinking. He will also drink shots of liquor whenever liquor is available.

On the night prior to our second interview, Jeff experienced his first blackout, in addition to passing out. He recalled that he had been at a party with friends and drank in excess of seven beers and smoked several joints.

He vaguely remembered returning home from the party but has no memory of being found passed out on the bathroom floor by his mother. He has no recollection of a conversation with his parents regarding possible hospitalization. Apparently eager to minimize this experience, he attempted to persuade me that he became sick for reasons other than drinking and taking drugs, and noted that he constantly loses his memory anyway, usually after smoking marijuana.

Along with his current pattern of drinking, Jeff's use of marijuana concerns me. He began smoking pot two to three years ago after being introduced to it by his sister. He admits that he liked to smoke from the start and says that he enjoys being "buzzed," silly, and stoned as a result. Jeff has experienced a marked increase in his tolerance to marijuana and stated "I have to smoke a lot to get high now." He currently smokes pot every day, usually after school, and prefers to smoke with friends. He claims that he generally does not drink or take drugs alone. He will occasionally smoke before school, but claims that this practice has decreased because his classes are more difficult this year. Overall, Jeff claims that his use of alcohol and marijuana has increased markedly over the past four years, especially this past summer when he began smoking pot every day.

He has experimented with several other drugs, including mescaline, acid, percodan, cocaine, and valium, "because they were there." He also said that he would probably continue to use these other drugs if they were readily available to him, although they are not.

Throughout the three meetings, I noticed that he became increasingly uncomfortable and embarrassed. The further we got into the evaluation, the more I noticed Jeff's use of the defense of denial as he repeatedly made the claim that "it does not affect my current lifestyle." He said to me on one occasion, "I'd like to change. I feel like I can, but I don't want to."

Questions for Class Discussion

1. Is Jeff's pattern one of moderate use, abuse, or dependence? (Refer to DSM-IV for criteria of abuse and dependence.)

2. Is additional information needed to verify this categorization? To elicit this information, what questions would you ask and in what way?

3. What are the next steps you would take in working with Jeff to address his drinking and drug use behavior? What would appropriate goals be, and how would you engage Jeff in working on them?

4. What is the most likely pitfall here in the worker's approach to Jeff and his situation?

5. Would it be important to involve Jeff's family, and if so, how? Who should be included in the sessions?

6. If the client were younger, would there be safety issues of concern to the worker? How should they be handled? What ground rules should be negotiated with him about safety? Should these ground rules apply to Jeff, too, even at his age?

7. How serious is marijuana use by adolescents? Should the worker be as concerned as she is about Jeff in this regard?

8. What should the assessment include when clients are adolescents?

Teaching Points

1. Jeff's alcohol and drug use may have passed the point of abuse and progressed to dependence. Symptoms include:
   - increase in amount of alcohol consumption and development of tolerance over a four-year period;

- daily use of marijuana and increase of tolerance;
- difficulty with school work, apparently related to drinking/drug use;
- minimization and denial;
- first blackout from alcohol and a possible repeated pattern of memory loss;
- experimentation with other drugs and tendency to use whatever drugs are available;
- early age of first use;
- drinking to achieve a mood swing, a possible indication of psychological dependence.

2. Questions to be asked include:
   - What physical effects occur during periods of non-use?
   - Have there been attempts to cut down or stop, and how effective have these attempts been?
   - What events precipitated Jeff's efforts to cut down or stop? Did he feel guilty, frightened, or disgusted with himself? Was there additional trouble with police, friends, money, driving, or other events that made Jeff aware that his drinking or drug use might be causing serious consequences?

3. A useful strategy would be to engage Jeff in one or more time-limited experiments (two to four weeks) to see if he could temporarily stop or cut down. This would help him see whether he had lost the ability to limit his use. The worker could help him monitor his responses to cutting down or stopping, to see if he experiences a sense of "need" or mental "preoccupation" to return to alcohol or marijuana use.

4. The worker's tendency may be to take charge of the situation and try to impose abstinence, telling Jeff that he is either heading toward addiction or is addicted and must stop immediately. This approach may mobilize more denial and defensive-

ness. Instead, the worker should engage Jeff in continued exploration of possible effects of the drinking and drug use, as well as other issues of concern to Jeff— for example, relationships with peers, parents, girlfriends. If Jeff sees that he can use therapy to address problems of concern to him, he will likely continue in treatment and be more receptive to examining his problem with alcohol and other drugs.

5. Jeff's family is key to helping him address his problem. The worker has already spoken with his mother, who expressed concern about Jeff's grades. She has acknowledged that Jeff's older sister has a history of drug use that worries her, and that her own father was an alcoholic. Thus, the worker could discuss with the mother the value of holding family sessions and use her assistance in involving other members.

   Family meetings for assessment purposes should include Jeff's mother, father, sister, and himself. If other relatives live in the household, are closely involved with the family, or are concerned about Jeff and his progress in school and life in general, they too should be included.

6. Workers should notify teen-aged clients that parents will be contacted if the worker learns that clients are jeopardizing their safety. Although Jeff is 18, he has had a recent incident where he passed out. His continued use of drugs may warrant outside intervention by adults. Confidentiality issues are especially important in working with adolescents. Many experts believe that a contract between the worker and the adolescent should include a statement that most of what is said will be confidential, but if the adolescent discloses something that would cause harm to oneself or others, confidentiality will not be preserved by the clinician (Kinney, 1991).

7. Experts differ about marijuana's potential to cause physical and psychological damage. Evidence suggests that marijuana is not as benign as once thought. It is now considered to be addictive, with a withdrawal syndrome characterized by irritability, anxiety, insomnia, nausea, and loss of appetite (Bloodworth, 1987; Group for the Advancement of Psychiatry, 1991). There is also evidence that chronic use will cause physical changes in the brain (Doweiko, 1993).

8. Morehouse (1989) stresses that the assessment process with adolescents should include:
   - obtaining as much information as possible from the referral source about alcohol and drug use;
   - gathering data from the adolescent on his/her social, psychological, physical, family, and school functioning, including contact with the courts and police and a specific drinking and drug history; and
   - obtaining urine screens, because adolescents will often deny drug use to keep the information from their parents.

References & Suggested Readings

Amodeo, M., & Drouilhet, A. (1992). Untangling a complex web: Countertransference with substance abusing adolescents. In J. Brandell (Ed.), *Countertransference in psychotherapy with children and adolescents* (pp. 285-315). Northvale, NJ: Jason Aaronson.

Bean, M. (1982). Identifying and managing alcohol problems of adolescents. *Psychosomatics, 23*(4).

Bloodworth, R. C. (1987). Major problems associated with marijuana abuse. *Psychiatric Medicine, 3*(3), 173-184.

Doweiko, H. F. (1993). *Concepts of chemical dependency.* Pacific Grove, CA: Brooks/Cole.

Group for the Advancement of Psychiatry. (1991). Substance abuse disorders: A psychiatric priority. *American Journal of Psychiatry, 148*, 1291-1300.

Kinney, J. (1991). Adolescence. In J. Kinney, *Clinical manual of substance abuse* (pp. 207-223). St. Louis, MO: C. V. Mosby.

Klitzner, M., Fisher, D., Stewart, K., & Gilbert, S. (1992). *Substance abuse: Early intervention for adolescents.* Bethesda, MD: Pacific Institute for Research and Evaluation.

Milman, D. H., Bennett, A. A., & Hanson, M. (1983). Psychological effects of alcohol in children and adolescents. *Alcohol Health and Research World*, 50-53.

Morehouse, E. (1989). Treating adolescent alcohol abusers. *Social Casework, 70*(6), 355-363.

Nelson, D. D. (1978). *Adolescent chemical use.* Minneapolis, MN: Compcare Publications.

Bobby and Susan Enact a Play about Children Affected by Alcohol and Drug Abuse

This process recording illustrates the use of an innovative drama activity to help children identify the roles they play in their families and explore the effects of their parents' alcoholism. It illustrates a way clinicians can use expressive methods as part of group treatment.

Group purpose: To provide education about addiction and encourage the expression of feelings related to addiction in the family

Group members: At the meeting described, the group consists of a pair of siblings: Bobby, age 9, and Susan, age 14. Their mother has recently been discharged from the inpatient detoxification program and is involved in outpatient treatment. The family is white and working class, with five children.

Worker: Graduate social work student who learns the 12-step model of recovery through weekly attendance at AA meetings during his field placement.

Setting: Outpatient office of a chemical dependency treatment agency that uses a 12-step model. Although the agency recognizes the need for services to children, this group is the only program offered. The group is open-ended, accepting children whose parents are currently in treatment.

Background Information

Bobby and Susan's mother reported that before and since the children's birth, she used alcohol, benzodiazepines, and marijuana; the father reportedly used marijuana consistently. At this point, the mother attends AA meetings daily and considers herself "in recovery." The father is an active marijuana user. The mother entered treatment after a serious traffic accident involving children (not her own) whom she was transporting. She was arrested and convicted of driving under the influence, and the case received substantial local press attention—much to the embarrassment of Bobby and Susan. Although the accident and their father's drug use were discussed at the intake interview, Bobby and Susan had been reluctant to talk about either of these issues, and discussions had been limited to a focus on their mother.

Worker's Comments

Directly before I introduced the activity, Bobby and Susan had divulged that their father had moved out of their home the previous week at the request of their mother. They both denied feelings about this, reporting several times when asked that it was "fine."

The play appears exactly as dictated by Susan and Bobby, who were enthusiastic about the project and worked quickly. The children in the play, Molly and Tim, both were described with similar characteristics as Susan and Bobby. Susan particularly seemed to identify with her character; several times during the dictation she referred to Molly as "I" or "me." Bobby and Susan also described their mother as being similar to the mother in the play.

I commented that it seemed like their father's departure was hard to talk about, which they both denied. After a long pause, I asked if they would like to begin the activity for the session, offering to talk more about their father if they wanted to later. They both agreed. I then explained that I thought we might be able to do something with drama this week, because

both siblings had participated in school plays in the past, and Susan was currently rehearsing a major role in her school's production of *Charlotte's Web*. I said that a play is an especially good way to think about roles, like roles with an alcoholic or addicted parent. I illustrated this by referring to a discussion about roles that we had during an earlier session. I asked Susan if she was allowed to act like herself when she was performing in *Charlotte's Web*. She said she was not, that her director was always telling her to "get into your role." I said that this was what roles are like: You feel like you have to act out a role even if you sometimes don't want to. I asked if this made sense and they nodded.

I then asked if they thought that they could make up a scene from a play, with the only rule being that it must somehow involve a family and drugs or alcohol. They said they thought they could, and began dictating enthusiastically as I wrote. We began with the list of characters. As they added dialogue, I asked them to identify the feelings of the characters. I wrote these feelings next to the characters' lines.

The O'Tarlaga Family
by Bobby and Susan T.

Cast of Characters

Tim O'Tarlaga: Brother/son, age 12, likes sports.

Molly O'Tarlaga: Sister/daughter, age 15, likes talking on the phone, going shopping, and being with friends.

Bill O'Tarlaga: Father, age 31, alcoholic (sometimes drinks, not in recovery), works but skips.

Vanessa O'Tarlaga: Mother, age 31, works, cleans, cooks.

Frank: Friend, age 13, likes sports.

Alison: Friend, age 15, likes talking on the phone, going shopping, and being with friends.

Worker's Comments

After the father was identified as an alcoholic, I asked what this meant—whether he was actively drinking or "in recovery." Earlier in the group we had discussed these terms, so I felt it was a good chance to review them. Susan replied that the father "sometimes drank, but that he's not in recovery." When I asked her what this meant, she said, "He hasn't really decided to try to work on changing things, like going to AA." I compared this to the difference between Bobby and Susan's mother before and after she entered treatment, and they both agreed it was the same.

While deciding on characters, Bobby and Susan argued repeatedly about ages, names, and other details. We had to leave several blank spaces at first because they could not agree. During one intense argument about how often the father skipped work, I stopped them to "take a break" and talk about the arguing. I said that this was a bit different from earlier sessions, because they usually don't have such a hard time agreeing. They replied that they were "always like this." I asked how it felt when they argued, and they both denied caring. Since Susan had resorted to calling Bobby names, I asked Bobby if that hurt his feelings. He said no. I asked Susan if she really meant those names, because she had been smiling when she said them. She said she was serious, smiling again rather affectionately at Bobby. I pointed this out and we all laughed. Susan then explained that although Bobby "gets on her nerves," she is "mostly" just joking with him—like with her friends. I asked Bobby if he knew this and he said yes.

I asked them why they thought it was harder to agree this week, and they said theydidn't know. As a follow-up, I asked if they might be thinking about their father leaving the house, since they had just talked about this before the meeting. They both denied this. I said that sometimes people have a harder time getting along when other important things are happening.

After this discussion, they went back to fill in the blanks we had left, and were able to propose and agree to compromises. Susan especially was more flexible. One example was the last name of the family. Earlier, they could not decide between an Irish or an Italian name, but they now agreed on a hybrid: O'Tarlaga.

Scene I

Home around dinner time. Father is one hour late getting home, and he just got there.
Mother: Why are you late?
Father: I had to work late, and then I went to the bar afterward.
Molly: Is it all right if I go over to Alison's house? (Molly doesn't want to see her parents argue.)
Tim: Can I go to the basketball court and shoot some baskets? (Tim wants to get out of the house.)
Mother: Yeah. (Mother knows they don't want to see an argument.)

Worker's Comments

I asked if this was like them, because Susan often said that she spent all her time at her friends' houses, and Bobby spent a great deal of time playing outside. They agreed.

Since we had gone over the roles often found in an alcoholic family in earlier sessions, I asked them what roles these kids might be playing. We had defined 4 roles: "Mom or Dad, Jr."; "Rebel"; "Invisible Child"; and "Family Clown." They said that they were both playing the "Invisible Child" role: trying to get out of the way and not be noticed.

Kids leave stage left and right.
Father: Why are you always picking on me? (Father feels mad.)
Mother: Because you need help. (Concerned.)
Father: I don't need help, I'm fine. (Father is talking like a big shot.)

Worker's Comments

I asked why the father was so mad, and Bobby said, "Because he doesn't want to admit he's an alcoholic." I asked what we had called that before, and they said "denial" in unison.

Mother: Yes, you do need help.
Father: No, I **don't**! I'm going to the bar.
Mother: **Don't go!**
Father: **I'm out of here!**

Father storms off the stage, just as Molly comes back. Alison is with her and they get there just as Dad speeds off in the car.
Molly: What's up with Dad, Mom? (Molly knows where he's going—feels worried.)
Alison: Yeah, he looks madder than a bull on a rampage! (Alison knows what is going on because Molly tells her. Feels worried and anxious.)
Mother: He just had an argument with one of his friends, and he's going to talk it out. (Mother feels sad because she knows he's going to get drunk and she's lying to Molly.)

Scene II

One hour later, Tim is home watching television while Alison and Molly are in Molly's room listening to music. Mother went shopping. The phone rings, and Molly turns the music down to answer. They are both still dancing.

Molly: Hello! (Happy.)

Cop: Is Mrs. Vanessa O'Tarlaga there? This is the Pine Valley Police.

Molly: She stops dancing and so does Alison. (Feels scared.) No, is there some sort of problem?

Cop: Yes, your father was in a serious accident and was arrested for drunk driving.

Molly: Did he hit anyone? (Feels angry at her father, sad because she realizes her father needs help, embarrassed because her father was drinking and driving.)

Cop: Yes, he hit a 10-year-old boy.

Molly: **Oh, my God!** Are they both all right? (Feels worried.)

Cop: The boy was hospitalized and your father has just a few scratches.

Molly: I'll have my mother call you as soon as possible. (She hangs up the phone and tells Alison what happened. She feels sad, worried, angry, confused.)

Alison: Are you all right? If you need anything, I'll be here for you.

Molly: Thanks, I'm all right. I've got to go to tell Tim. (Feels upset and ashamed, but doesn't want to worry Alison. She runs downstairs.)

Tim: How long were you on the phone? (Feels fine.)

Molly: Never mind that. Dad's been in an accident. (She tells him the story.)

Worker's Comments

I decided not to point out the clear similarity between this accident and their mother's accident. I felt it was too painful for them, and they both seemed tentative even including an accident in the play. Instead, I reached for the feelings of embarrassment and shame. I kept the discussion on the characters, rather than on Susan and Bobby. I asked if Tim and Molly were often embarrassed by their father's drinking. Susan said quietly, "Some-

times." I said that must be very hard for them. They returned to the activity rather quickly.

I also pointed out that Molly seemed to worry a lot about her friend's feelings. I asked if Molly had a chance to talk to her friend, like Susan had said she could talk to her friends. Susan said yes.

Scene III

Half an hour later, mother comes home. Molly tells her what happened, and they go down to the police station.

Mother: I'm Mrs. Vanessa O'Tarlaga. I'm here to bail my husband out of jail. (Feels angry and sad.)

Cop: Right this way.

(She goes to the cell.)

Mother: **Look what you've done!**

Father: I'm sorry, I need help. (Feels sad and ashamed.)

Mother: **Good.** I'm glad you finally realized that.

The father got help. He went to the treatment center and now he goes to AA meetings. The whole family is helping him deal with his problems. They deal with it too, by going to counseling and Alateen/Al-Anon meetings.

The father lost his job after the accident. He got a new one after one-and-a-half months. He wanted to take it "one day at a time." The family also takes things "one day at a time."

Worker's Reflections

Originally, Susan and Bobby ended the story on an even more rosy note. Bobby then doubted whether the father would be able to keep a job, and they added his job loss, plus the "one day at a time" statements. While they were talking about the father losing his job, I commented that it sometimes gets worse at home after an alcoholic gets sober. Bobby and Susan agreed to this tentatively. I asked if this was the case in their family, and they said no. I pointed out also that the whole family seemed to be working on taking care of themselves.

At this point their sister arrived to pick them up. I told them what an excellent job they had done, and said we would talk more about the play at our next session.

Questions for Class Discussion

1. What are some of the effects of parental alcoholism on children? What are some of the roles children play in families when there is alcohol and other drug abuse?

2. How can groups for children be beneficial? Compare this method to individual work.

Teaching Points

1. Many children affected by parents' substance abuse share particular coping patterns or functions in the family. Wegscheider (1981) described these patterns as family roles: the hero (overachiever); the rebel (scapegoat); the mascot or clown (placater), and the lost child. Children confused by their parents' behavior often try to make sense of the inconsistencies and often feel responsible. They may feel compelled to keep the "family secret" to the extent that they don't even talk to siblings about their worries.

2. In a group, children realize that there are others like themselves; they feel less isolated. They get information about drugs and alcohol that helps them make sense of their parents' problems and behavior (and perhaps feel less responsible). This information is also helpful in preparing them for their own decision making about drugs. They may get acquainted with self-help groups for children and adolescents through group participation.

In a group, there can be a range of coping styles and expressions. Children can learn from each others' opinions and questions, and can observe different reactions and experiment with new behaviors. They can get to their feelings at whatever level is safe—through play, through others, or through direct expression. Children learn to help each other, to make decisions together. These experiences build competencies for life. Drama (and other expressive methods that use symbolic and indirect means) can help children release painful feelings, integrate information, test new behavior, and gain self-confidence.

Suggested Readings

Black, C. (1981). *It will never happen to me.* Denver, CO: M.A.C. Printing and Publications Division.

Brown, S. (1985) Children with an alcoholic parent. In N. J. Estes & M. E. Heineman (Eds.), *Alcoholism: Development, consequences and interventions* (3rd ed.). St. Louis, MO: C. V. Mosby.

Children of Alcoholics Foundation, Inc., P.O. Box 4185, Grand Central Station, New York, NY 10163-4185. Tele: (212) 754-1656.

Duffy, T. (1985). Psychodrama in the beginning recovery from substance abuse. *Alcoholism Treatment Quarterly, 7*(2), 97-109.

Johnson, J. L. (1991). Preventive interventions for children at risk: Introduction. *International Journal of the Addictions, 15*(4), 562-586.

Macgowan, M. (1992). *Group work today to prevent group work tomorrow: Practice and research approaches to working with latency age children of substance abusers.* Paper presented for the 14th Annual Symposium of AASWG, Atlanta, GA, 1992 (Florida International University).

Sher, K. (1990). Psychological characteristics of children of alcoholics: Overview of research methods and findings. In Galanter (Ed.), *Recent developments in alcoholism, 9,* 301-326.

Wegscheider, S. (1981). *Another chance: Hope and health for the alcoholic family.* Palo Alto, CA: Science and Behavior Books.

Using Groups for Education, Support, and Stimulating Motivation for Change

Carter: Helping a Recovering Inmate Face Loss

Individual change often begins in groups, when clients let others help them with decision making. Participating in a recovery group can alleviate the pain of losses, help with the expression of ambivalence, and instill hope for finding a place in the larger community. Such a group can be particularly meaningful for men who have traditionally been undervalued and stigmatized in our society. Here, the worker facilitates a group culture of respect, client autonomy, and peer support.

Setting: Medium security, short-sentence men's prison.

Group members: Group of 12 self-selected prison inmates who are polysubstance abusers (50% primarily alcohol, 25% cocaine, and 25% heroin) with a median age of 26 and a racial composition of 7 white, 4 African American, and 1 Puerto Rican.

Client: A 30-year-old African-American male dropout, dependent for 16 years on alcohol and cocaine, with a record of five prison sentences.

Worker: A white male social worker who has specialized in group work, and who has extensive experience in corrections and substance abuse treatment.

Presenting problem: Deciding whether to separate from intimate partners who continue to abuse substances.

Case Record

The "Elmwood" House of Correction is a medium security, short-sentence men's prison in a predominantly white working class area. Under contract to the Department of Corrections, I led a substance abuse education-and-support group at Elmwood for self-selected members of the prison population. The group met for two 90-minute sessions weekly and focused on primary substance abuse issues. Members learned about the nature of addiction and recovery, were introduced to treatment resources such as halfway houses and self-help fellowships, and practiced the skills of active membership in a mutual aid group. The group was open-ended, with an average size of about 12 members.

Carter, the group member who is the focus of the critical incident analyzed in this study, is a 30-year-old African American whose father and grandfather were both violent alcoholics. Carter dropped out of school during the eighth grade at the beginning of his 16-year history of addiction to alcohol and cocaine. Over the course of this history, he served five prison sentences amounting to almost seven years. The arrest that led to Carter's current imprisonment was for distributing ("dealing") cocaine. Carter's wife of 12 years, who is also a cocaine addict, was arrested at the same time, but was released on probation.

Except for a month of spotty attendance at a Narcotics Anonymous meeting at a community center in his neighborhood, Carter has never been in treatment. Although he is a very bright, attractive, and personable man who has expressed a desire to "get ahead" and be a "real father" to his two daughters (ages 8 and 12, currently living with Carter's mother-in-law), Carter has never held a job.

During his first month in the group, Carter had been cynical and rarely participated. At the beginning of his second month, Carter's father died. Carter missed the two sessions following the death, but he came to the third and wept openly about his loss. He said that the actual loss of his father "woke up old feelings of loss." He explained that his father "died for us many years ago when he left us for the bottle." He then expressed sadness about repeating his father's pattern: "I've done the same thing—lost myself and my family to the bottle and the [freebase] pipe."

During the ensuing months, Carter gradually became a regular, high-participating member of the group. Increasingly, he viewed his losses as consequences of out-of-control substance abuse, and he seemed to accept the necessity for abstinence as a condition of recovery. He enrolled in both a GED high school program and a college-level computer programming course. During his third month, Carter began to formulate a post-release plan that included counseling, job training, and support from an uncle who is a longtime AA member. He also identified returning to his actively addicted wife, "Carla," as his most likely "pitfall" and "craving trigger." With the group's help, he began questioning his plan to return to the apartment he shared with Carla.

Throughout months four and five, Carter struggled with this decision. He told the group in detail about telephone calls and letters in which he tried unsuccessfully to persuade Carla to enter treatment. With the group's support, Carter had contacted a halfway house, but he had not made a decision to enter it. With his release date two weeks away, Carter seemed unusually withdrawn and preoccupied, and the following critical incident took place.

The group was discussing the need for planning the recovery. I said, "You seem deep in thought, Carter. What's happening?" Carter just shook his head. I allowed the silence to stretch on for about 15 seconds, then said, "You're getting out in two weeks, how's your planning going?" After another long silence, Carter said, "It seems like every time I talk about Carla here, everyone's saying I've got to leave her. That pisses me off, because I don't think you all understand what that means. Drugs or no drugs, the bitch has done a lot for me. We've been through a lot together. She helped me when no one else would, had my kids, . . . I can't just run out on her to save my skin." Red replied, "Well, maybe that's the best you can do is save your skin. The best for you and your kids. Better for your kids to have one parent alive than none." Carter's expression didn't change. After a brief silence, I said, "I think Carter's saying that it's easy for us to say, 'Save yourself,' but we're talking about leaving someone he loves. Is that right?" Carter nodded. I continued, "Well, I can understand that, and I admire the up-front way you've been struggling with this. I know what you went through when your father died, and now you're deciding to give up drugs and a whole way of life. You must be asking yourself how much loss is enough." Again, Carter nodded soberly. There was another silence.

Sensing some uncertainty in the group about how to be helpful, I decided to model an approach. I said, "I don't know about the others, but I'm not saying, 'You've got to leave her.' That really isn't my decision. It's much too tough a decision to make for someone else. You know yourself and Carla best. And deep down you probably know your own needs. Our role is: if you're having trouble with the decision, we can share our experiences and you can decide what applies and what doesn't. We can also let you know we care about what happens to you. But it's your decision, not ours." Tony said, "Anyway, I don't think we're telling you to do anything, man. Seems to me you're the one who's been saying you can't go right back to Carla. We just sort of backed you up on it." Others indicated agreement. I asked Carter if that was his impression. He answered, "Well, yes and no. I mean, I was testing out the idea, I was saying . . ." Red interrupted, "You were saying you were scared to go back to her. Which I don't blame you for. I've been there, man." Carter responded, "You been with your woman. How the f--- you know what's what about my woman? Carla has cut her using way down because she knows I'm coming home." Red said, "Calm down, man, I know it ain't the same. I know you're hurting. But let me ask you this: You've been asking Carla to go to detox for almost three months. Now it's only two weeks until you wrap up. Has she gone yet?" Carter shook his head no. Red asked, "Does it look like she's gonna go?" Again, looking somber, Carter shook his head.

I said, "You seem really worried about this," and Carter nodded. Joe said, "I hear that. I'd be worried too. But I can tell you this: You can't make another person recover. I've tried. Think about it. What if Carla had told you to go to detox before you were ready? Would you have gone?" "No way," said Carter. I glanced around the group and everyone looked engaged. I said, "It seems like a lot of people can relate to Carter's situation." Red said, "Right. My situation was . . . my last time out of jail I was really trying to make it, trying to stay clean and all, going to work, going to meetings every night. But Lisa's using, all the time saying, 'You care more about those Holy Rollers at meetings than you do about me.' But she won't go to a meeting. So I get home one night and she's really loaded. You can see it, her eyes, the slow way she moves. You can hear it in her voice, sort of pebbly. You can even smell it. And I'm having that sick gut feeling and thinking, why her and not me? I'm full of resentment. I know she's probably gotta a package right in the flour jar or some f---ing place. And I'm wondering who she got it from, and what she did for him to get it." [sympathetic nods]. Joe said, "It made you

lonely, right?" Red said, "Right. And I felt like I couldn't even get it on with her unless I got high too. I was remembering the few good times when we were both high and forgetting all the other times." Tony said, "You don't know if you're remembering the sex or the high." Carter asked, "So what happened?" Red said, "What happened? What do you think happened? I got high, I got laid, and next thing I knew, 'Heere's . . . Red!' Red's back in Elmwood for a return engagement." Tony said, "By popular demand." Carter joined the general laughter and then said, "I know what everyone is saying. I know you're trying to help." After a pause, he added, "Deep down I know you're right." Red said, "I knew we were right when you yelled at us, man. How many times have I yelled at you when I knew you were right?" [laughter]

I said, smiling, "What's your next step, Carter? Without trying to sway you [laughter], I want to point out that at the halfway house you could probably find people who could relate to you, like here." Carter said he would send the halfway house another note. I said that the group would follow up next session, and I commended members for pulling together on a difficult problem.

Carter arranged to go to the halfway house, but only after another session during which members, once again, used their own experiences to help him think through the consequences of returning directly to Carla. Members also continued to express great empathy for Carter's sense of loss, and toward the end of the session, Tony helped Carter rehearse breaking the news to Carla: "Just tell her it don't have to do with love. It has to do with what drugs do to you. Tell her you need to stay alive for your kids, and later, if she gets into recovery, well, who knows?"

I do not want to be overly optimistic about Carter's prospects. Although he has remained in the halfway house for almost a year, his situation indirectly points to gaps in social services for poor addicts. Carter was lucky indeed to find group support for continued treatment and to secure a bed in a halfway house. Even so, given the depth of Carter's attachment to Carla and to the old way of life, and given a dearth of health, housing, and employment services, further difficulties are likely.

Questions for Class Discussion

1. What is known about the impact of an intimate partner who continues to use drugs on the continued recovery of the clean partner?

2. What role does grieving over losses due to one's own addiction play in recovery? What are the kinds of losses people tend to experience due to their own addiction? How might other losses be connected to difficulty in recovery? What methods are useful in helping people to grieve these losses?

3. What challenges might a member of an undervalued group face in maintaining recovery?

4. What theoretical frameworks can be applied to this case?

Teaching Points

1. Abstinence is a precondition for recovery once clients have moved into substance dependence. Recovering individuals must put priority on abstinence in early recovery lest their ability to fulfill other roles be undermined (Brown, 1985; Hester & Miller, 1995; Washton, 1989). For many addicts, drugs, love, and sex are intertwined (Logan, 1992; Washton, 1989). Newly released inmates may be starved for intimate contact and comfort and therefore vulnerable to relapse.

2. Most substance abusers are brought to the threshold of recovery by losses, and then,

in the recovery, they must confront the likelihood of further losses, especially related to drinking and drug-using family members and associates. Resistance and false starts are expected in the grieving process.

When clients feel pressured to make separations before they are ready, resistance is driven underground. This is often true of clients who have been alienated from social supports and who distrust authority. When these clients feel coerced or when they suspect that their deepest feelings are not being respected, they are likely to respond by fighting, clamming up, or projecting a veneer of compliance, which is more deadly than open anger to productive group work. Thus, the first task in the case just described was to tap Carter's unexpressed feelings. This helped create a safe atmosphere for the expression of ambivalence. Once Carter's distress was out in the open, the other members were able to demonstrate their understanding and comfort him in loss.

3. The following is a partial list: poverty, losing structured time for meetings previously provided in prison, fewer services, no work history, friends who may be using, differential enforcement of laws by police and courts, actual and imagined intimidation by a formal treatment system, lower expectations regarding the prognosis for recovery, presence of drug dealers.

4. The group's understanding of Carla's status as a "craving trigger" owed something to a behavioral approach—specifically, to explanations of conditioning theory in some earlier sessions. The overall emphasis on peer support and modeling is consistent with social learning theory (Bandura, 1977), and turning to a concrete "next step" at the close of the session derives from cognitive-behavioral modalities

(McAuliffe & Albert, 1992; Zackon, McAuliffe, & Ch'ien, 1992). A number of theoretical frameworks inform the approach to Carter's case. An ego-developmental perspective probably heightened the leader's sensitivity to the death of Carter's father and its relation to Carter's own attempts to achieve fatherhood. This allowed the leader to make the connection for Carter and the group between the loss that first made Carter active in the group and the losses that he was currently facing. The unifying theme of his losses was the necessity of taking responsibility despite feelings of abandonment. Carter feared that being responsible would mean being lonely. By supporting his responsible decision making, the group showed Carter that taking responsibility might result not in loneliness, but in social acceptance.

5. The worker can be particularly effective in reaching for the client's ambivalence about leaving the partner, and in encouraging peer support rather than trying to force the client into an unwanted decision. Individuals who have become chronically dependent, whether upon substances or social agencies and institutions, require active support for autonomy, but this must also be responsive to the client's developmental level. Workers must show consistent respect for clients' intelligence, decision-making abilities, and good will. In addition to empathy for the difficulty of Carter's situation, the worker conveyed confidence in Carter's ability to select the appropriate help from his peers. The worker was demonstrating his confidence in the abilities of the other group members to supply the needed support. The members responded with sensitivity and with vivid personal stories such as Red's.

Their responses, partly because they *were* from peers, addressed with special relevance and force most of the points a worker might have made in individual case work with Carter. The main points included:

- that recovering individuals must put recovery first to be able to fulfill family roles;
- that for many addicts, drugs, love, and sex can become deeply intertwined;
- that the newly released inmate, starved for heterosexual contact and comfort, might be highly vulnerable to relapse;
- that a recovering person cannot take responsibility for another's recovery; and
- that separating from a loved one for the best of reasons can be very painful and can cause feelings of divided loyalty.

An additional overriding principle is that intensive support and repeated reminders of the reasons for therapeutic separations can make the separation process easier.

References

Bandura, A. (1977). Self-efficacy: Toward a unifying theory of behavior change. *Psychological Review, 84,* 191-215.

Brown, S. (1985). *Treating the alcoholic: A developmental model of recovery.* San Francisco: Jossey-Bass.

Hester, R. K., & Miller, W. R. (1995). *Handbook of alcoholism treatment approaches: Effective alternatives* (2nd ed.). Boston: Allyn and Bacon.

Logan, S. M. L. (1992). Overcoming sex and love addiction. In E. Freeman (Ed.), *The addiction process* (pp. 207-221). New York: Longman.

McAuliffe, W., & Albert, A. (1992). *Clean start.* New York: Guilford.

Parad, H. J. (Ed.). (1965). *Crisis intervention: Selected readings.* New York: Family Service Association of America.

Washton, A. M. (1989). *Cocaine addiction: Treatment, recovery and relapse prevention.* New York: Norton.

Zackon, F., McAuliffe, W. E., & Ch'ien, J. M. N. (1992). *Recovery training and self-help: Relapse prevention and aftercare for drug addicts.* Rockville, MD: National Institute on Drug Abuse.

Time Out: A Support Group for African-American Grandmothers Rearing Their Addicted Daughters' Children

A young mother's dependence on crack cocaine can have a pervasive impact across generations. Mothers and "crack babies" are only part of the picture. Grandparents, extended families, and neighbors may be burdened with the care of the children. This case illustrates the importance of support groups in helping grandmothers cope with their caretaking tasks and demonstrates methods for empowerment. It reflects the historic resilience of the African-American kinship network and shows the worker reflecting on his awareness of racial oppression and gender issues.

Setting: The group met at a neighborhood health clinic for two hours, once a week.

Group purposes: To support grandmothers who, because of their daughters' addiction to crack cocaine, were left with the rearing of their grandchildren. To help the grandmothers develop resources and strategies for meeting their responsibilities without jeopardizing their own survival.

Group members: Nine African-American grandmothers, ages 39–65 with low incomes, who were raising their grandchildren, ages 2–12. (Many of the children had emotional problems; some had significant medical problems due to their mother's drug use during pregnancy.) Initially three grandmothers approached the worker and asked for help in starting their own support group. They recruited other grandmothers.

Group leader: African-American male, with 28 years of clinical social work experience, who volunteered his time for three years to work with this group.

This case study began when the three grandmothers contacted me, stating that they needed assistance in starting their own support group. Their lives had been deeply affected by the entry into their homes of grandchildren whom they loved, but did not know—grandchildren who now depended on them. We agreed that I would work with the group, that we would meet for two hours each week at a local health clinic, and that the women would recruit as many new grandmothers as possible.

First Phase

At the initial meeting, the women arranged themselves around a table. I asked each to identify herself and tell the number and ages of the children in her care. As they spoke, it became clear that they had strong feelings of pain and anguish. Many became so emotional that they could not complete their introductions. All defined themselves as alone. Isolated from friends and extended family, they had no one to whom they could turn when the burdens of care became overwhelming or when their physical energies weakened. Mrs. Fort, a 39-year-old grandmother of three, shared her feelings with the group:

> It isn't right. My daughter is out there in the streets taking no responsibility for her kids. I'm at home with her kids, which is where she ought to be. This is supposed to be my time and your time. Look at us, old women before our time, and I hate it. [She started to cry, but

quickly resumed her composure.] Who said this was my job, why me? We must be fools. I sometimes wonder if my mind is gone.

As the weeks progressed, the group became a place where the women received emotional support, where their feelings were recognized as important and they could express them without fear of ridicule. Mrs. Greene, a 45-year-old grandmother of five, was not too talkative initially, but during the fourth group session offered the following comments:

> I don't have nobody I can talk to; I called my mother and she didn't want to hear my problems. Your mother is supposed to be there for you—not mine. I love my kids. As bad as they are with those drugs, I am there for them any way I can. My mother knows, but it shames her that she has a granddaughter on the streets, who has 3 babies to show for it. Why should I be the one? Nobody cares. If they do, they have a mean way to show it.

After several months, the women began to feel more comfortable with me and with each other. On one occasion, they discussed how easy it had become for them to talk together and how they enjoyed knowing that they would meet each week. Mrs. Adams commented:

> I resisted coming here because I have never been close to other women, including my sisters and my mother. Yet in here we look so much on how we feel and I can handle saying I did something wrong without feeling somebody would not like me because of what I said. Several times I thought about not coming back because when some of you started crying, I was about to go off, too. I have always been by myself. I did not think I would ever say to other people what I said here. I feel OK with you now, I guess I belong here.

Mrs. Amos added:

> I feel the same way. Some of you know how I resisted coming here. I don't like talking about my business, but sometimes you got to talk to somebody, it gets too heavy. The stomach can only take so much and no more. I even went to my church and tried to talk to my pastor about it. He made me feel like two cents' worth. Talked about how God's pleased and this was my cross to bear. I have to admit to you, I did not go back, and my church is important to me. It was all I had; one or two friends would let me talk to them, but even they got tired. Here, you all let me say everything and I don't worry so much now.

The women began to trust each other to the extent that they allowed each other's pains to be expressed. During one session, Mrs. Lomax, the acknowledged leader of the group, expressed feelings that generated a powerful exchange. Mrs. Lomax usually appeared in control, but it was clear this day that she was not functioning well. She had lost one daughter after five brain operations and was angry about the situation with her other daughter.

> The social worker who placed my daughter's children with me did a number on me. She said that my daughter was not a real addict, she was just experimenting, and I wouldn't have the three kids long because she'd be home soon. Well, three years later, I still got the kids and she's still more out than in treatment. She's struggling hard to die. My other daughter fought hard to live and still died. My husband left me when my daughter first got sick. He wouldn't help me with her or the other one. He split real quick. When she died, some of me died too, but I had to live for my other daughter. Look what she's doing to her life, my life and the kids' lives. When I first got my three grandkids, my sister told me I was a fool for taking them.

I should give them back to the social worker who brought them. But these are my grandkids and my mother would roll over in her grave. I can't let them go someplace else. It might eventually kill me, but so what?

Her comments stunned the group. Many proceeded to cry, including Mrs. Lomax herself. I commented that it was obvious she was experiencing some very real pains surrounding her losses, including a child and a husband, that her surviving daughter's behavior only extended her pain, and that it took real courage to bring those feelings forward.

At that point, two women went around the table and put their arms around Mrs. Lomax, who then really allowed her feelings to emerge. Her anguish was so intense that everyone in the group proceeded to ventilate their feelings. This outpouring lasted for several minutes, and eventually Mrs. Lomax said:

Something happened here to me tonight. I been hurting so long for so many things, but nobody would let me say them. Sometimes I feel like a nervous breakdown is about to happen. But tonight I couldn't hold it in any longer, you all wouldn't let me. Our children are killing us and it looks like only us can stop it. I love my daughter, but sometimes I really hate her, deep down inside. But I couldn't say that before, because nobody would understand, so I kept it inside, and it's been killing me slowly. But you ladies have been helping me and even I didn't know it. Mrs. Jackson over there called me one night after we left here and we talked for one hour about things, but mostly about our kids. Mrs. Fort came by my house one day and left some clothes for my two-year-old grandson. You all care about me and my cup is full right now. Something is happening to us right in front of our eyes. And I want to thank you. Sisters, I want to thank you.

Several women expressed their feelings about the group and how it helped to hear what the others had to say. Mrs. Jackson, a very quiet woman in her late 50s who had seven of her three addicted daughters' children, made the following comments, crying through most of it:

When I came the first time, I wasn't coming back because it was too painful to hear what everybody had to say. I told one of my friends that I get too stirred up and I already have a heart condition and maybe I shouldn't go back. But as you know I made all the meetings. My plate is full and sometimes it almost runs over. We all have our problems, but I know now that I'm not the only one. I now have a place where I can go just for me and that feels good. My husband died three years ago and I miss him a lot. He helped me so much with the kids. He did everything including cooking and changing diapers, anything that would help me, and he was a real man too. He worried about our daughters and asked where we did wrong. He had a heart condition, also. I think the worry and stress killed him and I hate my daughters because he died taking care of their children. I'm quiet and scared and shy, and I couldn't say that to people. Here I can and I thank you all. I feel better for the first time since I lost my Bennie.

Worker's Comments

My underlying assumption was that the women in the group could help each other and that it was my role as the social worker to help that process—not to do the job for them. I continued to state that the group really belonged to them, and that I would help them do whatever they wished to accomplish. I tried to establish an accepting, open atmosphere where they could feel free to talk with each other.

I offered to do some stress reduction exercises with them. They agreed, but seemed fearful until I explained that they would not be hypnotized but would be taught how to relax. After trying the exercise, they acknowledged how relaxed they were and decided to do it before each meeting.

Within a few months, the group had developed strong bonds. Being able to share their feelings openly and without shame or fear of ridicule, the women discovered the reason for the group's existence. They began a new process of self-discovery in the unfolding of their stories. Many of them functioned under great hardships that had begun to affect their physical and emotional health. They had too many responsibilities and too little support; they were required to provide care for too many children without any rest and relaxation. Some of the feelings they identified were depression, anxiety, hopelessness, helplessness, low self-esteem, and a sense of alienation and abandonment. It was important to help the members see the value in having those painful encounters with the past; the pain experienced in recalling those traumas would become part of the healing process.

In the group, the women developed meaningful relationships, which would serve as sources of strength and solace to draw upon whenever needed. As African-American women in similar situations, they could truly understand and support each other. I encouraged them to maintain their attachments outside the group, extending the interdependence they had built together.

Second Phase

The support group created an opportunity for the grandmothers to identify ongoing problems created by their current role as parent substitutes for their grandchildren. It also provided a forum to discuss problems created by life circumstances, poverty, race, and gender.

The grandmothers discussed their norms as Black women of their generation: they had been told that they had to be strong, that Black women have so many people depending on them that they have to keep their emotions "on hold," never letting anyone see them cry or appear weak. They were also told that anger was an emotion they could not express.

In the group, I encouraged different norms. I acknowledged the importance of being able to express their feelings, of being themselves. I invited them to talk about the significance of the African-American woman's life experience. The response was immediate, with several women expressing opinions:

Mrs. Lomax: Black women have always had it tough. I don't know a Black woman who has not had more than her share of sorrows, most times because we are women, and poor Black women at that. Racism took our sons and husbands from us, through drugs and alcohol. Our men can't get jobs, so they take it out on us and themselves. They sometimes kill us. And we have to be strong through all of that. I had a good job for 13 years before my daughter took sick; I lost my job because I had to take time off too many times to take her to the doctor. That could happen to anybody, but when it happened to me, I took it personal because I'm a Black woman and not too important.

Mrs. Fay: My husband was a good man, but he lost jobs because he was Black and did not belong to a union; we couldn't afford it. We didn't have food on the table sometimes because once people found out he was Black, the job suddenly disappeared. I had to be strong for him when the world stepped all over him. He stood up for me, but nobody else did. There were times when I wanted to hit somebody because he hurt so bad. When I cry now, it's for more than you see. Now I can cry openly and not be afraid of looking ugly and have makeup run down my face [everybody laughs].

We always take care of everybody else and put our needs last. Our mothers did it, their mothers before them, I do it, and if our daughters were OK, they would do it also. But I want out of this. I got pains that belong to someone else, and this is supposed to be my time. It ain't fair.

Something new had started to happen within the group. The women were beginning to identify specific feelings, some of which frightened them, as well as some deep-seated issues that they had not allowed before into their consciousness. Now they recognized that they needed to find new ways of coping.

One particular event catapulted this group into action at a different level: three women whom they had tried to recruit into the group died as a consequence of heart attacks. These attacks were brought on by malignant hypertension, unmanaged diabetes, and extreme obesity, all of which had developed since the placement of their grandchildren in their homes. The grandmothers were devastated when they learned of the deaths, and Mrs. Lomax expressed the sentiments of the group:

Is this going to happen to the rest of us? We tried our best to get them to join. How did we fail them? That could be one of us. We tried, but things were stacked against them and they didn't make it. They were prisoners in their own homes. Are we going to sit back and let this devil called crack cocaine take us down with our daughters? I had started to get to Mary, the one whose daughter attacked her for the food stamps to buy drugs. She would have liked us because she was so alone, where we were before we found each other. We have to stop doing things the way we have. We have to let our daughters go—turn them loose, and focus on how we can do better for ourselves and our grandkids.

That meeting marked another pivotal point in the group's progress. I shared my observation that the members had overcome their original inhibitions, and said it was wonderful to feel their bonding with each other and their respect for each other. They had grown closer and stronger and were now empowered to move on to other areas of concern.

Third Phase

It was very painful to accept, but the grandmothers agreed that they would always have primary responsibility for these children, because many of the daughters would never come back to resume care. The women prayed that the Lord would take away the craving for crack from their daughters before it killed them.

The women continued to put their grandchildren first and to make sacrifices for them. They worried that they might not live long enough to keep the children drug-free and get them ready for independence. They knew that if they did not take care of themselves, however, they would lose the children. They began to recognize what they could and could not do, to take responsibility without jeopardizing their own survival. They also asked for help in meeting the children's needs. Eighteen months after the group started, the women asked me to start a support group for their grandchildren. Mrs. Lomax once again voiced the concerns of the group:

Our grandchildren are very depressed. They don't understand why their mothers left them, and the other children at school make fun of them. They see us on television talking about their "bad" mothers. They love their mothers but they live with us, old women who are mad or sad most of the time, no money and no energy to do things with them. They have nightmares all the time and they lash out at each other. They need help real bad.

Mrs. Johnson, the 65-year-old great-grandmother commented:

My 12-year-old grandson is really troubled. He came home one day saying that the kids at school told him that his mother didn't want him and didn't love him. It was so sad to listen to him crying at night when he thought I was asleep. I tell him that his mother loves him, but she isn't well and can't take care of him. That's all I can do. He needs a man in his life to help him over these bad times. We don't know who his father is, never did know. His little sisters are very rebellious and angry all of the time. I don't know what to do anymore. One night, the 6-year-old girl asked me, "Granny, do you hate keeping us?" I almost died. How do you answer her truthfully so she won't hurt? I finally told her, "No, it is hard sometimes, but I love each one of you and I will always take care of you." That's OK for awhile, but a week or so later, she will ask me again. She needs therapy and I know it hurts her to be without her mother, but it's not my fault. It's not my fault. I can say that now, but not before this group took me in.

These and other comments by the grandmothers reflect their coping skills, their learning to assess their capabilities and resources, to reject blame, and to set limits.

Mrs. Jackson very timidly shared with the group an event that was very meaningful for her and was an indication of her own change:

My 38-year-old daughter called me today from the county hospital. We heard from her last year around this time. I have her five children and they saw her once last year. You didn't know if she was dead or alive. Out of the blue she calls. She has a new baby but it was born too early and she wanted me to bring it home. Can you believe it? I said, "No, hell no" [the women loudly applauded her]. A year ago, I couldn't say that. I never felt good about saying no to anybody. But I did this time, and all because of you here, I could say no, and mean it [she started crying and two women went to her]. I

feel sorry for the baby. Sounds like he is pretty sick if he came early. But I can't take him. I feel bad, but I guess I might feel worse if I took him. I guess if I felt like this before, I wouldn't be in the situation I am now. I love my grandkids, but I love me a little more now. I hope it lasts and I don't go weak.

This was an important moment for Mrs. Jackson and the other women in the group. Learning to say "no" for all the right reasons was hard, but possible. I used this opportunity to remind the grandmothers how far they had come individually and as a group since we started years ago. In their own struggles to survive and through their sharing and understanding of each others' pain, they had become focused and empowered.

Fourth Phase

A recent development in the group is the recognition that the members have something to offer to other women who are struggling with the same issues. The women are currently seeking community funding to develop a refuge for grandmothers, similar to respite care programs for battered women. They wish to establish an outreach program for women who are alone and are suffering silently. They have moved to a level of advocacy on behalf of all women who become surrogate mothers late in their lives and at a time when their resources are limited.

The Role of the Social Worker

In this case study, the reality of race and gender was apparent and had to be acknowledged. As an African-American male therapist, I had to confront my own awareness of the historical and contemporary issues pertinent to African-American women, and, secondly, I had to establish for them my own relationship with and respect for African-American women.

After joining the group and eventually developing some confidence and trust with the women, I invited 16 of them to dinner at a local restaurant. I set no limits to their choices, and we enjoyed ourselves immensely. When we met the following week in group session, they were effusive in their thanks to me for a night out on the town. One of the women voiced a group consensus: "You have to excuse us, but we are not used to Black men being nice to us, and you made us feel special."

That statement reminded me that these women are indeed extraordinary. They have survived unspeakable traumas by some men in their lives and were left with little hope of acquiring the admiration, love, and respect of other Black men. My response to them was that I had high respect for Black women and, because I had enjoyed excellent relationships with Black women in the past, I did not expect our relationships to be any different.

As an African-American male, my awareness of racial oppression is firmly imprinted in my consciousness. I am also culturally aware of the oppression of women. In my work with this group, I made every effort to use this knowledge and to interact in a way that showed my caring and my regard of the members as equals. I value greatly the opportunity to have worked with these powerful women.

Questions for Class Discussion

1. What does the case illustrate about the impact of drug addiction across generations? Who was affected and in what way?

2. What are the characteristics of crack cocaine that make it such a worrisome drug?

3. Why is crack cocaine so ravaging in low-income neighborhoods? Relate the socioeconomic and political factors to the crack epidemic.

4. What stress is inherent in the caretaking role imposed on these grandmothers at this stage of their lives? Do they have particular health risks? How is their role reinforced by traditional expectations for African-American women? What would be true of expectations for other socioeconomic and ethnic groups?

5. Assess the role of the worker in this case. What values and skills did he demonstrate that have particular relevance for working with families affected by substance abuse? For working with a support group?

6. How was this group beneficial for the grandmothers? What phases did they go through in their work?

7. How important was it to provide members with information about addiction? Would you have recommended Al-Anon to these members? Instead of the group, or in addition to the group? Discuss.

8. How do you see the worker's self-disclosure here? Does his socializing with the clients raise boundary issues? If yes, how? If no, why not?

Teaching Points

1. Drug-dependent parents cannot care properly for their children, both because they are high on drugs and because they are preoccupied with securing them and the money to pay for them. Children may be left at home unsupervised for long periods, with no daily routines for eating, bathing, or going to bed. Physical safety is often an issue in that they may wander outdoors, allow strangers into the house, hurt one another, or hurt themselves in household accidents. Grandparents, extended family, and neighbors may be burdened with the care of the children, despite their own needs and limited resources.

2. "Crack" is a smokeable form of cocaine. This "route of administration" of the drug

into the lungs creates a more intense "high" than cocaine used in crystalline, which is administrated nasally. Unfortunately for the user, this more intense "high" is short-lived (often only 10–15 minutes) and leaves the person craving more crack almost immediately. This property of the drug is thought to create a powerful psychological dependence in the user. "Drug-seeking" behavior also becomes a central dynamic for the crack user and eclipses all other concerns.

3. The crack cocaine epidemic creates numerous survival problems for African-American and other families, especially in low-income neighborhoods. Parents find it very difficult to keep their adolescents from succumbing to the lure of drugs from the streets. The quick and intense high of crack is seductive, and it has been made readily accessible. It is inexpensive (often less than $10 for a chunk or "rock"), easy to use (empty plastic soda bottles can be used as "pipes" for smoking), and distributed widely in poorer communities preyed upon by drug dealers. Poverty, unemployment, oppression, and a sense of hopelessness contribute to drug use and drug dealing. Related crime and deaths, especially for teens and young Black males, are tragic consequences.

4. Traditionally, African-American women have been the stronghold of the family. In the midst of poverty and oppression, they have nurtured and supported everyone, generally without complaint. Extended, demanding child care responsibilities for grandmothers, however, can take an emotional and physical toll. Risk of heart disease is high for African-Americans; according to *Boston Globe* stories (July 6, 1993, and September 7, 1993), the risk is 68% greater for Black women than white women, and life expectancy is about seven years less.

5. In this case, the worker demonstrated principles of self-determination, mutual aid, and respect for human dignity and worth. These principles are vital in combatting the stigma of drug addiction, especially when coupled with experiences of oppression. The worker in this case was sensitive to racial and gender issues and sociopolitical history. He was flexible, respectful, and responsive to the evolving phases of individuals and the group. The purpose of the group was to help develop coping skills, making it a support model. (Therapy and support groups have a number of therapeutic factors in common.) The worker recognized that the healing process for these grandmothers involved the release of feelings, self-reflection, reworking of past experiences, as well as support, affirmation, consciousness-raising and, eventually, social action.

6. The group helped the grandmothers feel less alone in their unexpected life task. They gained support from each other. They explored their role within the sociopolitical context. As they told their stories, they became empowered to act on their behalf and to advocate for their grandchildren and other grandmothers.

Group phases: The group formed a relational base through the expression of their common pain and burden. They experienced a period of empathy and support. They shifted into consciousness raising around their role as Black women in the family and society. They shared experiences of oppression. Finally, they moved into a phase of social action, in which they developed a program of respite care for grandchildren and grandparents.

7. Information about addiction could help the grandmothers understand their daughters' problems and guide them in their responses and obligations. In particular, AA could help in relieving the women's sense of responsibility and guilt for their daughters' addictions. The group was unique, however, in its ability to bring African-American women together. Having a common history and a common task, they could understand and support each other fully, as no other fellowship could.

8. The worker, an African-American man, responded to the group's request for sponsorship and structure. He helped build an environment where the members could express feelings without judgment. He demonstrated his care, respect, and belief in these women to manage their affairs. He worked to understand their roles and their experiences as African-American women. By taking them to dinner, he helped them celebrate their success and their grace. The worker maintained his function in the group, combining closeness and formality.

Suggested Readings

Berrick, J. D., Barth, R. P., & Needell, B. (in press). A comparison of kinship foster homes and foster family homes: Implications for kinship foster care as family preservation. *Child Welfare Review*. New York: Columbia University Press.

Garvin, C. (1987). *Contemporary group work*. Englewood Cliffs, NJ: Prentice Hall.

Gitterman, A., & Shulman, L. (1994). *Mutual aid groups, vulnerable populations, and the life cycle* (2nd ed.). Itasca, IL: F. E. Peacock.

Hines, P., & Boyd-Franklin, N. (1982). Black American families: A clinical perspective. In M. McGoldrick, J. Pearce, & J. Giordano (Eds.), *Ethnicity and family therapy*. New York: Guilford.

National Black Child Development Institute (1989). *Who will care when parents can't? A study of Black children in foster care*. Washington, DC: Author.

McKay, N. Y. (1992). Remembering Anita Hill and Clarence Thomas: What really happened when one Black woman spoke out. In T. Morrison (Ed.), *Racing justice, engendering power*. New York: Pantheon.

Toseland, R., & Rossiter, C. (1989). Group interventions to support caregivers: A review and analysis. *The Gerontologist, 29*, 438-448.

Vardi, D., & Buchholz, E. (1994). Group psychotherapy with inner-city grandmothers raising their grandchildren. *International Journal of Group Psychotherapy, 44*(1), 101-122.

Psychodrama in a Residential Treatment Center: Working with Ambivalence

This vignette can be used the whole way through, along with the discussion questions, or it can be read only to the point where the asterisks appear. In the latter case, students can then be asked to take on the role of the worker and respond to the questions: How do you feel? What do you think? What do you say? Students may also be asked to stand in Jack's shoes, or in the shoes of other group members, using the same questions. The vignette captures the ambivalence that often appears when clients are challenged to "work" in treatment. It also illustrates the worker's ability to modify therapeutic tasks to make them more manageable.

This incident occurred at the beginning of a psychodrama session that was mandatory for all members of the residence. The psychodrama director/worker described the group as using drama to help them explore their AODA use and to learn skills for getting and staying alcohol-and-drug-free. The worker said psychodrama could be an interesting and powerful method, but added that she would not put people on the spot to perform. She did encourage them to participate as much as they could and asked what they thought of what she said.

Jack: How come when people leave this group, they're depressed? I've never been to this before, but last week when people came downstairs it looked to me like they were depressed.
Worker: Hmm, let's see. [to the group] Those of you who were here last week: What do you think about this? Were you depressed?
Group: [noncommittal]

Worker: Well, let me remember last week. The drama was about someone who really didn't have anybody in his life to help him in his recovery. He didn't have much of a family. It was kind of depressing.

But it's not always sad. The drama comes from the group, from the stories of your lives as you work on recovery.
Annie: Can't we do what they do in the music group?
Worker: What do they do in music group?
Annie: Well, you lie down on the floor and they play music.
Lisa: And you fall asleep . . . .
Worker: Well, I suppose sometimes you *need* to fall asleep. This is hard work. Sometimes, you need to plow right in and . . . [hopeful].
Jack: Well, I guess I rained on your parade.

*   *   *   *   *

Worker: [enjoying the metaphor] I don't think you did. I think you put up the umbrella.
Group: [sighs—visibly relaxed]
Worker: Let me make a suggestion of what we can do today. What if you each thought of one thing you wanted to accomplish in the next day or two, something that would move you along in your recovery. Find a partner that you would like to talk to about this. You may talk in here or go out in the lounge area outside. I'll call you back in 15 minutes and we'll decide where to go from there.

The energy of the group increased as members talked together in pairs. After 15 minutes, the group came back and one member agreed to rehearse his action—making a phone call and asking someone to be his sponsor. He chose someone from the group to play his potential sponsor, dialed the phone (prop), and nervously started talking. The group members identified with his difficulty in asking for help and were very involved.

Questions for Class Discussion

1. What do you think the worker felt when the member challenged the effect of the group? How do you understand this member's behavior? Is this resistance? Denial? Explain.

2. Should the members be confronted with their avoidance of the reason they are there—their drug and alcohol problems?

3. Did Jack play an important role for the group? If so, explain.

Teaching Points

1. The worker probably felt on the spot. She may have felt annoyed, angry, or scared about the criticism of her group (and her competence). As a result, she could have become more authoritarian ("You have to be here"), retaliatory ("It's your problem"), or defensive about the importance of psychodrama or the group. Resistance usually stems from apprehension about a situation. It can take many forms—confrontation of the worker, joking, distractions, horseplay, etc. It is usually a means of protection from pain or fear. It can also be a way of testing the safety and limits of the group. In this case, attendance was mandatory, but members had a choice about their level of participation as well as the direction of the drama(s).

2. The worker asked them to examine their resistance and to negotiate a way that work could be done. This was a confrontation that demanded work, but was not coercive. Work on substance abuse problems can be done in a variety of ways—not always serious or intense. Suggestions for work in dyads and for enactment of vignettes both respected the members' fears and helped them accomplish tasks that they could put into action for their recovery.

3. Jack might be a spokesperson for the group. Although he looks like a troublemaker and a spoiler, he can be an ally to the worker insofar as he expresses the feelings of the others. If the worker is attentive to him, others will see her respect, which can be generalized to them. In addition, her exploration of his issue and its universality can address the concerns of the whole group (alcoholism is depressing; recovery can be depressing). The worker explored Jack's feelings with him and the group. It became clear that the other members were exhausted, scared, or depressed and were not willing to participate in a "heavy" drama that day. They were able to take on a task that was broken into smaller, more manageable pieces and come together around the enactment of a vignette at the end.

Suggested Readings

Breton, M. (1985). Reaching and engaging people. *Social Work with Groups, 8*(3), 7-21.

Duffy, T. (1992). Psychodrama in beginning recovery from substance abuse. *Alcoholism Treatment Quarterly, 7*(2), 97-109.

Kellerman, P. (1983). Resistance in psychodrama. *Group Psychotherapy, Psychodrama and Sociometry, 32*, 30-43.

Milgram, D., & Rubin, J. (1992). Resisting resistance: Involuntary substance abuse group therapy. *Social Work with Groups, 15*(1), 95-110.

Shulman, L. (1992). The skills of helping: Individuals, families and groups (3rd ed.). Itasca, IL: F.E. Peacock.

Brazilian Immigrants:
An Outpatient Alcohol Education Group

The following process recording is of a mandated alcohol education group conducted in Portuguese and attended by four Brazilian men. The participants tell their stories in an engaging, straightforward manner. The recording highlights the interface between cultural issues and substance abuse, the special circumstances of immigrants, and the implications of national policies and law enforcement. It challenges the student to think of group dynamics, the role of the group leader, and working within different cultural contexts.

Description of the Group

This is a court-mandated 16-week alcohol education program for first-time DUI offenders. Participants were four male, middle-class Brazilian immigrants, ranging in age from 22 to 56, who have lived in the U.S. between two and seven years. The members were attending a Portuguese-speaking, all-Brazilian group after four weeks of participation in a Spanish-speaking group. The main issues addressed were the cultural identity of the group and the cultural aspects associated with alcohol use. Differences between American and Brazilian laws regarding the use of alcohol were discussed, as were such shared experiences as the migration process, culture shock, economic and social status in the U.S., and the struggle for employment. (Most Brazilian immigrants work as dishwashers, janitors, or waiters. Most of them intend to make some money and then return to Brazil.)

This group model reflects the theory and methodology of "conscientization" of the Brazilian educator Paulo Freire. This method is characterized by the use of group discussion to increase autonomy and to empower individuals through the sharing of common history and discussion of different points of view.

Background of Session

This is the first session since the group became all-Brazilian. It took place at a large table in the basement of the local substance abuse agency. The group leader, who is bilingual and bicultural, opened the session, presenting himself as a Brazilian psychologist and a doctoral student currently doing research on the local Brazilian community. He invited the participants to talk about themselves and about their experiences as immigrants.

The first to talk is Pereira, 32, a very articulate man with an expressive voice and youthful appearance.

Pereira: I was born in Belo Horizonte and before coming here I had a small business with some friends, selling beer. It went well for some time, but the speculation with the prices of beer made it impossible for us to compete with bigger companies and we went into bankruptcy. I was in despair. I was at a party one night and an uncle of mine was saying in a loud voice that he could bring anyone to the U.S. without a passport. I bet with my friends that I would be the next one to come, so I am here. I thought, well, I'll go to the U.S., stay for a year or so, pay my debts and return to Brazil . . . I had a tendency to drink, but in Brazil, I used to drink without getting drunk. Here, I drink too much. Life here is no life: women are difficult to meet and the ones you meet are willing to go with anyone. It's a new country, with totally different rules. One takes a punch in the face (*uma traulitada*) when one comes here.

The second person to talk is Joao, 56, born in Luz, Minas Gerais. Joao is the oldest of the group and speaks with the strong accent of the rural part of Minas. He says the reason he came to the U.S. was to grow financially.

Joao: I was born in an Adventist family, a very religious family, and I have not been successful in the U.S. First, I lost my daughter in an accident. Then, my wife left me. I had two accidents at work, breaking my nose and right arm. I have had surgery twice that cost me "blood and sweat" (*gotas de sangue misturada com suor*). Finally, Immigration went to my work place, going after all Brazilian workers, and I lost my job. I am a religious man, not an alcoholic, but the last year was a heavy and unlucky year (*foi o ano do peso, o ano do azar*). I was taking Holypinol prescribed by the doctor for insomnia and one night, while working, I took a pill with a bit of Kahlua, a woman's liquor, and then drove home. As I was parking the car, the police stopped me and I got arrested.

Antonio, 32, is a dark, tall man, with coarse features and a calm voice. He says he was born in Governador Valadares, Minas Gerais, "a city where everybody talks about the U.S. Believe me, it is a fever, a disease." He says he considers himself an alcoholic.

Antonio: I drink well (*Eu bebo ben*, meaning "I drink a lot"). Here in the U.S., there is a law against the use of alcohol. And with an arrest and without a driver's license, one cannot get a job in this town and this is difficult for Brazilian immigrants. In the town where I live, there is no public transportation. Here in the U.S., everybody has a car.

The fourth participant is a young man in his twenties, nervous and tense, talking fast and never looking anyone in the face. Carlos says that he has been drinking since age 14, adding that "different from the U.S., in Brazil everybody can buy alcohol." His talk is poignant and full of resentment.

Carlos: I was living well, going to college, preparing to be an engineer, working in a multinational company. I had a car, my own apartment, a credit card, and a good bank account. Then a new man was elected president and a new economic plan came. The factory where I was working reduced its employees from 1,300 to 600 and I lost my job. I would like it if the country had more jobs, more education, less corruption. I have a hard life here in the U.S. I am lonely, too, and the first impulse is to pick up the telephone and call everybody, family, friends, everybody back home. Here, I have no friends, I mean, healthy friends. Here, it is just work and work.

One night I was coming back from a party. I had some *cachaca* (home-brewed sugar cane alcohol) and the police stopped me. That's why I am here. But you see, in Brazil a truck driver can be so drunk that when the police stop him, he can't even stand on his feet. The greatest number of accidents happen there because of alcohol. If the law in Brazil was as tough as it is here, these accidents wouldn't happen. But, in Brazil, if someone has a good financial situation, he is not going to be arrested. Here in the U.S. the law applies to everybody. In Japan too, people don't drive drunk because they have moral principles. I am changing now. I believe I can change my way of life and I am happy to be participating in this program. It is expensive, very expensive, but it is worth the price, because I am paying for my education.

Group Leader: [Wondering if other group members perceive things the same] Is it true that the law against driving drunk in Brazil is different from the United States?

Antonio: That's true, I heard about a case last week in Brazil: a guy was driving drunk and killed three children. He posted bail and was free, without even losing his license.

Pereira: I agree. Here in the U.S. it can take some time, but sooner or later the police will arrest you if you are driving drunk. I cannot imagine a program like this one in Brazil. In Brazil, if you are poor, you cannot pay for the program, and if you have some money you pay a lawyer and escape the obligation of attending the program.

Carlos: In Brazil, people prefer to pay. See my case, I had a fight with a girlfriend of mine. She hit me; I hit her in the face, and she called the police. When the police came, I paid a bribe and was allowed to go free. I came out on top (*sai bonito da historia*). That's the way things are.

Pereira: An American friend of mine was asking me why I came to the U.S. and I told her I wanted to buy a house. . . . You have to work a lot, but if you do you can get what you want.

Group Leader: [curious about the participants' perceptions of U.S. values] So is it true that in the U.S., if you work hard, you can succeed?

Pereira: If you are a bachelor, if you left your family in Brazil [as he did], especially now with the *Plano Real*, it will take at least ten years for you to succeed. Here in the U.S. one has no life: you work and sleep, work and sleep. My goal now is simply to pay off the debts I made to come here and go back to Brazil. When I left Brazil I was crazy: now I am aware of myself, I know myself and I consider myself a new man. Mentally, I grew up a lot.

Carlos: You know, everybody has his personality, his way of doing things. My brother is living here in the U.S., too, living in Miami. He is married, has an apartment, a good

job, and he is doing very well. He has no bad habits and he has a goal. I am different. I am the only one in my family that drinks, and I spend all the money I earn. I like cars, I enjoy life, and I can't do physically hard work.

Group Leader: What do you think is the relationship between personal values, personal power, and recovery from alcoholism?

Joao: When I came here I took a beating (*chicotada*), but I believe that everything that happens to us has a meaning. I consider everything that happened to me to be a blessing of God. They say that alcoholism can't be cured, but I promise God that nobody will ever see me putting a drop of alcohol in my mouth anymore. I believe in the Almighty God, and nobody will ever have the privilege of seeing me drink again. God will not permit it, because He is the Light and the Power.

Carlos: I can say that I knew the law. Everybody told me to be careful, but you never think things will happen to you. People said to me, you're an alcoholic, and I laughed. Who, me? I got mad at people who said this. It is ugly, it is ridiculous, but you have to admit to yourself that you are an alcoholic.

Pereira: They say that alcoholism has no cure. One must learn (*voce tem que botar na sua cabeca*) that even if you spend three or four years without a drink, if you have the first one, you will drink too much. This is the truth.

Antonio: In Brazil, I spent three years in AA. I saw people who had been five years without alcohol who had a drink once and ended up lying in the gutter (*terminou na sarjeta*). Myself, I went to a party the other day and drank so much that I couldn't go back home. I know a guy from Valadares and he is an alcoholic. He is married to an American woman and has been living here for 12 years now. He has nothing: no documents (his wife has refused to sign any), so he can't go to Brazil to visit his relatives. That's no life. I think that alcohol is a drug, a stimulant like any other. When I drink a few beers, I am not the same person.

Pereira: It's like a drug, indeed. I went to a party and after the first beer I could feel I wasn't the same person. I entered into an emotional state. I got depressed. It was like a trip, I was back with my family again, could feel them next to me. Sometimes it is the opposite; if I drink, I forget my family. You see your body and mind as separate; you are in the air (*fica aereo*). You feel different emotions; you remember a song; you're tripping. I believe that the cure for alcoholism is the knowledge that there is no cure. When you don't fear alcoholism, you drink again. If you believe there's no cure, you're cured.

Joao: You must believe in God, creator of land and sky. In Him one finds the power to correct his mistakes, failures, illusions. If you ask God with faith and love, God will save you. In Him you can trust because He has the Power; every moment one must appeal to Him, because everything has a cure.

The session is over. We make arrangements for the next session and prepare a brief agenda of future issues.

Questions for Class Discussion

1. If you were the leader, which themes would you be trying to keep in mind?

2. How might culture and ethnicity influence the style of leadership and member participation?

3. How could the leader follow up on the contributions of each member? What could he say to seek clarification, to intervene on an affective level? Would a focus on affect be culturally appropriate?

Teaching Points

1. Four themes would be especially important.

Cultural Context

- Diversity within cultural group: age, race, class, reason for migration, legal status, degree of family fragmentation, stage of acculturation, future orientation (remain in U.S. versus returning to homeland).

- Impact of political and economic situations in Brazil: hyperinflation, underemployment, low wages, high cost of living, "pervasive uncertainty."

Immigrant Experience

- Migration as an adaptive response to economic/political/social and/or family situations.

- Migration as a traumatic experience with multiple losses: family members, language, culture, and support systems; perhaps also loss of status, profession, and religion.

- Initial culture shock; stages of acculturation (adjustment, adaptation, settlement); variations of acculturation (integration, assimilation, separation, marginalization).

Stressors

- Economic—finding employment, financial responsibilities for family in Brazil.

- Cultural—differences in mores, values, systems, pace of life.

- Social—isolation, loneliness, and "invisibility"; absence of family, friends, informal networks, social services.

- Legal—if undocumented, fear of deportation and risk of financial exploitation.

Alcoholism

- Differences in laws and enforcement in the two countries; need to educate immigrants regarding strict enforcement in U.S.

- Use of denial as common response of substance abusers; added complexity if

individual seeks to explain pattern of use in terms of cultural norms; challenge to practitioner to differentiate between cultural practices and denial.
- Catholic and Protestant attitudes toward abstinence and controlled drinking.
- Views of alcoholism as a disease and as a social problem; implications of failure/victory in addressing alcoholism; moral and cultural aspects of failure.
- Concept of shame in Latino culture; importance of honor, confession, testimony.

2. The worker was following a Freirian model. Underlying principles of Freirian theory and methodology state that all individuals have the capacity to think critically about their world and act creatively to transform it; education is not a "neutral" process, but should be one of empowering individuals to move toward new possibilities and a fuller life, both individually and collectively. This would probably result in a less directive and more reflective leadership style than that of many leaders trained in the U.S. with a "therapeutic," psycho-educational, or educational model.

3. The leader might help the group move forward by commenting on the type of interaction he sees in the group and how it could facilitate or impede group cohesion, individual autonomy, and critical thinking about the self, the world, and others. Moreover, asking clients for clarification about their statements (which leave many points implied but unstated in this process recording) would help them reflect on their beliefs and feelings in a deeper way. The themes identified in the first teaching point offer rich material for exploration by the worker.

Reaching for the affective content would be appropriate from a cultural point of view:
- Within the Brazilian culture, expressing one's emotions is considered both natural and healthy. Many Brazilian immigrants experience Americans as somewhat cold and distant, and miss the opportunity to speak freely of their feelings.
- The leader could explicitly acknowledge, normalize, and then further explore the pervasive themes of isolation, loss, and loneliness, which are experienced by most immigrants.
- The leader could explore how each of the men would feel or does feel accepting the label of "alcoholic," "problem-drinker," or "a person who has trouble when drinking occurs." What would have to happen in each man's life to lead him to this conclusion? Would the conclusion be associated with embarrassment or shame? How would others (family, friends, acquaintances) view the man, and how would that make him feel?

If the leader wished to use more clinical therapeutic interpretations and interventions, however, he would need to consider how the culture and class backgrounds of the participants might influence their understanding of formal mental health counseling.

Suggested Readings

Freire, P. (1970). *Pedagogy of the oppressed.* New York: Seabury.

Margolis, M. (1994). *Little Brazil.* Princeton, NJ: Princeton University Press.

Lynch, E. (1992). Developing cross-cultural competence. In E. Lynch & M. Hanson (Eds.), *Developing cross-cultural competence* (pp. 35-59). Baltimore, MD: Paul Brookes.

McLaren, P., & Leonard, P. (Eds.). (1993). *Paulo Freire: A critical encounter.* London: Routledge.

Philleo, J., & Brisbane, F. L. (Eds.). (1995). *Cultural competence for social workers: A guide for alcohol and other drug abuse prevention professionals working with ethnic/racial communities.* CSAP Cultural Competence Series 4, DHHS Publication No. (SMA) 95-3075.

Mandated Treatment: Working with Denial and Projection in a DWI Group

Involuntary clients often deal with their anger and fear by projecting their feelings onto individuals and events outside themselves. Though the worker's task is to help clients understand their feelings and accept responsibility for their behavior, timing is important—confronting clients too soon may have a polarizing effect. This case illustrates a critical incident when group members avoid discussion of another member's relapse and its consequences. Some strategies are offered for dealing with denial and projection.

Background

Josh explained to the group how he got caught driving while intoxicated and without a license over the weekend. He said that he was three blocks from his house, stopped at a light, when a kid who was hanging at the corner ran up to his car. (This corner was recently targeted by the police because of drug trafficking problems.) Josh stated that he told the kid to go away and then continued driving when the light turned green, but saw the flashing blue lights of the cruiser almost immediately. The police pulled Josh over to see if he had just been involved in a drug deal. They noticed that his breath smelled of alcohol and proceeded to test to see if he had been drinking. Josh said to the group, "I didn't put up a fight. I was drunk and I was caught."

Bart: Akron cops are such bastards.
Worker: It seems you have some anger toward the cops.
Bart: They are such idiots. What are they bothering Josh for? How come they didn't go after the kid selling the drugs?

Worker: What about the fact that Josh was driving while intoxicated without a license?
Bart: Well, he shouldn't have been driving, but the cops were looking for a drug bust, and they didn't even go after the people selling the drugs.

The worker asked the group members why they were focusing on the police instead of Josh's DWI arrest. The worker pushed them to acknowledge that a third such arrest was a real possibility for everyone in the group, and asked them how they could avoid this. The men said that they had stopped drinking, so they didn't have to worry about getting another DWI.

Questions for Class Discussion

1. What is your understanding of the dynamics or meaning "underneath" the group's dialogue?

2. What additional questions could the worker ask to help the group members gain insight into their own reactions?

Teaching Points

1. In the example that one of the men gave, members were faced with the reality of their problem. They projected blame outward onto others—the police, the drug-dealing kid—to avoid their own discomfort and responsibility. Their response may be understood as part of their denial, which offers self-protection from the gravity and shame of their problem. Denial involves an "alternative reality" or alternative explanation so that the person is protected from painful facts (Bean, 1981). The worker is confronting them with the real-

ity of what happened. She is asking them to look at their projection and to admit that this could happen to them.

2. The worker could sensitively ask them to consider their reaction to the incident and analyze their feelings and fears about it. She could do this by asking them to consider questions such as:

   - Why was it so difficult to look at Josh's part in this incident? Could they see themselves there? Under what circumstances?
   - If they had stopped drinking and using drugs, how had they done so? To what did they attribute their success?
   - When were they vulnerable? What could they do during those times?

This kind of exploration does not avoid the work of the group, but it allows members to save face. In other words, if one door won't open, rattle some other doorknobs—another door might open.

Suggested Readings

Bean, M. H. (1981). Denial and the psychological complications of alcoholism. In M. H. Bean & N. Zinberg (Eds.), *Dynamic approaches to the understanding and treatment of alcoholism* (pp. 55-96). New York: Free Press.

Hepworth, D. H., & Larsen, J. A. (1993). Enhancing motivation with involuntary and ambivalent clients. In *Direct social work practice: Theory and skills* (pp. 348-391). Pacific Grove, CA: Brooks/Cole.

Milgram, D., & Rubin, J. (1992). Resisting resistance: Involuntary substance abuse group therapy. *Social Work with Groups, 15*(1), 95-110.

Mantano, R., & Yalom, I. (1991) Approaches to chemical dependency: Chemical dependency and interactive group therapy—a synthesis. *International Journal of Group Psychotherapy, 41*(3), 269-293.

Vanicelli, M. (1992). *Removing the roadblocks: Group psychotherapy with substance abusers and family members*. New York: Guilford.

Treating Multiple Dysfunctions in Adults

Gloria: A Mexican-American Woman in Outpatient Treatment

Female alcoholics and addicts often have trauma histories, and both the substance abuse and the trauma may need to be addressed to ensure recovery. Workers may sequence the work or address the issues simultaneously. A sophisticated level of clinical judgment is needed to determine which approach best fits a specific client. The following case presents a detailed description of treatment over time, and highlights worker–client boundary issues, cultural influences, and trauma experienced during abstinence. The case also illustrates effective interagency collaboration. To support clients in maintaining abstinence, a variety of interventions may be helpful, including individual counseling, family 12-step participation, medication evaluation, and case management. A process recording of a specific contract is also presented, and can be used for a class exercise or to supplement the general case summary.

Nuestra Vida is a community-based agency providing individual and group counseling, prevention and outreach services, classes for DUI offenders, and violence prevention classes to the Latino community. The worker was in the role of alcohol/drug counselor.

Gloria, 35, had started receiving Supplemental Security Income (SSI) benefits due to a disability, her addiction to heroin. A stipulation of her receiving the SSI benefits was that she participate in weekly individual or group counseling to deal with issues of sobriety. The case manager thought I would be a good match for Gloria, since we are both women and of Mexican-American descent. The case manager informed me that Gloria was struggling to keep her appointments and would often cancel or "no show." She said Gloria understood that clients were not to attend appointments under the influence of liquor or drugs, but was having difficulty staying "straight" long enough to keep her appointments. Gloria was born and raised in the small town of Santa Clara and had recently returned to live with her mother and stepfather after four years of living with an abusive man in another town.

Gloria's presenting problems included an addiction to heroin and alcohol. When Gloria first started attending sessions with me she was using heroin daily, but only in small amounts so as not to appear "strung out." When Gloria couldn't "cop" drugs, she would often frequent the local bars with girlfriends and drink until she went home with someone or did things she couldn't remember. Gloria was studying to become a baptized Jehovah's Witness, and although she appeared to find strength in her belief in God, she felt that God saw her as a "sinner" and a bad person. She often expressed feelings of great remorse in our sessions.

When she first came to the agency, she was desperately missing Javier, her estranged boyfriend. Gloria mentioned on several occasions that he beat her frequently and that twice he chased her with a knife. Javier had been phoning Gloria, and she asked her family to tell him that they did not know where she was.

Now that Gloria had returned to Santa Clara, her two teen-aged daughters had returned to live with her at the home of Gloria's parents. Gloria informed me that she was on the waiting list for Section 8 housing and that she was not always comfortable at her mother's. She said her mother often treated them like they were burdens and seemed impatient for Gloria to get her own place.

In the initial interview, Gloria admitted that she was only attending sessions at Nuestra Vida to receive her check. She did not think I could help her with her addictions and thought it was something she had to work out on her own. She felt she needed support in dealing with the loss of Javier.

Our primary focus was helping her to achieve continuous sobriety from alcohol and drugs; I thought that progress would be otherwise difficult. I also found that Gloria was suffering from depression and felt she would benefit from a psychiatric evaluation. She also had endured many forms of oppression.

Gloria had no formal schooling beyond the eighth grade and was lacking in work skills and experience. She was struggling to get by with the small income she received from SSI. Her living situation was chaotic and stressful, and with the recent loss of her relationship with Javier and the added responsibility of finding housing, environmental and transitional stressors were high. Gloria appeared to be suffering from Post-Traumatic Stress Disorder, too, because she complained of chronic nightmares, depression, and despair, and admitted surviving ritual sexual abuse by her father, her brothers, and her uncles.

As strengths, I noted her faith in God and the support she experienced from the members of the Jehovah's Witnesses. She attended the local Kingdom Hall services and meetings a couple of times a month. Gloria also seemed to enjoy reading self-help books and would sometimes go to the library and check out John Bradshaw's books and other similar literature on recovery. She occasionally attended 12-step meetings including AA and NA, which she found helpful.

Our sessions were in English. Gloria did not speak Spanish very well, as is the common experience of many Mexican-Americans living in California.

Goals and Intervention Plan

I asked Gloria to start attending at least one 12-step meeting a week. After the three-month treatment plan review, she was to attend at least three AA or NA meetings a week, to have obtained a sponsor, and to be working on the 12 steps. I made a referral for her to see a psychiatrist. Gloria was diagnosed with depression and placed on antidepressants, but was inconsistent in taking the medication. By the next three-month review, Gloria was keeping regularly scheduled appointments with her doctor, but was not taking medication regularly. She agreed to discuss with me if the medication was not working.

Gloria and I did significant work concerning her cognitive distortions about herself as an inferior person. I also disclosed that I was a Mexican-American in recovery from addiction. I felt that I modeled effective and honest communication and coping skills.

For help with her children, I referred Gloria to a local agency that accepted Medicaid and provided counseling for adolescents and their families. The treatment plan specified that either Gloria would attend family counseling with her daughters or that her daughters would be in individual counseling with a therapist in the agency. Gloria decided that she would wait and see how the therapy went with her daughters before she talked to a family therapist there.

To address her educational deficit, the local school district had an excellent adult education program for persons working on their high school diplomas and GEDs. Social Security provided incentives for people receiving SSI in the form of scholarship assistance, monies for books, and living expenses. Gloria seemed excited by the idea, but felt she wouldn't be ready to attend school until she had achieved continuous abstinence from alcohol and drugs.

Gloria was already receiving the maximum benefits allowed under SSI and state disability, but we discussed the possibility of her daughters pursuing employment to alleviate some of the financial stress. I helped her work on a budget and brainstorm possible work options, but Gloria did not feel ready to reenter the work force. She was allowed SSI cash benefits for at least 24 months, which seemed right for Gloria at that time. When she had continuous sobriety, we could renegotiate work and her education.

Gloria continued to check with the housing authority, but things did not look hopeful. The waiting list was at least two years long. Gloria did not have any family she could stay with other than her mother. We devised "safe places" for her to go—the beach, the YMCA, an AA meeting, a friend's house, or church—when she needed emotional space.

Regarding the sexual abuse she experienced as both a child and an adult, I referred her to the local rape crisis center. To be honest, I referred her because I was not sure how to proceed in treating the PTSD. But I encouraged her to use positive self-talk, to release anger and sadness, and to reach out to friends in recovery.

Treatment Analysis

Gloria attended AA and incest survivors meetings once or twice a week. I felt she should go to AA and NA much more frequently, but I backed off because I didn't want her to become overwhelmed and quit therapy. Though I felt these meetings could be of enormous aid to her, she had not taken some essential steps in using the programs—for example, finding a sponsor and working on the 12 steps. I stopped asking her about it because I sensed that she was just not ready, but I also offered to work on the steps with her if she was interested.

Using the psychiatrist was not a successful intervention. Gloria would stop taking her medication as soon as she started feeling better. I didn't want to push her into taking it, because she was still using heroin about once a week. Gloria had overdosed once, and the doctor was very clear with her not to take the medication if she was still using narcotics. Eventually she stopped seeing the psychiatrist, feeling she received enough help in her weekly appointments with me and the woman at Rape Crisis.

It would have been wonderful to find a residential treatment facility for her, but no hospitals in the area had Medicaid beds. I was able to locate one about 100 miles away, but Gloria did not want to be that far from her children. She said she would consider it if one opened up in Santa Clara.

Gloria frequently made negative comments about herself, and I would reframe these. She was a very beautiful woman who was raised hearing comments like "stupid," "slut," and "no good." Gloria had internalized much of the abuse she had suffered at the hands of her oppressors. She seemed now to be participating in her own oppression, for example, by her maladaptive use of addictive substances. We would look at painful experiences from her past that related to her parents and others who had abused her. This cognitive work was instrumental in helping her take the blame off herself. I gave Gloria a lot of positive feedback for taking risks, by sharing with me and being willing to feel the pain.

During her time in treatment, both of Gloria's daughters became pregnant and had decided to carry their pregnancies to term. This was difficult for Gloria because she had been pregnant with both daughters in her teens and was scared they would follow in her footsteps. They did attend family therapy a few times, but neither was interested in continuing. Unfortunately, I could not provide them with family counseling as I was not yet licensed and our funding did not allow family therapy except by licensed clinicians. I did try to demonstrate new ways Gloria could express herself with her daughters that did not involve yelling or getting physical. I also served as a safe outlet for her to express her frustrations and anger about parenting and her daughters' behavior.

Gloria looked into the high school diploma program and realized she qualified for free classes and textbooks, but she wanted to wait another six months before enrolling. Although she wanted to get her diploma, the thought of returning to school after 20 years—while still in early recovery—terrified her. I respected her decision and agreed to discuss it only when she felt ready. Gloria was getting sober for the first time in 20 years and her recovery seemed difficult enough.

She continued on the waiting list for housing, but had developed a daily walking routine to keep her out of the house and into her own "safe place." Gloria was learning healthier coping skills in times of stress.

The referral to the Rape Crisis Center turned out to be an effective intervention. She was attending weekly counseling with a therapist with whom she had bonded quickly. She admitted treasuring her two weekly appointments with me and "Toni" from Rape Crisis.

When Gloria expressed feelings of shame and unworthiness, I admitted that I had had similar feelings during my drinking and drug-using days and in early recovery. I also reminded her frequently about the amazing job she was doing in therapy and told her she was a wonderful person to work with.

I experienced a lot of satisfaction in working with Gloria. She was eager and willing to grow, and her vulnerability and honesty allowed me to feel close to her. We had much in common as Mexican-American women who were both in recovery; in fact, she often said that she hoped someday she would accomplish what I had ac-complished. Sometimes Gloria would ask me if we could get together for dinner or a movie, and I would gently remind her that, as client and therapist, we could not socialize. She seemed to understand and said she just wished she had a friend like me who was sober and emotionally healthy. I knew, though, that Gloria was only seeing a small part of me and didn't realize that I too struggled and made mistakes.

I know that each client I work with will evoke different parts of me. My work with Gloria evoked the parts of me that I find most comfortable and loving. This, I realize now, is why I enjoyed working with her so much.

Worker's Observations

As a Mexican-American woman living in California, my work with another Mexican-American woman added a unique element to the therapeutic relationship because we shared a common history and experience of special holidays, foods, traditions, and possibly religious and cultural beliefs. One cultural aspect that I kept in mind during treatment was my client's experience of growing up in a patriarchal family. Gloria seemed to always look to the men in her life when considering important decisions. It would have been insensitive of me to disregard this and support her in being more independent if that was not what she wanted. Many people in the Mexican culture have a low opinion of women who drink and/or use drugs, and this cultural phenomenon could have contributed to Gloria's low opinion of herself and possibly undermined her recovery.

In terms of countertransference, I experienced some fear of identification because, although my father was an immigrant, I was raised in an upper-middle-class home. I think the transference/countertransference between us was positive and healthy and resulted from us being similar in age, in ethnicity, and in recovery. She told me that therapy allowed her to experience her first trusting relationship with a woman.

I offered to work on the 12 steps with Gloria, because I felt she was finding it difficult to connect with a sponsor for fear of rejection, intimacy, and the crowds at NA. Although not ideal, I felt Gloria could benefit from working on the steps with me. I would only recommend this intervention to other clinicians in recovery who had developed healthy boundaries with their clients and who would not feel burdened or resentful of the possibility of extra phone calls during the week. I had worked on the steps with clients before and had found it effective.

I did promote intimacy in our work by offering her a lot of positive feedback and nurturing. My self-disclosure, which I did because I felt I served as a healthy role model, helped with this. Women in recovery often find themselves dealing with feelings of shame and guilt around their sexual behavior and parenting abilities. It is healing for a woman to be able to work on these issues with a woman therapist who also happens to be in recovery. I am very aware of what and how much I disclose; it happens only after the therapeutic relationship has had a chance to develop and centers only on issues of addiction and recovery. My level of self-disclosure is different with every client.

Knowing when a client in recovery is ready to deal with issues of sexual abuse is a complex task. Gloria drank and used drugs in large part to escape these feelings, I believe. Because Gloria was not entirely clean from drugs when she started working on these issues, I communicated frequently with the other therapist to make sure she was not being overwhelmed.

Process Recording

Prior to this session, Gloria had canceled the previous week because she decided to visit her brother in Fresno. Her brother was also using heroin, and was recently released from prison. I was concerned about Gloria going to Fresno because this was also where her ex-boyfriend Javier lived.

Lisa: Hi Gloria, it's great to see you. I missed seeing you last week.

Gloria: [Appearing agitated.] So did I. I wished I had been here for it.

Lisa: What do you mean? Was your trip to Fresno OK?

Gloria: No, it wasn't, but I'd rather not talk about it.

Lisa: OK, I understand. But will you let me know if you change your mind?

Gloria: Yeah. I probably will in a while, but just not right now.

Lisa: That's fine, Gloria. Is there anything in particular you would like to talk about?

Gloria: Well, I blew it. I got high this week. It was terrible, I passed out and don't even remember very much of what happened.

Lisa: I'm sorry. Would you like to talk about it?

Gloria: Well, something really bad happened, but I feel like it was my fault so I kind of just want to put it out of my head and pretend it never happened and just move on. [Her eyes were welling up with tears.]

Lisa: I can understand that feeling, but you look so sad right now, do you think you really can just put the feeling behind you?

Gloria: No, I guess not. God, Lisa, so many terrible things happen to me. Sometimes I wish I could just die, do you know? [She began to cry.] Well, I went to visit my brother and his wife and my brother said, why don't we go by Javier's house and say hi. I haven't seen him in a long time and I don't know why I did, but I said yes and I went with him. Well, we went to Javier's and it was really weird, Lisa, to see him. He already had a new girlfriend and she was only about 18 or 19. It made me sick. I kind of wanted to warn her about him, but I didn't know what to say. He is such a pervert. And to think that my daughters might have moved in there with me. Remember I told you he was a child abuser? He made a couple of passes at one of my daughters when she was younger. That man is pure evil! He was arrested when he was younger for sexually abusing a little girl. Well, he was being real nice and flirting with me and asked me to stop back later when his girlfriend went home. I told him I didn't think so. After my brother drank a few beers, I asked him if we could leave and he said OK.

Lisa: You said earlier that you don't know why you said yes to visiting Javier. Do you think maybe you felt you needed to after leaving there so abruptly? I'm wondering if a part of you wants to let him know how you feel about the abuse and pain? Or possibly to let him see that you are a survivor?

Gloria: Yeah, I felt like I wanted to see him and let him know that he didn't affect me anymore. I also wanted to tell him that I think he's evil and that I could never forgive him for what he did to me, but that I wished him the best. And that he really needed some help. It kind of felt good to see him and know that I don't feel so obsessed with him anymore. Well, after Javier's, we went to my brother's house and my brothers and I got high and then they started talking about my dad like he was some great man or something. It made me sick and I told them so. My dad sexually abused all of us and they made it sound like he was a good father or something. Well, I told my one brother that I was going to wait for him in the car. I was staying with him and his wife. [She began to cry again.] Next thing I know, I'm waking up in the back seat, my brother is driving and my pants and underwear are around my ankles and my bra is pushed up and my breasts are hanging out. I asked him what happened and he told me to shut up. He told me he would kill me if I ever told anyone. I asked him why he would do that to me, that I was his own sister and he said it was my fault and that I shouldn't have been talking about my dad like that. He even took my money. I had had forty dollars in my back pocket. I think he went back and scored some more drugs while I was asleep, but he swears he didn't take my money. But he told me to shut up and stop whining and we stopped by his bank. He said I didn't take your money, but I'll give you $40 from my account for the money you must have lost. He's such a liar. I hate him and I hope I never see him again. I never want to talk to him again. But you know Lisa, he was right. It was my fault. If I hadn't gotten high, this would never have happened. I wouldn't have passed out or anything.

Lisa: Gloria, what your brother did was wrong and you are not to blame. It doesn't matter whether or not you were high, no one has the right to hurt you or take advantage of you. I am so sorry this happened to you and so honored that you could share such obviously painful feelings with me. It must have really hurt to experience such a traumatic event by your brother when you know that he too had been a victim of sexual abuse.

Gloria: Exactly. I can't believe he would do that to me. My father used to do that to him and I know he used to hate him for it. My brother abused me when I was younger, but I had forgiven him for it because I knew that it was all that he knew. But to do that now? I don't understand.

Lisa: Gloria, do you know that you have the right to press charges against him? What you experienced was rape. It doesn't matter that you were high or passed out. You did not consent to sexual intercourse and that is rape.

Gloria: Yeah, but what's some cop going to say? I was high and I have tracks in my arms. I don't want to talk to any police and I don't want my brother to be arrested. He's on parole, if he gets arrested he'll go back to prison. But who I do feel sorry for is his kids. I wonder if he will abuse them.

Lisa: Well, Gloria, I don't want to tell you what to do. But you have every right to press charges against him, even if it means that he goes back to prison. I know that would be hard for you, but sometimes I believe that is where some people need to be. I don't know about his children. But you know that people who were sexually abused often become perpetrators themselves. It sounds like your brother is in a lot of pain and needs some professional help. But that still does not make it right for him to have hurt you.

Gloria: I wish he would go to counseling. I have talked to my other brother about it, who just got out of jail, and he thinks he needs it. But this brother thinks he's OK or something. All the kids are so screwed up in my family.

Lisa: Once again, Gloria, I am sorry this happened to you. You deserve happiness and joy in your life. It is your right.

Gloria: Maybe not, Lisa. Maybe some people are just supposed to have miserable lives. Sometimes I really think that's true for me. Just when I start feeling a little better, something terrible happens to me, too.

Lisa: I could see how you might feel that way, but I truly believe that you are deserving of happiness. I see how your childhood could lead you to believe that isn't true. You are a loving, kind, and vulnerable person with a big heart. I see so much that is wonderful about you.

Gloria: [Crying softly.] You always say stuff like that. Do you really feel that way?

Lisa: Yes I do.

Gloria: You are so nice to me. I really appreciate it.

Questions for Class Discussion

1. How is the issue of oppression relevant to this case?

2. How did the worker respond to the trauma issues? Could she have done more, or done something different?

3. What are your speculations about what the future holds for Gloria's daughters? What would the goals have been in family therapy and how could they have been accomplished?

4. Was the worker overidentified with the client? What indications do you have for your answer? Do you think the worker might have experienced "survivor's guilt" in working with this client? If so, how did it express itself?

5. How significant is it that the worker herself was a recovering alcoholic/drug abuser?

Teaching Points

1. If the client is a woman, of color, and economically disadvantaged, then we have the classic triple oppressions related to gender, race, and class (Shulman, 1992, p. 7).

   Even though therapists need not be recovering alcoholics, it is imperative that they be thoroughly familiar with AA steps and traditions and with the AA experience: it permits them to harness the wisdom of AA in the service therapy (Matano & Yalom, 1991, p. 226).

   Repeated exposure to oppression, subtle or direct, may lead vulnerable members of the oppressed group to internalize the negative self-images projected by the external oppressor—the "oppressor without" (Shulman, 1992, p. 36).

   To understand our adult survivor clients, we must recall with them what it was like to grow up in a family where oppression, victimization, and secrecy were the norms of their daily lives, and how this atmosphere, as well as the larger society, has influenced their lives as adults (Schiller & Zimmer, 1993, p. 216).

   Like immigrants, newly recovering addicts must leave a familiar, all-encompassing way of life without a clear idea of how to replace it. Still shaken by their losses, they are beginners at many things that most people take for granted (Albert, 1994, p. 200).

2. Indications that the worker has done enough or that the timing was not appropriate for doing more include:
   - client was dealing with multiple other issues in her life that were draining her energy: housing, her daughters' behavior and pregnancies, PTSD, and depression;
   - client was not totally abstinent;
   - client was addressing trauma issues in individual counseling and by attending incest survivors' group once or twice per week.

   Indications that more could have been done:
   - Worker might have warned Gloria that abuse survivors may put themselves in situations where revictimization is likely and could have asked Gloria to anticipate where such situations might lead. This might or might not have been effective in heading off the later rape.

3. Unfortunately, Gloria's daughters may repeat various aspects of her pattern. However, if Gloria is able to recover from her addiction, and work through issues related to trauma, she will serve as an example of how such progress can occur. Goals of family therapy might have included:
   - facilitating communication between mother and daughters, including helping each of them discuss areas of disappointment, anger, and positive connection with one another;
   - assisting in developing a contract between mother and daughters about reasonable limits, discipline, and responsiveness to each others' needs.

4. Identification with the client seemed to have served a positive function. Further, the worker seems to have engaged in periodic self-reflection and self-monitoring to guard against overidentification.

   The term "overidentification" implies that the worker's level of identification with the client was unhelpful. Areas where the client's progress was impeded by this dynamic would need to be identified before use of the term would be justified.

   The worker may have experienced "survivor's guilt" based on the volume of positive feedback provided to the client. However, this feedback may have been essential to support the client in her arduous efforts to get back on her feet. Survivor's guilt would interfere with treatment if it led to the worker's failure to confront Gloria about her self-defeating behavior.

5. In this case, the worker's recovery history seems to have been used in a therapeutic way, in that:
   - discussion of her history did not dominate the work;
   - she did not draw conclusions about the client simply based on her own history;
   - she did not pressure the client to take certain steps because those steps had been helpful to her.

   It is likely, however, that a non-recovering therapist could have done similar therapeutic work. The content and texture would have been different, but could have been equally effective.

References

Albert, J. (1994). Talking like real people: The straight ahead prison group. In A. Gitterman & L. Shulman (Eds.), *Mutual aid groups, vulnerable populations and the life cycle* (2nd ed., pp. 199-214). New York: Columbia University Press.

Matano, R., & Yalom, I. (1991). Approaches to chemical dependency: Chemical dependency and interactive group therapy—A synthesis. *International Journal of Group Psychotherapy, 41*(3), 269-293.

Schiller, L., & Zimmer, B. (1994). Sharing the secrets: Women's groups for sexual abuse survivors. In A. Gitterman & L. Shulman (Eds.), *Mutual aid groups, vulnerable populations and the life cycle* (2nd ed.). New York: Columbia University Press.

Shulman, L. (1992). *The skills of helping: Individuals, families and groups* (3rd ed.). Itasca, IL: F. E. Peacock.

Pilar and Eduardo: Substance Abuse and Domestic Violence

The relationship between domestic violence and alcohol and drug abuse is a complex one. Drinking and drug use often exacerbate violence, but, for some men, abstinence or reduced use does not decrease violence and the need to control others. Safety issues for the woman and her children, financial problems for the family, and trauma issues are often intertwined. This case illustrates the intersection of all of these issues and will be useful for both foundation and advanced clinical courses, as well as those focusing on family therapy and/or cross-cultural practice.

Pilar and her husband Eduardo are immigrants from a fairly peaceful Central American country. They came to the United States about 12 years ago to improve their financial circumstances and are legal residents. Pilar was 19 years old and Eduardo 22 when they married. She is from a large middle-class family, and he is from a much poorer one. She had considered attending college, but instead got married to escape her parents' traditional restrictions on her freedom. Eduardo, for his part, fell in love with her. Pilar's parents had to give legal permission for the marriage since in that country one must be 21. The couple has a son, Ramon, born in Boston.

Eduardo has a charming, personable, intelligent, and confident manner, and is handsome. He has always been a responsible employee, first in Central America and then in the U.S. Being the sole family provider has been important to him, and by working two jobs he has earned a middle-class salary. He has actively discouraged Pilar from working, taking English as a Second Language (ESL) classes, or learning to drive.

Eduardo has always enjoyed drinking with his friends, but had usually confined his drinking to weekends. He has never used drugs. On some occasions in their early marriage, he was verbally and emotionally abusive; on rare ones, he was physically abusive or threatening. Once he ringed their house with gasoline while Pilar and Ramon—then a toddler—were inside, and threatened to light it. After they came to the U.S., his drinking gradually increased in frequency and amount, but he had no difficulty behaving responsibly on the job. The family's income was fairly stable.

Pilar, the primary client, was referred for psychotherapy by her primary care physician. This is her first time in treatment. She is ashamed about coming for help. She is energetic, straightforward, bright, and articulate. Pilar continued to be caring toward Eduardo until recently, but now she is fearful when he is abusive. Her style is feisty, even when she is afraid. She does not drink or use drugs.

Eighteen months ago Eduardo was injured on the job. His case is due to be adjudicated soon. During these months of not working, the frequency and amount of his drinking increased enormously, to the point where he has often used up their rent and food money, even though his Worker's Compensation from the two jobs provides adequately for Pilar and Ramon. He has had frequent blackouts and denies certain behavior because he cannot recall it. His level of verbal and emotional harassment has increased, as well as threats to kill Pilar. Most, but not all, of this behavior has occurred when he was drinking. Pilar has called the police three times, and he was arrested once after he had brandished a knife. However, she withdrew the charges. Eduardo has said he will kill her if she ever puts him in jail again, and she believes him. In fact, she feels sorry for him when he begs to come back to her after a night of drinking.

She worries about her son Ramon (now 8 years old) and his role as mediator, ally, and witness. She will not go to a shelter because she is unwilling to leave Ramon with Eduardo or others. She has no income of her own, and emergency assistance takes at least 30 days. She cannot drive nor speak English. She has sought consultation from Women's Protective Services, which urged her to leave Eduardo. She learns that there is no Spanish-speaking AA in the area, but there is a support group for abused Latino women. She does not understand the process of addiction and thinks Eduardo could stop drinking if he wished. She does understand that sobriety might not affect his abusiveness. She feels trapped and furious and has suffered symptoms of PTSD and major depression, with frequent suicidal and homicidal (toward Eduardo) thoughts. Her decision is not to stay with Eduardo, even if he becomes sober, but she must wait until she feels safe to leave.

Eduardo has been through detoxification three times in the past two months: the first time because he was tricked into it by a friend, and the other times of his own volition when he began to believe that Pilar would leave him. He does not wish to end his marriage. He was referred by the detoxification facility for outpatient substance abuse treatment, but is uncomfortable with the idea of therapy. Like Pilar, he thinks coming for treatment labels him as crazy. There is only one AA meeting per week in Spanish in his area, but his English is sufficient for him to attend English-speaking meetings. He has gone to many of them in the past. Nevertheless, he is in denial about the extent of his drinking and its emotional and financial impact on his family. He

agrees with Pilar's view that he can stop drinking if he wishes.

Questions for Class Discussion

1. What are the major problems/issues highlighted by the case?

2. What are the worker's first tasks in her work with Pilar?

3. Is there any evidence that Pilar is an enabler of Eduardo's drinking? What evidence would you look for? If there is a problem, how would you help Pilar identify/understand the consequences of her behavior?

4. If Pilar decides to leave Eduardo, what avenues might the worker pursue regarding the family's economic stability?

5. How would you respond to the couple's beliefs that coming for therapy is shameful?

6. This agency has a rule against couples' treatment where there is physical abuse. What are the pros and cons of the rule in this case?

7. Should the worker explore the couple's migration experience since there may be psychological effects?

Teaching Points

1. The case raises multiple issues: impact of migration; cultural values and concepts related to mental health and substance abuse; stages and progression of alcoholism; the lack of linguistically/culturally appropriate services; and the controversies surrounding concurrent substance abuse treatment, domestic violence intervention, and psychotherapy. Specific problems include:
   - the couple's lack of education about alcoholism;
   - Pilar and Ramon's safety;
   - Pilar's symptoms of depression and PTSD;
   - Eduardo's alcoholism;
   - Pilar's financial dependence on Eduardo;
   - Ramon's role as mediator;

- the family's isolation and lack of natural support systems.
2. First tasks for the worker would include:
   - Formulating a safety plan for Pilar and Ramon.
   - Educating Pilar about alcoholism: its progressive nature, its family consequences, the role of denial and other defenses, the need for treatment, the likelihood that promises of abstinence will not work without problem recognition, and some type of support or intervention to assist recovery.
   - Educating her about domestic violence and the legal realities/system in the U.S.
   - Discussing cultural issues related to assumptions around marriage, gender roles, substance abuse, violence, mental health, and shame.
   - Considering a psychopharmacological referral for Pilar.
3. Although she feels sorry for him when he begs to come back after drinking, no assumptions should be made about enabling behavior. Pilar needs education about Eduardo's condition and consistent support so that she comes to believe that she deserves to live in a nonchaotic, nonviolent environment. Her financial dependence should be considered as possible motivation for taking him back, rather than a need to protect him from the consequences of his behavior.
4. If Pilar does decide to leave, the worker could discuss the following possible economic/support resources with her: Emergency Assistance, shelters, subsidized housing, ESL classes, job training programs, and agencies/programs serving Central Americans.
5. Strategies for approaching the couple's belief that coming for therapy is shameful include:
   - Discussing confidentiality; explicitly exploring concern that somehow the Central American community will know they are receiving counseling.
   - Normalizing adjustment/acculturation issues of immigrants.
   - Differentiating/educating about "mental health" versus "mental illness."
   - Framing the counseling as an "adjustment crisis" rather than "being crazy."
   - Exploring how the couple might handle their difficulties if they were still in their homeland, and which natural support systems they might use. This might include acknowledging the lack of these support systems in the U.S. and framing the agency as trying to serve in this role.
6. There are both pros and cons to the agency rule prohibiting couples treatment when there is physical abuse.

Pros:
- Maintains the wife's confidentiality.
- Husband cannot use therapy hour to extend the range of his intimidation.
- Wife is not placed at greater risk for what she says in couples therapy.
- Problem of domestic violence is defined as his problem, not the couple's problem.
- Problem of alcoholism is defined as his problem, not the couple's.
- Therapist can support the wife's stated wishes to leave.

Cons:
- If wife is ambivalent about leaving, couples work might help her to clarify her feelings.
- If both members of couple are interested in saving the relationship, couples therapy could offer a supportive forum.
- Joint treatment would allow the couple an opportunity to develop a mutual safety plan.
- Couples therapy might be a way of engaging him in substance abuse treatment and/or treatment for batterers.
- Joint therapy allows both therapist and husband to educate the wife about addictions.
- If there is a decision to end the relationship, joint treatment may help the couple do this in a healthier manner.

7. Pilar and Eduardo came to the United States for economic rather than political reasons. Unlike many immigrants from Central America and other parts of the world, they were not fleeing from a civil war or an oppressive political regime. Thus, the clinician need not be as concerned about trauma suffered through the refugee and immigrant experience and the resettlement process. Relocations such as this one often happen in a more planned way, since people are not fleeing a dangerous, and possibly life-threatening, situation. There may also be members of the extended family who have already settled in the U.S. and can provide some orientation to the new environment.

Suggested Readings

Chambon, A. (1989). Refugee families' experiences: Three family themes; family disruption, violent trauma and acculturation. *Journal of Strategic and Systemic Therapies, 8,* 3-13.

Delgado, M. (1995). Hispanics/Latinos. In J. Philleo & F. Brisbane (Eds.), *Cultural competence for social workers: A guide for alcohol and other drug abuse prevention professionals working with ethnic/racial communities* (pp. 43-63). Department of Health and Human Services publication No. (SMA) 95-3075.

Dorrington, C. (1995). Central American refugees in Los Angeles: Adjustment of children and families. In R. Zambrana (Ed.), *Understanding Latino families* (pp. 107-129). Thousand Oaks, CA: Sage.

Lynch, E. (1992). Developing cross-cultural competence. In E. Lynch & M. Hanson (Eds.), *Developing cross-cultural competence* (pp. 35-60). Baltimore, MD: Paul Brookes.

Ragg, M. (1988). Differential group programming for children exposed to spouse abuse. *Journal of Child and Youth Care, 5*(1), 59-75.

Mrs. Sann: A Cambodian Mother Accused of Child Abuse

Alcoholism in an adult often leads to impaired parenting, but does not necessarily mean that the children will be abused or neglected. Cultural differences between worker and client, and between client and his or her neighbors, may lead to incorrect conclusions about child abuse, child neglect, and the parent's fitness for continued parenting.

Mrs. Sann, 35, left Cambodia with three of her children after living through the dramatic hardships of the Khmer Rouge. Her husband, two children, her parents, and other extended family members died during that violent political regime. Many months later, with the hope of rebuilding her life with a new family, she married Mr. Pok while in a refugee camp. Two more sons were born in the camp before they arrived in the United States. Her husband got a job as a technician at Honeywell. Her oldest daughter began working to help the family financially. The other two daughters began high school. Mrs. Sann began a catering business at home to earn extra money while taking care of the boys, ages 10 and 8. She was a good wife and mother.

After delivering the first son by Mr. Pok, she began drinking. She continued to do so for several years, but caused no trouble for the family. She believed she could stop at any time, but her drinking got worse, especially when she catered dinners and parties away from home. The stress of working long hours under pressure, coupled with the availability of so much alcohol, led her to drink even when she vowed not to.

Mrs. Sann drank whenever she found herself missing her parents, aunts and uncles, husband, and children who had perished in Cambodia. Sometimes her longing for them was so strong it felt unbearable. She used alcohol more and more to get her mind off painful memories that rarely came to mind when she first arrived in the U.S. Lately, she finds she is often drunk, and craves alcohol all the time. Cambodian neighbors have noticed this and blame her for being a woman who is always drinking.

She becomes nasty, overly talkative, and defensive when her husband tries to stop her from drinking. At one point, Mr. Pok became unfaithful and now spends time with other women. Sometimes he becomes so angry with Mrs. Sann that he strikes her. The house has become a battleground with the two blaming each other; fighting and yelling are common. One of their teenaged daughters ran away from home with a boy from her school. Mrs. Sann's catering work has diminished, thus adding to the family's financial problems.

Last week, a non-Asian neighbor saw Mrs. Sann discipline her 8-year-old son and reported her to the state child protective agency for child abuse. A social worker from the agency visited and the boys are now in danger of being taken into foster care. When Mrs. Sann's Cambodian women friends heard about this incident, they were upset because they have seen Mrs. Sann discipline her children and they know her disciplining is not child abuse.

Questions for Class Discussion

1. Given that people in the Cambodian community blame Mrs. Sann for her drinking, how do you think alcoholism is viewed by Cambodians who have resettled in the U.S.?

2. How serious is Mrs. Sann's drinking?

3. What effects would you think the experiences of escaping from Cambodia, staying in a refugee camp, and resettling in the U.S.

have had on Mrs. Sann's emotional condition? How might Mrs. Sann's drinking be related to this?

4. If you were a protective service worker, how could you intervene in a culturally sensitive way? What alliance building and assessment principles would you keep in mind when first meeting Mrs. Sann?

5. How would you distinguish between child abuse and appropriate discipline? What role might culture play?

Teaching Points

1. Traditionally, alcohol has been used as a medicine in Cambodia and other Southeast Asian countries. It provides the base for many herbal remedies for a variety of medical conditions. It is not seen as capable of causing an addiction or illness.

   Considerable stigma is attached to alcoholism among traditional Cambodians. It has not been viewed as an illness, but as a moral weakness or the consequence of "bad fate" visited on a family due to the transgressions of past generations. Prevention efforts in the U.S. have generated a slight shift in this view, but many Cambodians still do not think of alcoholism as a treatable illness.

2. Mrs. Sann is most likely alcohol dependent, since she "craves it all the time," drinks even when she has decided not to, and reacts defensively when her husband tries to stop her from drinking.

3. Mrs. Sann likely has a dual diagnosis—alcohol dependence and PTSD. Drinking may well have begun as self-medication.

4. Because Mrs. Sann seems to have suffered greatly in her life, the worker should be careful to avoid "retraumatizing" Mrs. Sann by approaching her in an aggressive or confrontational manner. The worker could instead begin by praising Mrs. Sann for her courage and fortitude, and acknowledging the hardships faced by many Southeast Asians who have resettled in the United States.

   The worker should get to know Mrs. Sann as a person—beyond her child-rearing practices or drinking behavior—by asking about traditional Cambodian customs and values, community resources for support of new immigrants, and how Mrs. Sann and her family have adjusted to the United States.

   Berry and her colleagues (1992) report that Cambodian families resettled in the U.S. feel isolated and responsible for solving family problems alone. Family members of addicted individuals are especially reluctant to discuss their problems for fear of bringing shame to the family and community by exposing their secrets.

5. For traditional Cambodians, the cultural belief is that parents own their children and can discipline them however they see fit. Corporal punishment is accepted, although the family and community elders are watchful to ensure that the parental discipline is not too extreme. In this case, however, Mrs. Sann seems isolated and without traditional family supports. She seems to bear the burden of child care alone and may have reached the point of excess.

   Consultation with a bilingual, bicultural Cambodian worker would be especially useful to determine how the culture defines appropriate discipline. Some factors for the worker to consider would be whether the parent loses control while disciplining, whether the children are in danger of physical harm, and whether Mrs. Sann's discipline is different from that of other Cambodian women in her community. The worker should also realize that parental alcohol or drug use, although often reducing the parent's ability to ensure the child's safety, does not automatically indicate child abuse or neglect.

Although AODA is becoming increasingly evident among the Southeast Asian refugee population in many parts of the U.S. (Berry et al., 1992; Community University Health Care Center, undated; D'Avanzo & Frye, 1992; Jenkins, McPhee, Bird, & Bonilla, 1990; TonThat & Grigg-Saito, 1988; Yee & Thu, 1987), few if any culturally specific substance abuse services are available. While clients receiving health, mental health, and social services have often had AODA problems, only the more visible presenting problems have been addressed.

References

Berry, L., Nil, S., Locke, N., McCracken, S., Seth, K., & Koch, V. (1992). *Cambodian oral history research: Preliminary findings on alcohol and other drugs in Cambodia and in the United States*. Chicago: Refugee Substance Abuse Prevention Project, Travelers and Immigrants Aid.

Community University Health Care Center. (undated). *Alcohol and drug abuse in the Southeast Asian community*. Minneapolis, MN: Community University Health Care Center, University of Minnesota Hospital and Clinic.

D'Avanzo, C. E., & Frye, B. (1992). Stress and self-medication in Cambodian refugee women. *Addictions Nursing Network, 4*(2), 59-60.

Jenkins, C. N. H., McPhee, S., Bird, J. A., & Bonilla, N. H. (1990). Cancer risk and prevention practices among Vietnamese refugees. *Western Journal of Medicine, 153*(1), 34-39.

TonThat, A., & Grigg-Saito, D. (1988). *Substance abuse services: Community input and programmatic change*. Unpublished manuscript.

Yee, B., & Thu, N. D. (1987). Correlates of drug use and abuse among Indochinese refugees: Mental health implications. *Journal of Psychoactive Drugs, 19*(1), 77-83.

Mr. Pines: A Difference of Opinion on the Treatment Team

When members of the treatment team disagree about the nature of the problem, the client is caught in the middle. This case illustrates how formulations of the problem can vary among team members. The case also illustrates methods for dealing with client intoxication and denial.

Setting: Public outpatient program providing mental health and substance abuse services to court-referred clients.

Client: 52-year-old, divorced, homeless white man.

Worker: Latino social worker with experience in both substance abuse and mental health who believes in the disease model of addiction; theoretical perspective used is "eclectic/cognitive."

Presenting problem: Client was referred by municipal court following his conviction for loitering and public drunkenness and his subsequent incarceration in the county jail.

Case Record

Most offenses in this program are misdemeanors, but the clients feel the pressure of the court to participate in treatment. The community is a city of approximately 500,000 known for its ethnic diversity and progressive political views. The multidisciplinary clinic staff consists of social workers, counselors, psychologists, and a part-time psychiatrist.

Mr. Pines is a 52-year-old Euro-American who was referred by the municipal court where he faced charges of loitering and public drunkenness. He was interviewed briefly in jail, was shaking and sweating, but spoke in a coherent fashion. A referral was made to the outpatient program.

Mr. Pines appeared on time for his intake appointment. He was moderately disheveled, smelled of alcohol, but did not appear intoxicated. He had recently served 20 days in the county jail for a series of misdemeanors, mostly alcohol-related, and had had one DUI conviction several years before. He described his problem with alcohol as having gotten worse during his past year of homelessness. Mr. Pines said he feels extremely anxious when he wakes and seems only able to calm down after his first drink, which on this morning was a half pint of vodka. He also has to drink himself to sleep at night; his general daily intake totals five half pints of vodka. He has been drinking heavily for most of his adult life, especially during the past 22 years. He denies use of any illicit drugs and complains about the stress of being homeless and the difficulty of obtaining services and breaking out of the cycle. He currently survives on General Assistance. Since being evicted a year ago, Mr. Pines has been homeless. Before that he had lived with a woman who supported them, but when she left, he could no longer afford the apartment.

Mr. Pines appears his age. He showed no signs of organic impairment, but appeared somewhat depressed and spoke of difficulties with concentration and short-term memory, as well as periodically feeling "worms crawling on the skin." He is not suicidal. He is a bright, articulate man who has some insight into his problem and whose judgment is mostly intact when he is not under the influence of alcohol. His most immediate complaint is not being able to sleep through the night. He was referred to the psychiatrist for a medication evaluation.

Mr. Pines was raised in another state with one sibling. Both parents are now deceased. He worked after high school for a few years, was married, and had two children. He worked for a large corporation while completing his bachelor's degree in chemistry. In 1970 he quit his job, feeling he "couldn't take the stress of corporate employment," and has worked only sporadically since. For several years he had custody of his two children, supported them on AFDC, and believes that he did rather well. He feels the responsibilities of child rearing allowed him to reduce his alcohol intake during that time. The children are both grown with families of their own and doing quite well. Mr. Pines denies any previous treatment for either emotional or substance abuse problems. He is not aware of any alcohol-related physical problems.

Worker Observations

The first micro level issue presented by this case was one of diagnosis. This is a fairly significant issue as many subsequent controversial issues flow from it. The social worker saw this client as being in significant crisis due to alcoholism, the stress of homelessness, and recent arrests. He diagnosed the client as suffering from alcoholism (including physical addiction). He saw the "worms" on the skin as a transient organic phenomenon, possibly alcoholic hallucinosis. The inability to sleep through the night, the social worker felt, was due to the fact that every few hours the client would begin to detox, have symptoms, wake up, and need a drink to go back to sleep. The psychiatrist, on the other hand, while certainly agreeing with the diagnosis of alcoholism, felt there was an "underlying depression" to which the alcohol abuse was secondary. She also felt Mr. Pines had some "psychotic process" as evidenced by the tactile hallucinations. She prescribed a low dosage of an antidepressant, and recommended that Mr. Pines start individual psychotherapy with the social worker.

The social worker faced the issues of what to do about his diagnostic disagreement with the psychiatrist. In his mind, the client's homelessness, transient depression, tactile hallucinations, and legal problems all stemmed from the client's alcoholism. He saw it as the primary diagnosis, not as a "self-medicating" behavior for depression. As a believer in the disease model of addictions, he felt the client was close to "hitting bottom."

In the worker's opinion, the only goal was abstinence. He recommended that Mr. Pines attend the weekly alcohol and drug group, whose focus was the breaking down of denial. Mr. Pines had detoxed completely only once—in jail—in the past 20 years, and did not want to go through this experience again. The social worker hoped to assuage these fears, and eventually get Mr. Pines to agree to go to the social model (no medications) detox. The worker saw the medications given by the psychiatrist as counterproductive, but felt that an all-out confrontation over diagnosis and treatment would not do any good. Instead he proposed a compromise: Mr. Pines would attend the weekly group and then visit the psychiatrist for neuroleptic medication. He agreed to see Mr. Pines for a few individual therapy sessions.

The diagnostic and social complications in this case also raised macro/ethical issues. Mr. Pines contended that the $660 per month he would receive on Supplemental Security Income (SSI) would allow him to get off the streets, reduce the concomitant stress, and surely help him to drink less. The worker knew that the chances of an SSI application being approved were much greater if it carried a primary psychiatric diagnosis like depression or schizophrenia. There is still more moral stigma attached to an alcoholism diagnosis than a psychiatric diagnosis. Though he didn't really believe it, the worker felt he had barely enough evidence to give a psychiatric diagnosis if the primary goal were to help Mr. Pines and his homelessness. This was within the worker's power to do, and the doctor would certainly co-sign the SSI evaluation form. To do this, though, would be contrary to the worker's beliefs about this case. In addition, a more general discussion ensued in the staff meeting about taxpayers supporting an alcoholic man through SSI who not only lacked immediate plans for entering recovery, but would not even accept recovery as an eventual goal at that point.

Second and Third Sessions

In the two subsequent individual sessions, the worker continued to assess further information on Mr. Pines, to search for "motivational hooks" to get him to detox, and to evaluate the effects of the antidepressants given to him by the psychiatrist. In the second session, Mr. Pines told the worker that the medications "knocked him out" too much. To sleep too deeply while homeless can be dangerous, as it deprives one of the vigilance needed to survive on the streets, and makes one too vulnerable. The client said he would ask the doctor to try some other medications. Meanwhile, Mr. Pines was noticeably under the influence. The worker told Mr. Pines that if he did not attend the 10-week alcohol and drug group, the court would be told that Mr. Pines was not "complying with treatment." In the third session, Mr. Pines informed the worker that he was going to stop taking the medications. The worker responded that it was a waste of everyone's time for Mr. Pines to come for individual therapy when he was intoxicated. The client then said that all he really wanted was for the worker to fill out the SSI evaluation.

Worker Observations

The issue arose about whether or not to see the client if he had been drinking. Most substance abuse programs would say no. The psychiatrist was now out of the picture, as the client did not want to take medication. The worker agreed to fill out the SSI evaluation with a psy-

chiatric diagnosis. He informed Mr. Pines that he expected him to come to the alcohol and drug group, but would temporarily suspend the individual sessions. Mr. Pines was subsequently asked to leave one of the group meetings for being drunk and disruptive. The court was told that the client had failed to comply with treatment. Mr. Pines was not heard from for about one month, after which he was re-referred by the court for a second chance. When he returned to the group he was much cleaner, wore new clothes, and had been drinking but was in no way disruptive. His demeanor was somewhat contrite. He announced that his SSI had been approved, "thanks to the worker," that he was living in a residence hotel, and that he had cut his alcohol intake from five half pints of vodka per day to three. He said that he wanted to complete the 10-week group and that his next goal was to reduce his alcohol intake to two half pints per day. From the worker's perspective, Mr. Pines was merely rationing his alcohol and avoiding the needed confrontation with abstinence, but he was glad that the client was off the streets and had a means of support. The worker felt that his own ideological flexibility had allowed the client to articulate his goals. After achieving a more positive relationship with the client, the worker felt he could slowly treat the client as long as the client continued to receive SSI.

Questions for Class Discussion

1. What evidence is there in the client's history to support a diagnosis of alcoholism? What evidence is there to support a diagnosis of depression? Does Mr. Pines meet the criteria for dual diagnosis? If so, what is the evidence?

2. What approach would you take with regard to the diagnostic disagreement with the psychiatrist?

3. Do you perceive ethical and clinical dilemmas, as described by the author, in providing a psychiatric diagnosis to enable the client to re-

ceive SSI, even though you do not agree with the diagnosis? If so, how might you have handled this ethical dilemma?

4. If you do not agree to a treatment "compromise," how would you have engaged this client in treatment, and what would your treatment plan have been?

Teaching Points

1. At this point, no evidence exists for two independent conditions (i.e., dual diagnosis). The depression is likely to be a consequence of the 22-year history of drinking and is likely to diminish markedly within three to six months of abstinence and the provision of social services, including housing assistance.

2. The worker might consider two approaches around the diagnostic disagreement. If he has a good working relationship with the psychiatrist, he could address the difference of opinion by providing her with readings by recognized authorities on the psychiatric symptoms that accompany late-stage alcoholism. He could also develop an educational program for agency staff on issues related to dual diagnosis, phases of addiction, and treatment and recovery. In this effort, he could use speakers, journal articles, books, and consultants in the AODA field.

3. A number of ethical and clinical dilemmas emerge if the worker agrees to provide a psychiatric diagnosis so that the client is eligible for SSI. First, in assigning a diagnosis with which he doesn't agree, the worker is compromising his professional judgment and presumably his professional principles. Second, although the worker might sympathize with the client's situation, it is important that

he model ways to problem solve that are consistent with his own ethical beliefs and with principles of good practice. Third, although Mr. Pines contends that he will get off the street and drink less if given SSI, there is no guarantee that he will not use the money to continue to buy alcohol.

The worker could, instead, work with Mr. Pines to find an alcoholism detoxification center or shelter program which would help him stop drinking, and which could offer a network of housing, income maintenance, health, and employment services.

4. The worker maintained a balance of focusing the client toward the long-range goal of abstinence, while providing support for his immediate needs in incremental steps. This is especially important in working with clients who are homeless, who are in a late stage of alcoholism, and who might also be chronically mentally ill.

Suggested Readings

Bean-Bayog, M. (1985). Alcoholism treatment as an alternative to psychiatric hospitalization. *Psychiatric Clinics of North America, 8*(3), 501-512.

Jaffe, J., & Ciraulo, D. (1986). Alcoholism and depression. In R. Meyer (Ed.), *Psychopathology and addictive disorders* (pp. 293-320). New York: Guilford.

Manoleas, P., & Roffmann, R. (1992). Should social workers accept a disease model of addictions? In E. Gambrill & R. Pruger, *Controversial issues in social work*. Needham Heights, MA: Allyn and Bacon.

Minkoff, K. (1989, October). An integrated treatment model for dual diagnosis of psychosis and addiction. *Hospital and Community Psychiatry*, 1031-1036.

Examining Family Dynamics

A Hot Case: A Crisis for Parents with a Dually Diagnosed Son

A fee-for-service worker about to go on vacation is assigned a family case that erupts into a crisis. This is the family's first request for professional help, and they seek an immediate solution after many years of problems. The parents are engaged in denial about their alcoholic son who has serious psychiatric problems. The worker's intervention, although coming too late to head off the crisis, helps the family explore and heal old wounds. Guidelines are offered for relapse prevention and facilitating referrals to 12-step programs such as Al-Anon.

Setting: A small, nonprofit, social service agency.

Clients: A retired couple and their four adult children.

Worker: Male, part-time, fee-for-service clinician with full-time job in another agency.

Presenting problem: Alcoholic son (gay, mid-30s) of retired couple has been living in the family home while parents have been at their retirement home in Florida. He is unemployed, drinking, fighting with and threatening his father, and refusing to get help with his problems. Parents want immediate help because they plan to return to Florida in three weeks.

Case Record

Events unfolded rapidly following the worker's initial involvement with this family and included the incarceration of the son and the total destruction of the family home by fire. This brief case report describes the first two visits with the family. It illustrates many features of the systems involved and the problem of having to make a number of quick decisions about how to proceed in a crisis situation.

The retired couple was referred by their pastor to this social service agency. They had just returned from their retirement home in Florida and complained that they did not know what to do about their son who was in the home, drinking, unemployed, and refusing to leave or to get help for his problems. He was getting into explosive arguments with them and threatening his father physically. The agency director offered the case to a part-time fee-for-service social worker who happened to have an hour available the same evening. He accepted the case and decided to begin by inviting the parents for a same-day appointment.

The parents arrived early for the first visit. The worker introduced himself and discussed confidentiality and the limitations regarding abuse and danger. The mother appeared anxious and tearful, and said she was at her wit's end. She said her son had been a problem since he was little. She described him as a "bad alcoholic" who is homosexual, has mental problems, and has been in legal trouble. He had been living with a lover until a few months ago when he lost his job and became homeless. He pressured his mother into agreeing to let him into the empty family home, although the rest of the family is angry at her for "bailing him out again." When asked how he felt, the father said he wanted him out of the house. He told stories about the son getting into jams and begging his mother for help, such as calling her from a restaurant with an unpaid check and seeking her credit card number. The mother gave it to him; the father said he would have hung up.

The worker asked about other family members. The mother described her other children as wonderful. The older son is married with children and is a police officer. Thus, it has often been embarrassing to him when his brother got into trouble with the law. An older daughter is a nurse who is married with children and living out of state. A younger daughter, who was very upset about her brother's situation, is a para-professional and married to a firefighter. The mother was worried about her daughter's "de-pression" and pulled out a piece of paper on which her daughter had listed things she wanted to be read to the worker. The mother read the list, which noted: the son has also had drug prob-lems; he was twice unsuccessfully prosecuted for murder; he had a conviction for arson; and he had been hospitalized for mental problems. The daughter's note elaborated on one hospi-talization during which a psychiatrist indicated that he thought the son had manic–depressive illness, but was "overruled" by a senior psychia-trist who viewed the son's problem as predomi-nantly alcoholism.

The worker asked about the family history. The mother described the family as imperfect, but said that they had done the best that they could. She revealed her husband's alcoholism. Upon questioning, he indicated that he had been sober for two years. Although his drinking years were bad, the family remained intact during their 40 years of marriage. The worker also learned that both grandfathers had been alcoholic.

When the end of the hour approached, the worker asked each of the parents what they thought needed to be done about the situation. The father was clearly in favor of kicking the son out. The mother became tearful and was concerned about her son having nowhere to go. The worker suggested other options for the son, beginning with detoxification, and added that afterwards the son might be able to get into a residential program. He knew of halfway house programs that involved gay men. The worker said that the parents had a tough decision to make. The mother asked about resources, whereupon the worker listed the detoxes and

discussed asking the police or district court for assistance. She was reluctant to involve the police, though, out of fear of embarrassment to the older son.

The worker told them that he would be avail-able by phone for the next several days, but that he would be on vacation the following week. He offered them his business card and gave them another one for the son, so that he could call the worker himself if he needed help get-ting into treatment. Finally, the worker gently recommended that the mother attend an Al-Anon meeting. He gave her a list of meetings and told her that it might help to be with others who have been in this situation and to learn how they manage their feelings about it.

The worker did not hear from the parents or the son for the rest of the week. He did not contact them that week nor during his vacation. On the last day of vacation, the worker received an urgent call from the younger daughter. She was crying and reported that the son had burned down the house on the previous afternoon. No one was hurt in the fire, but the son had been arrested. She was afraid that her father had gone on a binge, as he was missing, and she was also afraid that her older brother was suicidal. The worker asked some questions about the behav-ior of the father and the brother, but there didn't seem to be a need for legal intervention for their safety. He recommended that she ask as many family members as possible to attend a family meeting on the following evening.

When the worker arrived at his full-time job the next morning, among his pile of messages from the vacation week was one from the alco-holic son who had tried to contact him. On his way to meet with the family that evening, the worker stopped for coffee and noticed that the story was on the front page of the newspaper, including a picture of the son being taken from the burning house in restraint.

The second visit was attended by both par-ents, the older daughter who had flown in from her distant home, and the younger daughter and her husband, whose firefighting company had responded to the house fire. As the family arrived, the mother said to the worker, "It just didn't work." Upon sitting down, they explained that the oldest brother was too upset and angry to attend. The older daughter announced that she was also very angry. The father was quiet. The younger daughter said that she had tracked down by telephone the psychiatrist who had evaluated the son as primarily alcoholic rather than mentally ill. She said that she told him to look at the front page of the paper and asked, "Do you think he's bad enough now?" before hanging up on him.

The worker introduced himself to the daughters and son-in-law. With the parents' permission, he reviewed the content of the first meeting. The mother recalled that, after the first meeting, they consulted with their pastor and were surprised that he said many of the exact same things that the worker had said. They also talked to an AA "12-stepper" who had been trying to reach out to the son. He told them that if his own parents hadn't thrown him out years ago, he would be dead. The mother had been telling the son about detox. The son seemed to be trying to make arrangements for detox, but the mother found out he was lying. They decided to confront the son by telling him that they were returning to Florida and that he had four days to get out. The son acted "strangely," which worried his father, but the parents went out to return some Christmas gifts to a store. When they returned, the house was on fire and the son was in police custody.

The family members started talking about the son. The older daughter said that he had always been "weird," even as a child. He was impulsive and would often have tantrums. The mother added that he was not "macho" like his older brother and that she felt bad for him. The father admitted to favoring the older son by attending his sports games and other activities,

while frowning upon the younger son's homosexuality. The worker commented that there seemed to be a split in the parental relationships, with the father close to the older son and the mother close and protective of the younger son. The older daughter agreed, and complained that both daughters were left out in the process. She said that she couldn't handle all the tension and trouble in the family and therefore moved away. She added that she had become very active in programs for "adult children."

At this point the younger daughter, who had been silent, started to cry. She raised her voice and told her older sister that she was very angry at her for leaving. She said that everyone in town and in school knew about the son's prior murder prosecution, and she was mortified as a teenager. Now with the story in the paper, she was too embarrassed to return to work. She said that she just wants to stay under the covers all day. She cries all the time and cannot eat. She denied suicidal ideas, but said she is afraid that she might go crazy. The worker offered some reassurance that she did not seem crazy, and that the feelings she expressed seemed appropriate for the experience. The older daughter laughed and said that this family didn't "do" feelings. She apologized to the younger daughter for leaving, but said that she felt she had no choice at the time.

The worker asked the father about his drinking; he answered that he was OK for now. He said that his pattern was to stay sober in a crisis, but binge when things were going well. The worker then asked the family about the older brother. The mother said that he probably wouldn't come to a meeting because of concerns about confidentiality. The worker offered assurances in that regard.

As it was well past the planned time to stop, the worker asked if there was anything else the family would like to bring up. The older daughter addressed her father and said that, although his drinking had caused a great deal of trouble for her as a child, being his daughter eventually brought her to where she is now, healthy and aware. She stood up and embraced him. The younger daughter started sobbing and the older daughter embraced her, too.

The mother said that she felt guilty and to blame for all of the family's problems. The older daughter reassured her and started talking about "co-dependency" as the tendency to accept blame for problems that belong equally to other family members, and as a common pattern among adults who grew up in alcoholic families. The older daughter then wanted her mother to explain what actually went on in her home growing up. The mother seemed surprised and said that although her father was a "bad alcoholic," the family stayed together and did all right. The older daughter said that her maternal uncle tells a very different story. The mother said she was sorry for doing things that might have hurt the family, like bailing out the son too much. She said that she always worries about him, that even now she worries that he has no underwear in prison. The older daughter replied, "Frig the frigging underwear."

The worker said that it was time to stop and asked the family about plans for the near future. The parents said they would be staying with the older son until they get things settled with the house, and after that, they would return to Florida. The worker asked if they would like another family meeting, and they said they would. The worker set a time for the meeting and again suggested Al-Anon. He said that he was sorry that the family talking and decision making was attended by the loss of their home.

Questions for Class Discussion

1. What common family responses to alcoholism are evident in this case? How are these responses expressed in the behaviors of individual family members?
2. Related to the worker's decision about how to intervene in this crisis case, discuss the following choices, and the potential consequences and outcomes of each:
   - Should the worker have tried to see the son at the outset of the case?
   - Should the worker have seen the son prior to advising the parents about their options?
   - Given the parents' ambivalence and lack of consensus, should the worker have taken a more exploratory approach with the parents in the first session?
   - Could the worker have more actively facilitated getting the son into detox?
   - Should the siblings have been involved earlier in the treatment process?
   - Should the worker have contacted the family prior to leaving on his vacation when he did not hear from them?
3. What should be the goals of the second family meeting? How could the worker further explore the father's alcoholism? What recommendations might be made for follow-up treatment for this couple once they return to Florida? What recommendations might be made for follow-up treatment for other family members?
4. From an agency management point of view, should this case have been assigned to a fee-for-service worker about to leave on a one-week vacation? Assuming that there was no choice in assignment of the case, or that from the intake the case did not appear to be a "crisis situation," what kind of backup or crisis management resources does the agency need to have in place?

Teaching Points

1. Blaming and displacement of anger is apparent, currently directed at the mother and the hospital psychiatrist. Cultural shame and embarrassment is present, exacerbated by the family members in the police and fire departments. There is a wish to view the son as primarily mentally ill and victimized by poor professional judgment.

Co-dependency, which enables the son's destructive behavior, is seen particularly in the mother, where its origin is apparent in her family, and in the split parental relationship in this generation. Co-dependency is characterized by preoccupation and extreme dependence on a person emotionally, socially, and sometimes physically (Wegscheider-Cruz, 1985). It is the assumption of responsibility for meeting others' needs to the exclusion of acknowledging one's own (Cermak, 1986). The children seem to have been trying to manage their father's and brother's alcoholism by combinations of avoidance, manipulation, sublimation via entering helping and crisis occupations, and some self-help activity.

2. The father's pattern of staying sober in a crisis and binging when things go well suggests that he is at high risk for relapse when the couple returns to Florida. In developing a preventive plan with him, the worker needs to explore how the father has gotten sober and stayed sober in the past, so that a similar treatment plan can be created *before* relapse. Examples of questions might include:
   - Did the father get sober with the support of an inpatient or outpatient detoxification and/or rehabilitation program? Could he return to this program for help if necessary?
   - Had the father ever used AA as a support in getting and staying sober? If so, was he still involved?
   - Did he have a sponsor(s) to whom he could turn for help?
   - What supports, if any, had family members used while he was getting and staying sober?
   - What changes in his daily routine and social life (e.g., friends, leisure activities) did he have to make to support his sobriety?

3. Referral to Al-Anon and/or other groups should be explored further with the wife and children. In referring clients to 12-step programs, it is important to:
   - Make sure the client has a list of local meetings. These can be obtained by calling the AA or Al-Anon information number in the telephone book. Meeting schedules are also available at many substance abuse, mental health, health, family service, and other social service agencies.
   - Explore the client's previous experiences with or stereotypes about 12-step programs and reassure the client that not all groups and meetings are alike.
   - Encourage the client to attend several meetings, especially "beginners" meetings in different locations, before deciding which to join.
   - Offer to accompany the client to meetings, if that is clinically indicated.
   - Encourage the client to get a sponsor as soon as he or she feels ready.
   - Review the client's experience after several meetings to offer support and perspective.

4. Given that the case constituted a crisis for the family (irrespective of whether the son had acted out), it seems unwise that a fee-for-service worker who was about to go on vacation was assigned. Many agencies have an "on-call" system where a crisis worker is available, at least by phone, during evenings and weekends. The worker can assess the severity of the situation and choose appropriate alternatives such as:
   - Counseling and calming the client/family, and advising they wait until business hours to see a clinician;
   - Recommending they use another resource temporarily (e.g., relatives, friends, clergy, 12-step program);

- Sending them to the nearest emergency room for psychiatric evaluation and disposition;
- Arranging for the original clinician to contact them if necessary.

In this case, the son's arson and the massive property damage that ensued might have been avoided if such an on-call system had been available.

Suggested Readings

Ashenberg-Straussner, S. L. (Ed.). (1993). *Clinical work with substance abusing clients*. New York: Guilford.

Bean, M., Whitfield, C., & Williams, K. (1976). *Alcoholics anonymous*, A psychiatric annals reprint, 1-34.

Bepko, C., & Krestan, J. A. (1985). *The responsibility trap: A blueprint for treating the alcoholic family*. New York: Free Press.

Cermak, T. (1986). *Diagnosing and treating co-dependence.* Minneapolis, MN: Johnson Institute Books.

Dulfano, C. (1992). *Families, alcoholism, and recovery* (rev. ed.). San Francisco: Jossey-Bass.

Treadway, D. C. (1989). *Before it's too late: Working with substance abuse in the family*. New York: Norton.

Wegscheider-Cruz, S. J. (1985). *Choicemaking*. Pompano Beach, FL: Health Communications.

Ziebold, T. O., & Mongeon, J. E. (Eds.). (1985). *Gay and sober: Directions for counseling and therapy*. New York: Harrington Park.

The Chum Family: Refugees from Cambodia

The following case highlights the evolution of alcoholism in a Cambodian family, including beliefs and attitudes about drinking, cultural patterns affecting family life, and possible impacts of the refugee experience. Teaching points identify aspects of loss and trauma that may influence the family's ability to cope. Several methods are described for increasing the cultural relevance of services.

This case can be used in both foundation and advanced clinical courses, as well as in an elective focused on cross-cultural practice. Some familiarity on the part of the instructor with Southeast Asian cultures will be helpful.

Case Study

This year's Cambodian New Year celebration is a happy one for the Chum Family. Mr. Chum has been sober for 15 months. The family went to the temple to give thanks that Mr. Chum has a job and his health is improving. His wife, Mrs. Sokha, does not have stomach problems as she did before.

The children are growing up. Their oldest son is graduating from college this year and will attend medical school next year. The middle son has come home for the celebration, and this has greatly pleased his mother, who has not seen him in many months. He dropped out of school about two years ago, and his parents believe that he has become a member of a local gang. The young daughter is beginning to overcome her learning problems and is doing better in school; she is also beginning to talk a little. She has always been very shy.

The Chums arrived in the United States 11 years ago. Both Mr. Chum and Mrs. Sokha were able to get jobs almost immediately and, after several years, were able to buy a house. Over the past 5 years, however, the family has had many troubles.

When Mr. Chum drank, both in refugee camps and during his first few years in the U.S., he would always drink heavily, but he would do this only several times a year. He would be sick for a day or two and then make a commitment to stop drinking. Mrs. Sokha was not concerned except that these drinking bouts were expensive and took away from the family's food and rent money. She would learn to anticipate these problem times by secretly saving any money she could. Mrs. Sokha thought that it would be best not to complain because she didn't want to anger her husband. Besides, she felt she was lucky; some women she knew had husbands who drank all the time.

Within a few years, Mr. Chum's drinking began to occur every weekend. He would meet up with friends and sometimes stay out all night. When he did not return home at the end of an evening, Mrs. Sokha would be very upset, fearing that her husband was having an affair. She felt angry and ashamed—the community would think she was a bad wife.

Mrs. Sokha worked ten hours a day at her job and tried very hard to save money. Exhausted from her labor, she was frequently ill with stomach problems. To keep her husband home, she constantly cooked his favorite meals and had beer in the house at all times. She also warned the children not to disturb their father, for he was tired from working so hard. Mrs. Sokha had heard that this was what other wives did to keep their husbands at home and away from other women.

This all pleased Mr. Chum very much and soon he was drinking every night, which led to a great deal of stress and tension in the home.

Mrs. Sokha and the children would try hard not to anger him, but often to no avail. There seemed to be no reason for these changing moods. He would be upset that the children were so disrespectful one day, and the next day he would praise them for almost the same behavior. No one in the family knew how to please him.

As time went on, the oldest son graduated from high school and received a scholarship from a prestigious university in another state. He went to a local college instead because of the family's financial problems. Traveling back and forth, and affording books and other college expenses would have been difficult. More important, he was unwilling to leave his mother alone to cope with his father—as the oldest son, he was able to calm his father down better than anyone else.

The second son was having trouble in school and frequently got into fights with other students. He dropped out of school and became involved in a gang. He often stayed away from home at night, and when he did come home, he argued with his father. Several times his father beat him severely, and on one occasion the son fought back and caused injury to the father.

The daughter was a very quiet and withdrawn child who spent most of her time playing with her dolls. She had no friends. Her teacher was worried that she might have a learning disability. She was not able to concentrate or finish her schoolwork.

One day Mr. Chum had chest pains and was taken to the hospital. The doctors discovered that he had many medical problems, including high blood pressure, a damaged liver, and an ulcer. The hospital sent a Cambodian counselor to talk with him about how drinking was causing his medical problems.

Mr. Chum eventually stopped drinking with the help of this counselor and his doctor. At first, family members did not believe that Mr. Chum's sobriety would continue. But months went by, and soon they realized he had been sober for more than a year. Conflicts and tensions in the Chum household had eased. Eventually, the oldest son felt he could leave to go away to medical school.

Questions for Class Discussion

1. From the limited information provided, are there any cultural issues which service providers would need to understand?

2. Can Mr. Chum's refugee experience be relevant to his drinking problem? If so, how?

3. How do you think the Chums understand Mr. Chum's excessive drinking?

4. If assigned to the case, how would you proceed? What kind of resources would you seek out? What kind of cultural concepts or values might help engage Mr. Chum in treatment?

5. Some studies report that Asians experience a "flushing response" after drinking. To what extent is this a deterrent to further drinking and to the development of alcoholism?

6. To what extent have substance abuse services been developed for Cambodian or other Southeast Asian refugees and immigrants resettled in the United States?

Teaching Points

1. Cultural issues:
   - gender roles—dominance of husband in marriage;
   - filial role—responsibility of elder son to help mother;
   - importance of community—"good standing" and respect is important to the family, as the community can "sit in judgment";
   - concept of "face"—an individual's behavior reflects on entire family, can cause "shame" and loss of status/respect for family in the community.

2. Relevance of refugee experience:
   - trauma—related to war, acts necessary to survive, escape, rape, assaults in refugee camp, "survivor guilt," shattered assump-

tions about world and self, issues of trust and betrayal;

- multiple losses—family members who died, family members left behind, homeland, culture, job, status, religion, maybe hope;
- loss of control—being in limbo in refugee camps, not feeling in charge/competent as a newcomer in a new culture;
- delayed surfacing of emotional issues—possible emergence of PTSD and/or depression symptoms;
- changing roles—loss of status/power as a male in the U.S., women recognizing new rights and power, children "empowered" by early language acquisition, parental power and status of elderly possibly diminished;
- increasing Americanization of children—possible intergenerational conflict;
- changing political situation in Cambodia—possible sense of urgency to visit Cambodia and find relatives, and/or ambivalence about remaining in the U.S.;

3. Views of drinking and alcoholism:
- traditional view of alcohol: OK for men in social situations; heavy social drinking is endorsed, but alcoholism is stigmatized and shameful (Amodeo, Robb, Peou, & Tran, 1996);
- cultural conceptions of alcoholism and drug abuse, as well as conceptions of physical and mental illness, are different from Western conceptions; the "disease concept" may be confusing and may reduce the credibility of the worker;
- education about medical and social consequences and impact of alcoholism on the family system is essential.

4. Recommended aspects of the treatment plan and interventions:
- Use bicultural/bilingual staff, if available; agencies should pair a bilingual, bicultural Cambodian worker with a clinician with substance abuse experience to do assessment and counseling.

- If bilingual, bicultural staff is not available, use interpreters. Issues include ethical/practical issues of relying on family members to provide this service; availability of trained interpreters; necessity of pre- and post-conferencing with interpreter; recognition of both linguistic and "cultural" interpretation needs (Amodeo et al., 1996).
- Rely upon key cultural informants—formal/informal community leaders and bicultural human service providers who may offer essential information, insight, and resources.
- Consult and collaborate with existing agencies that are successfully serving Cambodian families.
- Involve religious leaders and/or traditional healers who may be helpful (Berry et al., 1992).
- Identify substance abuse programs that have cross-cultural experience.
- Focus on traditional roles and values (e.g., family loyalty, male head of household, value of education, importance of parenting, standing in community) when seeking to engage client/family in treatment.

5. Research on Asians and drinking has determined that Asians often experience a "flushing response," consisting of facial flushing, dizziness, headaches, rapid heartbeat, and itching. This syndrome results from a genetically transmitted alteration to the alcohol-metabolizing enzymes. When Cambodian research participants were asked about this response, some said they had seen it in their peers, but the symptoms did not deter people from drinking and did not seem aversive (Berry et al., 1992).

6. Although AODA is becoming increasingly evident among the Southeast Asian refugee population (Berry et al., 1992; Community University Health Care Center, undated; D'Avanzo & Frye, 1992; Jenkins, McPhee, Bird, & Bonilla, 1990; TonThat & Grigg-

Saito, 1988; Yee & Thu, 1987), few if any culturally specific substance abuse services are available in many parts of the country where refugees have settled. Although clients receiving health, mental health, and social services have often had AODA problems, only the more visible presenting problems have been addressed.

References

Amodeo, M., Robb, N., Peou, S., & Tran, H. (1996). Adapting mainstream substance abuse interventions for Southeast Asian clients. *Families in Society, 77*(7), 402-412.

Berry, L., Nil, S., Locke, N., McCracken, S., Seth, K., & Koch, V. (1992). *Cambodian oral history research: Preliminary findings on alcohol and other drugs in Cambodia and in the United States*. Chicago: Refugee Substance Abuse Prevention Project, Travelers and Immigrants Aid.

Community University Health Care Center. (undated). *Alcohol and drug abuse in the Southeast Asian community*. Minneapolis, MN: Community University Health Care Center, University of Minnesota Hospital and Clinic.

D'Avanzo, C. E., & Frye, B. (1992). Stress and self-medication in Cambodian refugee women. *Addictions Nursing Network, 4*(2), 59-60.

Jenkins, C. N. H., McPhee, S., Bird, J. A., & Bonilla, N. H. (1990). Cancer risk and prevention practices among Vietnamese refugees. *Western Journal of Medicine, 153*(1), 34-39.

TonThat, A., & Grigg-Saito, D. (1988). *Substance abuse services: Community input and programmatic change*. Unpublished manuscript.

Yee, B., & Thu, N. D. (1987). Correlates of drug use and abuse among Indochinese refugees: Mental health implications. *Journal of Psychoactive Drugs, 19*(1), 77-83.

The Chum Family–Vignette

The following vignette is a condensed version of the previous case. The same questions for class discussion and teaching points can be used when discussing it with students.

The Chum family, refugees from Cambodia, arrived in the United States 11 years ago. Both parents were able to get jobs, and through hard work the family seemed to be successfully rebuilding their lives. They were even able to buy a house. However, during the last couple of years, Mr. Chum has begun to go out regularly with friends and drink; he comes home drunk and angry. At first it was just on weekends, and his wife was primarily concerned about the money he wasted. She decided not to complain, though, so as not to give her husband any reason to be angry at her. Lately, however, he is out drinking every night. His wife is afraid he may be having an affair and that the community will think she is a bad wife. She tries everything to keep him at home: cooking his favorite foods, stocking up on beer, and telling the children not to disturb him.

So far none of this has worked. Indeed, other family members are now having problems. Mrs. Chum complains of stomach problems and exhaustion. The oldest son turned down a scholarship to an out-of-state college, because he was worried about leaving his mother to deal with his father. The second son dropped out of school and is believed to have joined a gang. The daughter's teacher observes that she is extremely withdrawn and unable to concentrate on her schoolwork.

Last week, Mr. Chum was hospitalized with chest pains and, to his and his wife's surprise, doctors have told him his medical problems are related to his drinking.

The W Family: The Effects of Alcoholism on the Family System

Working with one person in the family affects the entire family system, as illustrated by the W family. Individual treatment, couple counseling, and family therapy are used effectively to address the needs of this alcoholic family. The role of the mother's cultural background and the father's childhood sexual abuse are highlighted. The children express themselves poignantly by drawing pictures during a pivotal family session. Teaching points emphasize the healing elements of family therapy and the importance of educating the family about alcoholism.

Setting: Outpatient substance abuse clinic in an urban community.
Clients: Married couple, Ed and Rose W., and their children: Rebecca, 16; Gary, 12; Bill, 9.
Worker: Female intake worker with an MSW.
Presenting problem: Ed and Rose have requested counseling. The purpose of the initial contact was to explore their request for counseling and to complete a psychosocial assessment with each of them.

Rose: I'm worried about my husband's drinking. He went to detox two months ago. At first things were better, but he's drinking again. We have so many bills, and he doesn't seem to care. I had to go back to work because of our financial problems. I'm really worried about our children. I know their father's drinking is affecting them—they're angry with him and don't even talk to him anymore. Sometimes, I just don't know what to do. . . . Nobody in my family ever had a drinking problem. I thought he would be okay when he came back from detox.
Ed: I was in detox a few months ago and I have had a few slips since I came home. Things are

not too good at home right now. My wife and I are always arguing. She nags me all the time about my drinking and the bills.

Part I
Psychosocial History: Rose

Rose is a 39-year-old white female of Italian heritage. She describes growing up in a close-knit Catholic family as the youngest of three children. She has a 42-year-old sister and a 45-year-old brother. Her parents are still living and are in their eighties. While Rose was growing up, her father was a self-employed cabinetmaker, and her mother a full-time housewife. Rose denies any history of emotional, physical, or sexual abuse during her childhood.

Rose was quite close to her paternal grandmother, who lived with the family until she died during Rose's senior year in high school. Rose's grandparents had emigrated to the United States from Italy, and the Italian culture remained a strong influence in her family throughout her childhood and adult life.

After graduating from high school, Rose continued to live at home until she married Ed when she was 22 years old. Rose's siblings also remained at home until they married. Currently Rose and her siblings live in the same city as their parents.

Ed and Rose have a 16-year-old daughter, a 12-year-old son, and a 9-year-old son. After being a full-time housewife, Rose recently took a part-time job as a clerk in a retail store due to the couple's financial problems. Rose reports that she and Ed have frequent arguments about his drinking and their financial difficulties. She denies that the arguments ever lead to any physi-

---

cal violence. Rose reports that she stopped being sexually intimate with Ed some time ago due to her disgust with his drinking.

Rose reports no history of alcoholism in her family. Although wine was always present in the household, its use was never problematic. Rose began drinking socially at the age of 18, and she denies ever trying any drugs. She says she never particularly cared for alcohol and states that she is currently abstinent.

Psychosocial History: Ed

Ed is a 43-year-old white male of Syrian and French heritage. He is the third of four children. He has a 47-year-old sister, a 45-year-old brother and a 40-year-old sister. He says that he was raised primarily by his older sister and brother because his parents were always working. His father was a mechanic and his mother was a chef. Ed describes a history of emotional and physical abuse while growing up, but denies any sexual abuse.

Ed reports having difficulty in school. He repeated second grade, and later left school after completing the eighth grade at age 15. At that time, Ed went to work to help support his family. Eventually he obtained some training as a chef and has remained in that line of work.

Ed identifies himself as an alcoholic. He reports that he began using alcohol when he was 14 years old. His drinking increased over time until he was drinking a six-pack of beer and two glasses of wine every day. He reports that he is currently drinking nearly a quart of vodka daily. He has frequent blackouts and describes experiencing morning shakiness so severe that he cannot hold a cup of coffee. He has had two arrests for DUI in the past eight years and says that his drinking led to a 3–4 month separation from his wife last year. Ed says that his doctor has urged him to abstain from alcohol due to enlargement of his liver. He denies using any drugs other than alcohol and denies any history of substance abuse in his family except for one sister who used to drink heavily.

Ed states that he drinks when he is angry and depressed and to "settle his nerves." He feels isolated from his family and reports that his daughter is not speaking to him. He is angry that his wife has taken his car off the road and refuses to let him drive.

Ed reports that he is attending AA meetings several times a week and that he has a sponsor. His only substance abuse treatment was a 21-day detox a couple of months ago. This treatment was initiated by his sister. The longest period Ed has successfully maintained sobriety is about 30 days.

During the three-session intake process, the social worker discussed with Ed the possibility of inpatient treatment before initiating outpatient treatment. The worker spoke with Ed about the potential danger and difficulty of trying to stop drinking on his own considering his daily intake of alcohol. Although Ed realized that his drinking was causing problems in his life, he was ambivalent about abstinence and resistant to returning to detox. He stated his desire to try stopping on his own with AA meetings.

When this case was presented to the treatment team, the recommendation was for eight sessions of family treatment for Rose and the children. The team felt strongly that Ed would need to return to detox before he would be eligible to participate in outpatient treatment.

Questions for Class Discussion

1. Concerning Ed's alcoholism, is it significant that he started drinking at age 14?

2. What can we say about Ed's acceptance of his alcoholism? What should the worker's goals be with regard to this issue?

3. What are your thoughts about Ed's AA attendance and the fact that he has a sponsor? Could we expect that this would be a sufficient intervention?

4. What are the possible benefits of family treatment, and what should the focus of this family's treatment be?

Part II

Rose and the children had been attending family therapy sessions consistently. Following the fifth session, however, the family situation came to a crisis when Ed became intoxicated in the home and threatened to commit suicide with a butcher knife. At this point, Rose obtained a temporary restraining order. Ed was removed from the home and taken to a detox.

During the last three of the eight family sessions, there was much discussion of the family members' feelings about Ed being out of the home. The children expressed feelings of relief. They were less preoccupied with his drinking as summer vacation ended and they returned to school. Rose expressed feelings of concern over the future of the family and making ends meet financially as she increased her work hours. Though the family members had no contact with Ed during this time, they learned from Ed's sister that he had elected to go to a nine-month therapeutic community following detox.

In one of the final family sessions, the social worker provided Rose and the children with paper and markers and encouraged them to draw and write about their feelings. Rose drew two buildings on her piece of paper. She labeled one building "hospital" and she drew a picture of her husband inside, labeling him "dad." She drew a picture of "home" with the figures of mom and the three children on the inside. The figure depicting herself had first been drawn with a happy face, which she had changed to a sad face. The caption read, "Dad is away for a while. Will we ever be a family again?"

Sixteen-year-old Rebecca divided her piece of paper in half. On the left side she drew about "daytime," showing her father washing the car, cooking pizza, running errands. She wrote, "In the daytime he was very busy. He also kept talking about it over and over." On the right side of the paper she depicted "nighttime," with a picture of the family members in the living room watching television. An arrow pointed to her father. "He'd stumble around the house, then pass out in the rocking chair," she wrote. "At night he'd say that he needed cigarettes or needed to play the lottery. We thought we could trust him. We were wrong. Again. He got drunk!"

Twelve-year-old Gary also drew a picture of the living room, showing himself lying on the couch with a frowning face in front of the television. He drew his father sitting in a chair with blurry eyes, mussed-up hair and a cigarette in his mouth. His caption read, "I hate when he drinks and falls asleep with a smoke in his mouth."

Nine-year-old Bill drew a portrait of his father alone on the page. His father was drinking from a bottle and the word "alcoholic" was on his shirt. At the top of the page in large capital letters he wrote, "I hate when my father drinks."

Question for Class Discussion

5. What did the drawings show about family dynamics? What was the major benefit of this exercise?

Part III

At the end of the eight family sessions the social worker recontracted with the clients. The children agreed that they were feeling better. Because they were returning to school and would be busy with many school activities, they decided they would not continue in treatment at this time, but would be welcome to return at any point in the future. Rose elected to continue in individual counseling with the social worker.

Initially, individual sessions with Rose focused on her feelings that everyone in the family was "going in different directions" and her anxiety in tolerating the uncertainty of the family's future. She revealed that she felt isolated from her family of origin, as they did not understand why Ed had to engage in prolonged treatment and why he could not just stop drinking and come home to the family. At this time, Rose was attending Al-Anon sporadically and was able to relate some of the concepts she encountered there to her own situation.

As therapy progressed, the worker continued to provide Rose with educational information about alcoholism and its continuing effects on her and the family after Ed was out of the house. Rose began to have some limited telephone contact with Ed, who remained in the halfway house in another city. Rose began to struggle with the questions, "Do I want to take him back?" "Am I forgiving him too easily?" and "What if he does come home and has a relapse?" Sessions helped Rose to identify and talk about her emotions. Gradually, she became able to focus more on herself in sessions. Outside of sessions, however, she spent all of her time working, caring for the children, dealing with the financial burdens, and giving little attention to her own needs. During this time, she stopped attending Al-Anon, though she continued to attend therapy weekly and very rarely canceled a session.

About three months into the individual treatment during the Christmas holidays, Rose's mother was diagnosed with a terminal illness. Although Rose's family of origin did not understand Ed's alcoholism, they had been a main source of support for her, and Rose was particularly close to her mother. Rose began visiting her mother daily to help care for her. A new treatment issue arose as Rose began to address her grief over her mother's impending death. At the same time, Rose continued to work on how her husband's alcoholism had affected her and learned to identify and modify enabling be-

haviors. Rose began to allow herself to vent some of the anger and sadness she was feeling, crying in sessions for the first time.

As Ed's graduation from the residential program approached, the future looked somewhat brighter to Rose. Ed was doing well in the treatment program, had nearly ten months of sobriety, and was actively involved in AA. Ed came home on a trial basis on a couple of weekend passes and the couple decided that he would return home after completing the residential program. An appointment was made for aftercare counseling for Ed at the outpatient clinic. In treatment, Rose and her worker spent a great deal of time talking about challenges the family would still face even though Ed was sober. The possibility of relapse remained.

Two days after Ed graduated and returned home, Rose's mother died in the hospital with Rose at her side. In order to be with his wife on that day, Ed rescheduled his intake appointment. Although he continued to attend AA meetings, Ed had one relapse before his intake appointment (with a different worker). Ed was assigned to individual therapy with a female therapist and struggled to reestablish his sobriety.

In her own individual therapy, Rose began to deal with the grief and loss issues in the aftermath of her mother's death. She was also faced with the disappointment of her husband's relapse and the adjustment of having him home. Rose was able to explore her secret fantasy that her husband would return home and take all the responsibilities off her shoulders and care for her emotionally. Not surprisingly, Ed's return brought with it the reemergence of some of the old family dynamics, and once again Rose began having difficulty focusing on herself and her own feelings.

During this time, the worker urged Rose to return to Al-Anon. The worker had made this suggestion strongly several times since Rose had stopped attending several months before. Rose agreed that she should go back, but acknowledged that for unknown reasons she felt resistant to returning. Further exploration did not yield any definitive answers about Rose's reluctance to return to Al-Anon. Rose felt that resuming weekly church attendance would be a positive support for her. The worker encouraged this and helped Rose to expand upon that idea by adding a few other self-care activities to this plan. At this point, the worker felt somewhat frustrated and puzzled about Rose's resistance to Al-Anon, but hoped that they would be able to continue to address it in treatment.

Over the next couple of months, Ed relapsed sporadically and finally decided to return to detox. He revealed to Rose that he had regained intrusive memories of childhood sexual abuse which he believed were affecting his attempts to stay sober. Although Ed's relapses were causing her considerable stress, Rose chose not to tell her father and siblings, thereby cutting herself off from her main source of support.

As Rose wondered what Ed's most recent treatment attempt meant for their marriage, Rebecca entered her senior year in high school and expressed her preference to apply to colleges away from home. Rose became quite upset and thought that she was losing yet another person who was important to her. In one session, Rose told her worker that she caught herself telling Rebecca that it was more important for Gary, rather than Rebecca, to go to college because he would have to support a family. Rose said the minute she made the comment she "realized it was wrong." This exchange paved the way for a session exploring Rose's feelings of being caught in a "cultural time-warp" between her own traditional Italian upbringing and her daughter's own desire to be an independent woman. Rose was able to explore in greater depth how the cultural influences were related to her wish to be taken care of by her husband. That wish, however, was now in direct conflict with Rose's feeling that she could not depend on Ed and that she wanted to be able to support herself.

At this point in treatment, the worker really began to tune in to the cultural issues involved—the worker realized that she had not been fully aware of their impact. She educated herself about the Italian culture and understood in a different way the importance of family and marriage to Rose.

As Ed and Rose continued in individual therapy, their individual workers began providing biweekly conjoint couple's sessions to help the W's establish some communication, divide household responsibilities, and continue to function until they were able to decide whether or not to continue in the marriage. Currently the workers are helping Ed and Rose negotiate a written contract to cope with difficult aspects of living together.

Ed continues to work in individual treatment to stabilize his sobriety. Further work with his therapist has revealed that his sexual abuse history is severe and that Ed has felt confused about his sexual orientation for some time. Rose is aware of Ed's confusion and is beginning to address her own ambivalence about remaining in the marriage. She is now able to look back on the early years of the marriage and see the beginning signs of alcoholism. She is able to discuss the uncertainty she felt about marrying Ed because he was not Italian.

Rose continues to explore what marriage and family mean to her, with the worker now listening with an ear tuned to cultural influences. This work is particularly powerful in the context of the uncertainty of her marriage, her mother's death, and her daughter's upcoming departure for college. Rose has reached back out to her family by sharing more about her situation with her sister. Although she does not attend Al-Anon, she has two friends who do, and she calls them regularly to confide about family issues. She continues to make progress in focusing on herself and building her own interests. Recently she even grew confident enough to find a higher paying job that she enjoys.

Question for Class Discussion

6. What are some probable causes of Ed's relapse?

Teaching Points

1. The fact that Ed started drinking at age 14 is significant for several reasons. From a developmental perspective, Ed's use of alcohol at this age likely inhibited his ability to master some of the developmental tasks of adolescence. Additionally, when onset of drinking occurs in adolescence, alcohol becomes incorporated into the individual's ways of coping with and relating to the world, and it plays an ever more integral role in daily life. In terms of the progression of the addiction, Ed has been drinking steadily and increasingly for 29 years and is showing symptoms of later-stage alcoholism: blackouts, withdrawal symptoms, arrests for DUI, marital disruption, and liver disease.

2. Although Ed identified himself as an alcoholic, his behavior did not indicate acceptance of the need for abstinence and ongoing treatment. The worker's recommendation regarding medically supervised detox was based on the risk of unsupervised detox in late-stage alcoholism, and it is important for her to continue to underscore this. Recognizing that Ed may not yet be ready to change his drinking behavior, the worker does have the opportunity to explore with Ed his ambivalence about abstinence. By providing a supportive relationship and environment in which Ed's denial can be worked through, she can provide reality testing about the role and effects of drinking in his life, education about alcohol-

ism and treatment, and exploration of his feelings about what life without alcohol would be like.

3. Ed's attendance at AA and his relationship with his sponsor may not be sufficient in his efforts to maintain sobriety, but they are the supports he is currently willing to accept. For this reason, he should be encouraged to continue, along with individual outpatient therapy geared to the work identified in the previous teaching point. The therapist might gently suggest that Ed attend meetings more frequently, since he seems willing to use AA, and might also explore whether he is using his sponsor as a real support. In addition, the therapist could explore Ed's willingness to use an outpatient detox, which would provide medical supervision, but allow him to continue with AA and to remain home.

4. Family treatment would be useful for a number of reasons:
   • It would provide the children with a safe environment for expressing their anger and related feelings about their father's drinking. Common feelings among children in this situation are guilt (that their behavior has caused the alcoholism or a specific relapse), shame (that their friends, teachers, or neighbors might discover that their father acts inappropriately when drinking), loss and sadness (that he is unavailable to them emotionally when high or drunk, and that his relapses may be the precursors to a permanent breakup of the family), and fear (that he may injure himself when out of control, that they may be the object of his erratic behavior, or that they may be harmed living in a family that, in essence, has no father).
   • It would penetrate Ed's denial about the severity of his drinking problem and the need for a more intensive treatment plan. It might also help him see that his commitment to

the family has been overshadowed by the drinking behavior to the point where family members felt abandoned and betrayed.

- It could help the family learn that alcoholism is an illness that leaves the drinker unable to limit his/her use of alcohol and unable to reliably predict his/her behavior when intoxicated.
- It could help family members examine whether they were engaged in enabling behaviors that inadvertently supported or promoted the drinking behavior.

During the first five family sessions, the worker presented Rose and the children with a variety of educational materials, including information about: the disease concept/progression of alcoholism; the concept that family members can't control, cause, or cure the alcoholism; detaching from the alcoholic; family roles; enabling; and the use of AA and Alateen as supports. The worker also facilitated discussions about the difference between what family members were feeling on the inside and what they were showing on the outside, and about setting limits with the alcoholic and following through on those limits.

5. The exercise of drawing feelings related to the family was useful in many respects. In particular, it helped reveal some of the thoughts and feelings Rose and the children had not been able to verbalize. As each family member shared his/her picture, the others commented on similar feelings as well as their surprise to realize others had felt the same. For example, all of the members had worried about Ed falling asleep with a lighted cigarette, but they did not realize the others had worried about the same thing.

6. Several stressors could have contributed to Ed's relapses in the time following his discharge from the halfway house:
   - Postponing the intake appointment for aftercare at a time of high stress and adjustment left Ed without a critical support as he made the transition from halfway house to home.
   - Ed returned home after a 10-month absence to a family that had been through many changes, as had he. His wife had begun to take care of herself emotionally and financially and was more aware of her tendency to take care of others at her own expense. His daughter was making plans to leave for college, and his sons had been able to express many feelings about their father's drinking. These changes called for Ed and his family to relate in new and different ways. He may not have been prepared for these challenges and did not have sufficient supports in place to help face them without drinking.
   - Ed may have experienced Rose's grief following her mother's death as both a loss of support to him and a demand on him to take care of Rose.
   - Ed may have turned to alcohol (as he likely did in adolescence) to manage the feelings accompanying his intrusive memories of childhood sexual abuse.

Suggested Readings

Black, C. (1979). *My dad loves me, my dad has a disease.* Denver, CO: MAC Publishing.

Brown, S. (1985). *Treating the alcoholic: A developmental model of recovery.* New York: Wiley.

McGoldrick, M. (1982). Italian families. In M. McGoldrick, J. Pearce, & J. Giordano (Eds.), *Ethnicity and family therapy* (pp. 340-363). New York: Guilford.

Steinglass, P., Bennett, L. A., Wolin, S. J., & Reiss, D. (1987). *The alcoholic family.* New York: Basic Books.

Treadway, D. (1989). *Before it's too late: Working with substance abuse in the family.* New York: Norton.

Wegscheider, S. (1981). *Another chance: Hope and health for the alcoholic family.* Palo Alto, CA: Science and Behavior Books.

Ana: Substance Abuse in a Central American Immigrant Family

Alcoholism affects all members in a family system. Some members develop patterns of "overfunctioning" to compensate for the underfunctioning of alcoholic members. Those who are overfunctioning are often unable to meet their own needs in healthy ways. Children are particularly vulnerable. This case is suggested for use in both foundation and advanced clinical courses; it may also be incorporated into policy and/or cross-cultural practice courses. It raises issues of trauma and substance abuse; transgenerational patterns of alcoholism; and the impact of gender, language, and culture on accessibility and acceptability of services.

Ana is a 40-year-old woman from a war-torn Central American country who came to the U.S. nine years ago with her mother and daughter to escape the violence of a civil war.

Ana was born into a rural, poor family and does not speak English. Her mother, Mrs. Vega, was told when Ana was born that Ana was in danger from black magic hovering over her future, and she took Ana as an infant to a spiritualist to prevent this. Ana's father was an abusive and alcoholic man who died when she was a teenager. A few times he threatened his family with a gun while drunk. Mrs. Vega was hard working and frugal and held the family together. Ana worked in a factory. She became pregnant at age 22 by a married man whom she saw as kind. Ana's daughter, Gloria, was raised as much by her grandmother as by Ana, since Ana continued to work. The baby's father visited weekly and took an active role in parenting, but was killed by a bomb when Gloria was five.

Still in her home country, Ana began drinking, and her drinking increased in severity over two years. She became psychotic and suicidal while drunk after being threatened at work by a man who tried to rape her. After she emerged from a brief hospitalization, she was referred to Alcoholics Anonymous. Almost all those in attendance were men, but a sprinkling of women helped her feel safe. She used AA well, remaining sober for three years.

The pressures of the war and a worsening economy caused Ana to decide to come to the U.S. with her daughter, her mother, and her sister. Once in the U.S., Ana began drinking only a few drinks per day, primarily on weekends. Despite her lack of English, she used connections with old family friends to get a job and worked for two years at an electronics factory, where she became involved with a fellow worker. She became pregnant. This man was killed in an unexpected accident early in her pregnancy, and she began drinking in greater quantity and frequency, often getting drunk.

Her daughter Gloria was bright and did well in school. Gloria often took care of Ana, but they argued bitterly about Ana's drinking and Gloria felt humiliated by her mother's drinking and verbal abuse. Mrs. Vega tried to cover up Ana's drinking, but eventually the neighbors and family knew. Ana's son, Jose, was born with fetal alcohol syndrome, and Mrs. Vega and Gloria became primary caregivers. The state's Department of Social Services was called in when Gloria felt overwhelmed by Ana's verbal aggression, shortly after Jose's first birthday. The DSS worker spoke minimal Spanish and Gloria acted as translator. Ana was forced to begin outpatient therapy for substance abuse.

Ana successfully hid her continued drinking for four months. In addition to mood swings and cognitive difficulties, she also had nightmares.

She often dreamed of amputated limbs and saw signs in the cracks in the ceiling. She seemed deeply ambivalent about Jose's care, as well as overwhelmed and ignorant about his basic needs. In a family meeting, Mrs. Vega told the outpatient therapist about Ana's continued drinking. Ana was deeply hurt and humiliated, but entered a detoxification center. After two months of sobriety, she began drinking again, and this time Gloria revealed it to the DSS worker. The worker found an appropriate residential treatment program available for Latinas in another state; it was a three-month program about three hours away. DSS gave Ana a choice of attending residential treatment or having Jose removed. Two more months passed before a bed opened up in the facility. Meanwhile, Mrs. Vega was certified as the foster care provider.

While this was happening to Ana, Gloria became heavily involved with a boy from school and became pregnant. When the baby was born, Gloria and Mrs. Vega cared for Gloria's own infant, as well as Jose. At 18 months, Jose was enrolled in an English-only early intervention program for children with special needs. He seemed unusually irritable and, due to a serious feeding problem from birth, was very underweight. Jose's cognitive skills were somewhat compromised, but his motor skills were on target for his age.

He was extremely aggressive with Ana, however, and she avoided touching him or dealing with him whenever possible. Nevertheless, she showed concern and love toward him. She was able to connect his developmental difficulties with the many family disruptions he had experienced. She understood, to some extent, that he had greater difficulty dealing with stimuli than other children did.

Ana remained sober for the year following her termination from the residential treatment program, even though she did not attend AA. There was only one Spanish-speaking AA group per week in her area, and only men attended, many of them as a condition of their probation. The one time she tried to attend, she felt fearful and uncomfortable. She continues to be isolated socially. She has trouble parenting Jose, even with a Spanish-speaking family worker visiting regularly. She continues to see her therapist, and is considering medication.

Questions for Class Discussion

1. How would you describe the impact of alcohol on this system?

2. What issues might a family therapist focus on in working with this family?

3. Discuss the case from a psychodynamic, sociocultural, and "disease-concept" perspective. How might each perspective inform your work with this case?

4. If you were assigning Ana an individual diagnosis, what would it be? If more than one diagnosis, what would they be?

5. Were there specific services you would have liked to have had available to Ana which were not there? If so, what? Why might these have made a difference in her life and treatment?

Teaching Points

1. Impact of alcohol:
   - Serves as a buffer against loss and trauma;
   - Has resulted in Ana's inability to provide adequate mothering for either Gloria or Jose;
   - Has forced Gloria to become a parent, as she assumed increasing responsibility for her mother and brother;
   - Has contributed to Mrs. Vega's increased responsibility for her grandchildren in attempting to keep the family together.

2. Family therapy issues include the strengths of the culture, including the helping networks; roles and responsibilities with mechanisms to ensure that Ana fulfills some of her duties as a mother and as an adult. In the past, both Gloria and Mrs. Vega have had to subordi-

nate their own needs. Ana's recovery should involve the goal of establishing more balance in these relationships.

3. Perspectives:
   - *Psychodynamic.* Trauma is a major dimension. Ana suffered abuse from her violent, alcoholic father. Then the man who had fathered Ana's first baby was killed after five years of involvement with the baby. When Ana suffered an attempted rape at work, she became psychotic and suicidal due to the triggering of previous trauma experiences. After coming to the U.S. and becoming pregnant a second time, her new partner was also killed. Early abuse and traumatic events may have led to Ana's inability to keep herself out of relationships or environments that replay the trauma, or an inability to invest emotionally in her children, especially Jose.
   - *Sociocultural.* Ana must work after her father dies, leaving the care of her child to her mother. The family is forced to emigrate and seems to become socially isolated in interacting with the dominant culture—after nine years Ana still does not speak English. Having been raised in a patriarchal culture, Ana may seek out men who are not wise choices because the culture emphasizes that women need men to survive.

     Social systems in the United States seem to operate to diminish the family's sense of cultural identity and integrity. Jose will go to an English-only program. Although Ana goes to a program for Latinas, it is more than two hours away from her family. There is only one Spanish-speaking AA group per week in her area.
   - *Disease-concept.* This case suggests intergenerational transmission of a genetically and biologically based condition. Ana's father was an alcoholic. Gloria may well develop alcoholism as she matures into womanhood. Jose was born with fetal alcohol syndrome. Without specific societal approaches involving proactive prevention and early intervention methods that target children from alcoholic families, this intergenerational pattern may continue.

4. Ana's diagnoses include:
   - alcoholism;
   - probable PTSD; and
   - possible history of psychosis and suicidal behavior (the most tentative of the diagnoses).

   Further investigation may well rule out these latter two diagnoses. The history tells us that Ana was psychotic and suicidal while drunk. Judging the mental status of someone who is drunk or intoxicated is very difficult. For example, hallucinations may be experienced, but they may be part of alcohol withdrawal (alcoholic hallucinosis), rather than a psychotic disorder. Similarly, talk of suicide may not be related to suicidal intent.

5. Freeman (1992) argues that a more cohesive form of interagency collaboration will be needed to provide services to such addicted women and their children. In her view, no single agency or organization will be able to provide the broad range of intensive and complex services needed; organizations that typically work with families at particular stages should become involved much earlier. Turf battles and competition will need to take a secondary place to building working relationships across agencies.

Suggested Readings

Comas-Diaz, L. (1986). Puerto Rican alcoholic women: Treatment considerations. *Alcoholism Treatment Quarterly, 3*, 47-57.

Cook, P. S., Peterson, R. C., & Moore, D. J. (1990). *Alcohol, tobacco, and other drugs may harm the unborn.* U.S. Department of Health and Human Services, DHHS Publications No. (ADM) 90-1711.

Flores-Ortiz, Y., & Bernal, G. (1990). Contextual family therapy of addiction with Latinos. In G. W. Saba, B. M. Karrer, & K. V. Murphy (Eds.), *Minorities and family therapy* (pp. 123-142). Binghamton, NY: Haworth.

Freeman, E. (1992). Addicted mothers—addicted infants and children: Social work strategies for building support networks. In E. Freeman (Ed.), *The addiction process: Effective social work approaches* (pp. 108-122). New York: Longman.

Inclan, J., & Hernandez, M. (1992). Cross-cultural perspectives and codependence: The case of poor Hispanics. *American Journal of Orthopsychiatry, 62,* 245-255.

Rosett, H. L., & Weiner, L. (1984). *Alcohol and the fetus: A clinical perspective.* New York: Oxford University Press.

Zambrana, R. (Ed.). (1995). *Understanding Latino families.* Thousand Oaks, CA: Sage. (Particularly chapter 6, "Central American refugees in Los Angeles: Adjustment of children and families," by C. Dorrington, pp. 107-129.)

Intensive Family Preservation

A woman who has a problem with alcohol or other drugs faces considerable stigma from society, as she may be judged as loose, immoral, or a poor mother. If a woman denies the problem or does nothing about it, she may be unable to care for her children and may eventually lose them; if she admits it and seeks help, she still may be judged unfit and separated from her children.

Setting: Urban Child Guidance Clinic, Intensive Family Preservation Program (IFPS).

Client: Robin, a 27-year-old Irish-American woman with two boys, Thomas, age 5, and Leonard, age 4 months. The family lives in an adequately furnished duplex and receives income from AFDC. Each child has medical insurance through his father's employee benefits. Robin is covered by Medicaid. Thomas' father lived with the family until Thomas was 3 years old. He has since married and has two other children; however, he has maintained a strong relationship with Thomas through frequent visitation on weekends. Leonard's father is 52 years old, divorced with several adult children. He has been involved with Robin for one year. Recently, his job with a defense contractor has taken him to Israel for months at a time. Robin was raised in a working-class neighborhood near her present home. Her father died when she was in high school. Her mother died 3 or 4 years ago of senile dementia. Robin has an older sister who lives in the area, but they have limited contact.

Family team: A 35-year-old white male licensed social worker with nine years of preservation experience in direct practice with children and families, and a 48-year-old Italian-American female family support worker, indigenous to the client's neighborhood.

Case Record

The referral to the IFPS came on a Monday morning. On the previous Saturday night, the police were called to Robin's duplex when her neighbor became concerned about the family's well-being. The neighbor complained that "something was wrong" because Robin would not answer the door. When the police arrived, the lights were on in the duplex, the door was locked, the car was in the driveway, but no one answered the door. Looking through the windows, the police saw Robin lying face down on the living room floor. She was surrounded by empty beer cans. The police officers entered the duplex by breaking the window and opening the lock. Upon entry, they found both children in their beds asleep. The children appeared to be well nourished, clean, and dressed in pajamas. The police officers found that Robin was unable to come to a conscious state. They called for emergency medical services and Robin was immediately transported to the emergency room of the closest hospital. She was admitted to the hospital when her blood alcohol level was found to be exceptionally high. Medical personnel felt that Robin was in need of inpatient care as she had arrived in a life-threatening state.

Meanwhile, police notified the on-call Child Protective Services worker, as the two young children had no one to care for them. After obtaining some information from the neighbor, Thomas' father was contacted and the situation was described to him. He immediately agreed to take Thomas. As no family members could be found to care for Leonard, the worker placed him in foster care. Because placement was sought for a 4-month-old child at a late hour on a weekend, the only available licensed foster home was nearly 100 miles away. This home had been approved to accept HIV-positive infants, but since there was an "open bed" and no other placement option could be found, Leonard was placed in this home. It was also learned that Leonard was connected to an apnea (sleep) monitor during the night. This was unexplained at the time of placement.

As Robin sobered up, the gravity of the situation became apparent to her. She was concerned with the whereabouts of her children, and was distraught that she was in the hospital. She was also physically ill and weak from her episode of heavy drinking. The CPS agency assigned a worker to the case and filed for Order of Temporary Custody for both children. Hospital personnel felt that Robin should be immediately transferred to an AODA treatment program; in fact, a bed had already been secured for her at a local inpatient program. The CPS worker met with Robin and said that if she wished to be reunited with her children, she would first have to demonstrate changed behavior. The first step in this process was inpatient treatment for alcohol abuse.

As the hearing for the Order of Temporary Custody was held, the judge ordered that an attorney be assigned to represent the "best interests of the children." This was done, and the attorney argued that the mother was in need of alcohol treatment if she expected to be reunited with her children. A review of state protective services records revealed that one previous complaint had been investigated when Thomas's father had reported that Robin's alcohol consumption was affecting her ability to care for the children. (After a brief investigation, a case was not opened as no evidence of child neglect or abuse could be found.)

Because Robin wanted to be reunited with her children, she consented to inpatient treatment for alcohol abuse. Meanwhile, the foster parent caring for Leonard complained that the child was extremely distraught and could not be comforted. An HIV-positive infant was in need of placement at this foster home, so after only a few days, Leonard was transferred to another foster home about 30 miles from Robin's home. The foster parent at this home also complained of the child being inconsolable. Eventually, Leonard was taken to a pediatrician who, after finding no physical symptoms, concluded that the child was reacting to separation from his mother.

Further assessment of Robin revealed the following:

- Leonard's father had stayed with the family for three weeks, but had left the day prior to Robin's binge to return to Israel for several months.

- The children had excellent health care records that were up to date. Leonard was using an apnea monitor as he was felt to be at risk for SIDS (sudden infant death syndrome). A sleep study at a local hospital had been scheduled to determine if he needed to continue on the monitor. It was revealed that Robin had another child that had died from SIDS approximately two years earlier. This female child, Jennifer, had been approximately four months old when she died. Her death from SIDS was confirmed by the state medical examiner.

- Robin did not consume alcohol on a frequent basis. She appeared to fit the profile of a binge drinker. When she consumed alcohol, however, she drank to the point of unconsciousness.

- Robin had experimented, but had never regularly used, any other substances.

- Robin had completed high school and had waited until she was 21 before she had her first child. This was partly because she had stayed in the family home and cared for her mother who eventually died from senile dementia.

- The state protective service worker was committed to working toward family reunification and took the initiative to involve the IFPS.

• The alcohol treatment program was agreeable to working with the state protective service department and with the family support service toward the goal of reunification.

The family preservation program agreed to accept the case, and a social worker and family support worker were assigned. The initial intervention involved meeting with Robin and the state protective service worker to explain the services. Robin agreed to work intensively, as she completed inpatient treatment and was discharged from the hospital.

As soon as Robin agreed to work with the IFPS program, arrangements were made for the children to visit with her at the inpatient program. She appeared to be greatly relieved after their visits, but continued to be worried about their well-being. Thomas's father was agreeable to keeping him in his kindergarten program, even though this required that he transport him to and from the school each day. Thomas expressed great concern about his brother and asked that he be permitted to visit with him, as well.

Robin was involved in a wide range of services at the inpatient program. As she entered a 12-step program, she began to learn more about alcohol abuse. She also began to uncover her own feelings of loss and desperation and how they related to her drinking episodes. Robin began to work through the intense grief from the losses of her father, her mother, and especially her daughter. She was successfully discharged from the inpatient program in time to accompany Leonard to the hospital for the sleep study. This took place over a weekend and revealed that he no longer had irregular breathing. Nonetheless, Robin requested that he continue to wear the apnea monitor at night. The state protective service worker and the attorney representing the children agreed that Leonard should be returned to his mother's care upon discharge from the hospital. The return was contingent upon the IFPS program providing intensive, home-based services for the family. Robin would also have to demonstrate competence in providing care for one child (Leonard) before the second child (Thomas) would be returned.

Over the next 12 weeks, Robin was seen on an almost daily basis by the IFPS workers, either as a team or individually. As part of her recovery program, she began attending AA meetings every day, as well as returning to the hospital for aftercare groups. She also spoke at length to the social worker and family support worker about the losses in her life. Most of the content, however, focused upon Jennifer's death. Describing the circumstances, Robin revealed that she had finished feeding Jennifer and that they both had fallen asleep. When Robin awoke, she found that Jennifer had died in her sleep. The pain and agony that she had felt had been bottled up since the baby's death. Robin also revealed her fear that Leonard would die from SIDS, as well. When Leonard's father left for Israel, she felt so much pain at this loss that she began drinking to the point of unconsciousness. She did not begin drinking until she had bathed, fed, and tucked the children into bed.

After 4–5 weeks of caring for Leonard, Thomas was returned home, as well. Although Thomas had been well cared for by his father, he insisted on going to his mother's. He was especially concerned about being separated from his brother and while separated had actually telephoned each day to talk to him.

As Robin became invested in AA, and as she worked through the grief and pain of her losses, her parenting improved. Even though she had always cared for the children's physical needs, it was unclear whether she had ever been able to meet their emotional needs. Her approach to the children changed as she became more aware of both of these components. She was very receptive to the "coaching" of the IFPS workers as they encouraged her to express feelings of anger, pain, and loss, and as they helped her to learn new behavior management techniques for dealing with her children and with her own feelings and behavior.

Thomas' father was skeptical of Robin's changed behavior, but he agreed that Thomas should return to live with his mother and brother. Leonard's father returned from Israel to find that Robin's changes were too dramatic for him. When she requested that he not drink in her presence, he became very angry. His history and behavior suggested that he also was in need of treatment for alcohol abuse. When he was approached by the social worker and offered help with getting services, he became furious and left the family, stating that he did not need nor want help. As he became aware that Robin was sincere about not drinking, he left the relationship. *Loss*

Except for one brief (one day) relapse, Robin has been sober for three years. The Orders of Temporary Custody expired after 90 days and her case was closed at the state protective services agency. Termination took place over many weeks, as the loss of the social worker and family support worker had the potential to evoke many strong feelings. After three years, she still contacts them every now and then to report on her progress. Thomas and Leonard are both healthy and developing appropriately. There have been no further reports of alleged neglect or abuse.

Questions for Class Discussion

1. What are the particular problems for mothers in getting treatment for drug and alcohol dependence?

2. At what point might infrequent drinking be a problem for someone? What questions need to be asked in an assessment interview to get at this information? What does this case illustrate about binge drinking?

3. What is the idea behind intensive family preservation work, and how does this fit with treatment of alcohol and other drug problems in the family? Evaluate the effectiveness in this case.

Teaching Points

1. A woman might delay treatment because, for instance, she does not have adequate alternatives for child care. Although improvements have come, a gap has existed in substance abuse treatment services for women with children, and for families as a whole. As in this case, a crisis situation often threatens the loss of the children and compels a mother to enter treatment. The crisis period is a window of opportunity if comprehensive services for the family are available.

2. A person does not have to drink on a daily or frequent basis to have a substance abuse problem. Binge drinking is often unrecognized as a problem, particularly if the person functions adequately and responsibly at other times. In an assessment, the pattern of drinking is critical (quantity, frequency, duration, consequences). Does the person drink large quantities to the point of blackouts, as in this case? Does the person repeatedly get into trouble or danger when on a binge? Do there seem to be particular precipitants for the episodes? In Robin's case, her drinking seemed to be related to losses. Some theorists might explain her drinking on the basis of "self-medication"—that is, she used a substance in an attempt to regulate her feelings of pain, guilt, anger, anxiety, or depression. The treatment concentrated simultaneously on helping Robin (a) develop skills for sobriety and (b) develop skills for coping with painful affect.

3. The IFPS uses a multisystems approach to advocate for the family, while protecting the best interests of the child. The charge to IFPS workers is to make "reasonable forts" to prevent unnecessary out-of

placement of children. If no alternative exists but to place children in foster care, the worker's goal is family reunification, when possible. Services are intensive, home and community based, and 8–12 weeks in duration.

In this case, due to the crisis situation, one out-of-home placement was necessary, but the other child was placed into kinship care (with the biological father). The actual and threatened loss of the children appeared to be the turning point for the client in her acknowledgment of her problem with alcoholism and her acceptance of treatment. The alcohol treatment program, the state protective service department, and the IFPS team worked collaboratively with this family. The IFPS became engaged while Robin was in inpatient treatment and continued on a daily basis for 12 weeks after her discharge. The children were returned as carefully and as soon as possible. Along with AA and outpatient alcohol treatment services, the IFPS team provided constant support for the family and remained available for long-term follow-up.

Suggested Readings

Adnopoz, J., Grigsby, R. K., & Nagler, S. (1991). Multiproblem families and high-risk children and adolescents: Causes and management. In M. Lewis (Ed.), *Child and adolescent psychiatry: A comprehensive textbook* (pp. 1059-1066). Baltimore, MD: Williams and Wilkins.

Adoption Assistance and Child Welfare Act of 1980, Public Law no. 96-272, H.R. 3434, 94 Stat. 500 (June 17, 1980).

Barth, R. P. (1990). Theories guiding home-based intensive family preservation services. In J. K. Whittaker, J. Kinney, E. M. Tracy, & C. Booth (Eds.), *Reaching high-risk families: Intensive family preservation in human services.* Hawthorne, NY: Aldine de Gruyter.

Finkelstein, N., Duncan, S., Derman, L., & Smeltz, J. (1990). *Getting sober, getting well: A treatment guide for caregivers who work with women.* Cambridge, MA: Women's Alcoholism Program of CASPAR, Inc.

Goldstein, J., Freud, A., & Solnit, A. J. (1973). *Beyond the best interests of the child.* New York: Free Press.

Grigsby, R. K. (1993). Theories that guide intensive family preservation services: A second look. In E. S. Morton & R. K. Grigsby (Eds.), *Advancing family preservation practice.* Newbury Park, CA: Sage.

Solnit, A. J., Nordhaus, B. F., & Lord, R. (1992). *When home is no haven: Child placement issues.* New Haven, CT: Yale University Press.

Ms. C: Asking the State to Take Child Custody

When a mother is cocaine dependent and afraid of harming her child, child welfare practice requires a comprehensive procedural approach, including assessment of the family situation, determination of the risk to the child, evaluation of child maltreatment, assessment of the need for out-of-home placement, and development of a service plan to eliminate risk factors. In the case below, risk factors and appropriate goals are outlined.

Setting: County Department of Human Services, Child Protective Services Unit.

Clients: Ms. C, a single 30-year-old black Protestant female dependent on cocaine, and her daughter Tiffaney.

Worker: Child welfare worker.

Case Study

Ms. C was referred to Child Protective Services (CPS) by a psychiatric social worker in a hospital emergency room, where she was both seeking admission for crack cocaine dependence and asking the state to take custody of her child for fear she would harm her. The slightly built Ms. C is originally from the South, where she resided with her mother and two sisters. She moved to a city in the Midwest four months ago to be with her daughter's father, Norman, who is unemployed and lives in a housing complex. She, Tiffaney, and Norman occupied a one-bedroom, rat-infested apartment with no utilities located next to a crack house, where Ms. C spent a majority of her time. During the assessment, I spoke with Ms. C two times in person, and an estimated 15 times on the telephone within a five-day period. Ms. C used a pay phone on the corner of her block.

Ms. C was referred to CPS when it was determined that she was not in control of herself and felt she may cause harm to her child because of her crack cocaine dependency. Ms. C said that, because of her addiction, she was requesting to be admitted for inpatient treatment, but if there wasn't a bed for her she would like CPS to take custody of her child. No bed was available, and the child was taken into custody at that time.

Part I

Questions for Class Discussion

1. What is known about the impact of substance abuse on parenting?

2. What approach might you take in your first interview with the mother? What areas/topics would you want to cover?

3. How would you assess risk in this case? What information would you need/want?

During my first interview with Ms. C, she explained why she gave her daughter up for placement. She stressed it was only a temporary placement until she could get herself into inpatient treatment and get well. I assured Ms. C that her daughter was well and in good care. I went on to explain about the foster parents and said that Tiffaney had been given clothing and would also go to the doctor to start receiving her shots. Tiffaney had not previously received any shots.

Concerns Presented by Client

Ms. C noted that because of her drug addiction, she has no money, no food stamps, and no place to live. Her apartment was trashed and looted by the neighbors that ran the crack house because Ms. C owed them money. She was also concerned that she would no longer be able to see her child fed or clothed or get proper medical care. She was curious to know exactly how CPS could help her and ensure her child's safety. I explained to Ms. C that, first of all, Social Services would file a Temporary Custody, and we would appreciate her appearance at the hearing. I also told her that she is guaranteed visitation and input into her child's care and that she will be made aware of any medical care her child receives. Income Maintenance would have to be contacted and advised that her daughter is in CPS custody, therefore preventing the family from receiving Aid for Dependent Children. Nevertheless, Ms. C could apply for General Assistance. She said she understood and only wanted what's best for her daughter. An application was made with her Income Maintenance worker.

Ms. C feels that she has totally lost control of her life. She has no money, no job, no home, and no friends able or willing sincerely to help her. She has very low self-esteem. When she looks in the mirror, Ms. C says, she sees a person with ugly skin, pimples, rashes, and a scrawny body. She wants to get off crack, yet feels too weak to do anything about it. Ms. C associates with other addicts, pimps, prostitutes, and pushers, and if necessary stays in the crack houses for periods of time and performs sexual acts to hit the pipe. Because most of her money goes to sustain her habit, Ms. C stays in her poor neighborhood. Ms. C feels she has no one, not even Norman, who is in a depressed state of his own.

Part II

Questions for Class Discussion

4. Would you substantiate child maltreatment in this case? Why or why not? What type of maltreatment?

5. Would you have removed the child from the home? Why or why not?

The assessment indicates that this is a dependency case with neglect indicated by Ms. C failing to provide her child with a safe, nurturing environment in which to grow. Ms. C failed to provide food, clothing, and proper medical care for her child. The county has temporary custody of Tiffaney.

Goals:

a. Ms. C will enter drug counseling at the agency, and enter a three–day detox program within 30 days.

b. Ms. C will attend classes on parenting skills that are offered by a local support group.

c. Ms. C will sign a waiting list at agency and, in the meantime, join outpatient support group and complete the program.

d. Ms. C will secure adequate housing within three months in a safe and drug-free environment.

e. Ms. C will cooperate with Social Services in keeping all appointments and will call if appointments have to be canceled. She will also provide all information as requested by the social worker.

f. Ms. C will maintain weekly contacts with her child.

g. Ms. C will provide a care plan for her child upon Tiffaney's return (reunification).

h. Ms. C will provide medical information and/or authorization to obtain medical information.

Part III

Questions for Class Discussion

6. In your opinion and based on your knowledge of child welfare practice, what are the advantages and disadvantages of the case plan?

7. How would you ensure culturally sensitive services in this case?

8. What are the larger (macro) social service issues represented in this case?

Teaching Points

1. Parental substance abuse can produce low birth weight, fetal alcohol syndrome, fetal alcohol effect, and learning disabilities. Other impacts of substance abuse on parenting:
   - bonding can be impaired if the abuse occurs when the child is very young;
   - drug-seeking behavior (with crack in particular) can take the parent out of the home and away from the child;
   - money spent on drugs is money diverted from basic needs;
   - judgment and emotional availability are impaired;
   - during drug withdrawal, parents are physically unable to respond to emotional and physical demands and potential crisis situations;
   - children are often forced to "fill in" for the dysfunctional parent;
   - there may be a bad crowd of people in the house;
   - household accidents are common;
   - drug use leads to unpredictable emotional response, including explosiveness, violence, and depression.

2. For single parents, knowing the child is safe is usually a precondition to treatment for the mother; the worker needs to ensure the child's safety first. Recovery issues are different for mothers. Fear of losing the child may be an incentive for the mother getting treatment, but fear that the child is not receiving good care and/or that the child will be taken permanently by CPS may be disincentives to treatment (Finkelstein, Brown, & Laham, 1981).

3. Different stages of child development carry different risk factors. Several major parameters should be considered in assessing risk: drinking and drugs (the kind of drugs used, pattern of drug use, stage of the parent's addiction, and the number of chemically dependent parents); child development characteristics (the child's age, health, personality, and location in the birth order); and environmental supports (adequate housing, socioeconomic status of parents, employment, the presence and number of other relatives).

4. A strong case for neglect can be made based on living arrangements that include a rat-infested apartment with no utilities located next to a crack house. Ms. C's addiction creates a dangerous situation for the child: when the mother is at home, she may be disoriented and unpredictable. Further, she is involved with drug users and pushers who may show up and demand money, drugs, or sex. Involvement in illegal activity puts mother and child at risk for police intervention.

5. Removing the child would probably be the best option. Although Ms. C is obviously concerned about Tiffaney and wants what is best for her, Ms. C is unable to act on her own or anyone else's behalf at this point. Norman also seems unable to serve in a parental capacity at this point.

6. Advantages of the case plan:
   - It is specific.
   - It is comprehensive; for example, it addresses substance abuse, housing, finances, child contract, sharing of information between agencies.

   Disadvantages of the case plan:
   - Time frames and phases of work are not indicated for several goals; this could be a problem in that some of these goals need to precede others.
   - How much input the client has had in the development of these goals is unclear. Are they her goals or the worker's? This will have a strong impact on the client's ability and willingness to work on them. Some goals that are important to the client may have been left off;
   - Some of the goals seem too rigid.

7. Poverty, race, and gender affect treatment outcome and need to be figured into the construction of the treatment plan.
8. Macro issues:
   - Underfunding of substance abuse treatment system: scarcity of treatment beds for detoxification, scarcity of residential programs for women and their children.
   - Lack of substance abuse training for child welfare workers.
   - Tension between the mission of the child welfare system and the substance abuse treatment system. The latter sees abstinence and recovery as precarious in the first year or more and recommends that substance-abusing clients focus their energy on establishing their lives as sober/clean individuals. The child welfare system would like parents to return to their parenting role as soon as possible. If safety for the child can be established, the child is often returned within the first six months of abstinence, when the likelihood of relapse is still high.

Suggested Readings

Azzi-Lessing, L., & Olsen, L. J. (1996). Substance abuse-affected families in the child welfare system: New challenges, new alliances. *Social Work, 41*(1), 15-23.

Finkelstein, N., Brown, K. N., & Laham, C. Q. (1981, Fall). Alcoholic mothers and guilt: Issues for caregivers. *Alcohol Health and Research World*, 45-50.

Finkelstein, N., Duncan, S., Derman, L., & Smeltz, J. (1990). *Getting sober, getting well*. Cambridge Women's Alcoholism Program of CASPAR Inc.

Tracy, E. M., & Farkas, K. J. (1994). Preparing practitioners for child welfare practice with substance abusing families. *Child Welfare, 73*(1), 57-68.

Wallace, B. C. (1989). Psychological and environmental determinants of relapse in crack cocaine smokers. *Journal of Substance Abuse Treatment, 6*, 95-106.

Zuskin, R., & DePanfilis, D. (1995). Child Protective Services: Working with CPS families with alcohol or other drug problems. *The APSAC Advisor, 8*(1), 7-12.

The Story of Phoung and Thi:
Fear of Losing Face in the Community

This case summarizes the progression of a husband's alcoholism and highlights the impact of alcoholism on the family system, particularly the "family rules." The case also challenges the reader to reflect on the couple's culturally influenced response to his alcoholism. Teaching points describe traditional Southeast Asian views of illness and mental illness and suggest methods for motivating families to accept help. The case can be used in both foundation and advanced practice courses, and is appropriate for class or small group discussion.

Case Study

Phoung and Thi, both refugees from Vietnam, met in college and married in their early twenties. Their parents approved of the marriage. Phoung was from a good family and worked for a prestigious company. He was a polite, sincere young man who treated Thi like a queen. Phoung's family was delighted that he had married a beautiful and smart woman from an equally good family. Their future was bright.

Phoung worked hard and was a good provider. He received promotions frequently and often traveled in his job. Soon after their marriage Thi had a baby boy, and the couple bought a house in a nice neighborhood. Thi stayed home with the baby, while Phoung continued to work hard and advance his career. About four or five times a year, Phoung would stay out late with his friends and come home intoxicated. The next day he would be sick and unable to go to work. Thi eventually worked up the courage to ask him to stop drinking so much. Phoung promised her he would cut down and did for a while. They were happy during the times he was not drinking.

As the years went by, three more children were born. Thi was a devoted mother. She found herself worrying about Phoung when he stayed out at night. The number of business meetings in the evenings seemed to be increasing along with the travel. He always came home smelling of alcohol, and his personality seemed to change when he was drinking. He would become nasty and critical of her, and he would accuse her of spending too much money and being too indulgent with the children. The next day he would be remorseful and tell Thi he didn't mean what he said.

Problems in the family and at work slowly increased. First, Phoung was passed over for an expected promotion at work. He blamed his disappointment on a new manager who promoted a woman. Thi then started to notice that household bills were not being paid on time. Overdue notices came in the mail. Thi took over this responsibility, because Phoung said he was too exhausted after a full day at work, and eventually straightened out the bills.

One night Phoung was arrested for driving under the influence of alcohol. Thi had used up most of their savings to pay overdue bills. When Phoung needed money to pay for a lawyer, Thi arranged for a loan and went to work to pay it off. The couple was too ashamed to borrow money from other family members. Phoung lost his license, and Thi started to drive him to work every day. Fortunately, the children were now old enough to get themselves off to school.

Thi found herself getting frequent headaches, and felt tired all the time. She started taking vitamins but that did not help. Thi realized that she could not bring Phoung to weddings and other social events. He would always drink too much and insult someone. Thi started to turn down invitations or go only with her children, saying that Phoung was on a business trip.

After 25 years of marriage, Thi was not even 50 years old but she felt like 80. She was very angry at her husband and made sure there was never any alcohol in the house. She worried about money and how she was going to pay for the children's education. She felt bad that her older children had to work every day after school. Thi found that she was often irritable and angry when she did not mean to be. Life seemed so difficult. Nobody knew just how difficult it was. It was her duty to protect Phoung and the family so they wouldn't lose face in the community.

Questions for Class Discussion

1. What key concepts about alcoholism are illustrated in this case study?

2. What attitudes about drinking do you feel are implicit? Do you think these are related to traditional Vietnamese views, or attitudes prevalent in the "mainstream" culture in the U.S.?

3. What cultural values are reflected that might be important in working with this family or other Vietnamese or Southeast Asian families?

4. What impressions do you have of the scope of alcohol problems among the Vietnamese resettled in the U.S.?

Teaching Points

1. Key concepts about alcoholism:
   - progression of illness—cycle, patterns;
   - a family problem—impact on finances, roles, family time together;
   - role of the enabler—adaptation, protection for the alcoholic, protection for the family as a whole;

- family rules—centrality of issue, blaming, silence (Wegscheider, 1981).

2. Cultural attitudes about drinking:
   - It is only a problem when a person cannot work or behaves inappropriately in public.
   - It can be controlled if the person is of good character.
   - It is shameful in the community.

3. Values and norms in Vietnamese families:
   - importance of the extended family and thus potential source of influence;
   - importance of education, possible motivation for father to stop drinking;
   - importance of saving "face" in community;
   - possible somatization of depression.

Among traditional Southeast Asians, the individual's needs are subordinated to the needs of the family and community. Shon and Ja (1982) note that personal actions reflect not only on the individual and the nuclear and extended families, but also on all the preceding generations. Whereas in mainstream U.S. society individuals are held responsible for their actions, in Southeast Asian families the family accepts and feels deserving of blame for trouble caused by family members, be they children, adolescents, adults, or elders. Mental illness is seen as familial and hereditary, and illness in one family member is seen as related to past family transgressions and therefore damaging to the reputation of the family as a whole (Gong-Guy, Cravens, & Patterson, 1991). Once the family's name is damaged, the stigma lasts for generations.

These values and beliefs contribute to the family's tendency to cover up an AODA problem and tolerate the destructive behavior of an alcoholic or drug-dependent individual until the problem is severe. From another vantage point, however, such values and beliefs may provide a motivational tool. Protecting the honor of the family and community is such a strong value that emphasizing the risk of loss-of-face for the family and community if AODA problems continue may be a culturally appropriate and effective method for convincing clients that behavior change is necessary (Amodeo et al., 1996).

4. There is little research on this topic—most information comes from small studies and anecdotal information. A Massachusetts study (Fontanella & Williams, 1993) found that 72 of 100 Vietnamese respondents knew some Vietnamese adults who had experienced problems resulting from AODA, and 10 knew many adults who had experienced physical, social, or legal problems because of AODA. The same survey showed that more respondents knew teens than adults who had experienced AODA-related problems. Of the Vietnamese respondents, 81 knew some teens and 23 knew many teens with such problems.

References

Amodeo, M., Robb, N., Peou, S., & Tran, H. (1996). Adapting mainstream substance abuse interventions for Southeast Asian clients. *Families in Society, 77*(7), 403-412.

Fontanella, M., & Williams, C. (1993). *Vietnamese and Cambodian community resident survey results*. Prepared for the Southeast Asian Family Empowerment Project, Metropolitan Indochinese Children and Adolescent Services, a Program of South Cove Community Health Center, Boston (unpublished).

Gong-Guy, E., Cravens, R. B., & Patterson, T. E. (1991). Clinical issues in mental health service delivery to refugees. *American Psychologist, 46*, 642-648.

Shon, S. P., & Ja, D. Y. (1982). Asian families. In M. McGoldrick, J. K. Pearce, & J. Giordano (Eds.), *Ethnicity and family therapy* (pp. 208-222). New York: Guilford.

Wegscheider, S. (1981). *Another chance: Hope and health for the alcoholic family*. Palo Alto, CA: Science and Behavior Books.

Phoung and Thi—Vignette

This vignette summarizes the progression of a husband's alcoholism. It highlights the impact of alcoholism on the family system, particularly the "family rules" and the role of the enabler. It also challenges the reader to reflect on the couple's culturally influenced response to his addiction. The vignette can be used in both foundation and advanced practice courses and is appropriate for class or small group discussion.

Phoung and Thi, and their respective families, came to the U.S. as refugees from Vietnam. When they married in their early twenties, both families were very pleased. Phoung was a polite, educated young man, and Thi was beautiful, smart, and from a good family. For a while, everything went well. Phoung worked hard, received promotions, and traveled on business, while Thi stayed home to take care of their children. The couple saved carefully and were able to buy a house. About 4 times a year, however, Phoung would stay out late drinking with his friends. He would come home drunk and the next day feel so sick he wouldn't be able to go to work. This worried Thi, so she finally asked him to stop. He promised to cut back and for a while did so.

However, over the years both the business trips and the drinking increased. When he came home drunk, Phoung would become angry and critical of Thi and the children, though he would apologize once he sobered up. Phoung gradually began having problems at work, being passed over for a promotion that he and his family expected him to get. Thi also began noticing that bills were not getting paid on time and so quietly took over this task.

One night Phoung was arrested for drunk driving. The couple was too ashamed to borrow money from family members, and so got a loan to take care of the legal expenses. Thi got a part-time job to pay this back. She tried to make sure there was never any alcohol in the house. She also started declining social invitations, since she knew Phoung might get drunk and insult people. Thi began to suffer headaches and felt tired all the time. She was angry at her husband for not behaving more responsibly and sometimes even lashed out at the children. She was constantly worried about money and how they would pay for their children's education. She felt that no one knew just how difficult her life was, but felt she couldn't talk about it for fear her husband and the family would lose face in the community.

Setting Goals and Implementing Treatment

Annette: A Mental Health Professional with Cocaine Dependence

Professionals often see themselves as invulnerable to the development of a drug dependence. Because they maintain control over so many other aspects of their lives, they believe they will be able to control drug use. Teaching points emphasize counseling approaches, circumstances prompting the need for abstinence, and triggers to relapse.

Setting: Private general psychotherapy practice.

Client: A 34-year-old single white female administrator in a community mental health center.

Worker: A clinician experienced in treating substance abuse and mental health problems.

Presenting problem: Supervisor suggested she seek therapy for a gradual decline in work performance. Client felt emotionally depleted and depressed about where her life was going, and a general malaise about her job.

Case Record

Annette was a 34-year-old single white female, employed as the director of a psychiatric day treatment program in a community mental health center. She initiated individual psychotherapy for herself at the suggestion of her supervisor who didn't know what was troubling her, but had seen a gradual, subtle decline in Annette's management work over a 6–8 month period. Her performance had become an issue in supervision. Annette had held the position for three years and had distinguished herself in terms of program development and creative ideas for expansion.

During the initial evaluation session for therapy, Annette described her problem as a general malaise related to burnout from working in human services. She felt emotionally depleted, depressed about where here life was going, and determined to change careers but confused about what she wanted to do next.

She was unmarried and described "relationship problems" as an additional source of stress and discouragement. Her relationships with men tended to last 3–6 months with great infatuation and sexual chemistry, but the men then disappeared or the relationship moved in a negative direction.

Following a family, educational, employment, and medical history, the therapist asked a series of routine questions regarding drinking and drug use. Given that Annette's previous participation in the assessment was very open, the worker was struck with how much Annette's discomfort seemed to surface around these questions. The therapist was able to elicit only a few specific answers and decided to postpone further exploration until a subsequent session.

The second session focused on relationship issues and eventually moved back to drinking and drugs. As the therapist explored relationships in high school, college, and graduate school, Annette acknowledged heavy drinking through college and graduate school. Annette's view was that it had never been a problem, although she described a few incidents that she acknowledged had been worrisome at the time. She loved to "party," then as well as currently, describing it as one of her greatest pleasures.

Before the close of the session, Annette admitted to some marijuana use, and to the worker's question, "Have you ever used cocaine in the past?" Annette, seemingly in a debate with herself about whether to answer the question truthfully, finally said "yes."

The third session began with an exploration of Annette's current social network, including women friends from childhood, friends from work, and neighbors in her apartment complex with whom she felt close. She had several long-standing friendships and talked about these relationships with animation, humor, and affection. The issue of "partying" as a form of recreation came up again, and the therapist used this issue to return to the discussion of Annette's past cocaine use. The therapist explained to Annette that she felt it was important because cocaine was a drug that "had a tendency to sneak up on people." People often found themselves more "attached" to the drug than they had intended to get, so the therapist thought it was important to explore Annette's "relationship" with cocaine to help "head off future problems."

Annette acknowledged that she had been using cocaine "on and off" for about three years. When the therapist asked how she used it, Annette said "intranasally." She had never tried free-basing or crack, although people at the parties she went to sometimes "were into free-basing." She originally started using cocaine with a man she'd been dating. After the relationship ended, she continued to get cocaine from his supplier.

With gentle probing by the therapist, Annette acknowledged that her use had escalated lately to almost every weekend and, when she had her own supply, a night or two during the week. She was working part-time on weekends as a cocktail waitress for extra money. After extensive probing by the therapist, she admitted that she was spending about $150 per week on cocaine, but she was using other people's cocaine at parties too. Because the therapist found that Annette's cocaine use was so consistent, she

asked systematically about a range of other drugs, and ways Annette dealt with unpleasant feelings following occasions of cocaine use. Annette disclosed, again reluctantly, that during the days following cocaine use she would often have 3-6 glasses of wine in the evenings and would use xanax if she was feeling restless.

In her view, there were no discernible negative consequences from her cocaine use. The men she dated generally liked to drink and "weren't opposed to drugs"—they were often heavy users themselves. In response to the therapist's question of whether Annette's relationship breakups might be related to the role of drugs in artificially enhancing the qualities of the men she dated, Annette guardedly acknowledged perhaps this might be so.

Annette's plan was to quit her job and change professions—take a year off and waitress full-time. The therapist said she believed that the cocaine/alcohol use played some role in the difficulties, and might even be a major precipitant, and encouraged Annette not to make major changes until this could be sorted out. In an effort to clarify the nature of the difficulties, the therapist reviewed the issues Annette had brought to therapy and concurred that they were issues worthy of attention by therapist and patient. These difficulties included increasing feelings of malaise about her current work situation, declining work performance, and confusion about another career path. Relationships with men were of equal or greater concern, and Annette despaired of finding a stable, exciting, and fulfilling relationship with a man who possessed some maturity.

The therapist also stated that Annette's increase in cocaine use, from monthly to more than weekly during the past six months or year, was an issue that required attention because of the tendency of cocaine users to develop a powerful psychological dependence.

The therapist explained that she was not certain about the seriousness of Annette's cocaine use, although she suspected it might be a serious problem, and encouraged Annette to engage in a time-limited experiment: to stop using it for a while to see if this might provide important information for both of them.

The therapist recommended that Annette try one month of abstinence from cocaine to help clarify her thinking and better evaluate the related issues in her life. The therapist's goal was to explore the role of drug use in Annette's life. She did not define this as the sole problem—it had been the therapist's experience that clients dropped out of treatment almost immediately if they had come for help with one problem, and the therapist immediately defined the problem as something else. Helping this client see her situation in all its facets would require the therapist to build a relationship, develop trust, and give Annette the sense that she was being understood. The therapeutic work involving cocaine use was defined as exploratory for both client and therapist.

In addition, the therapist recommended that Annette consider the following:

- seeing the therapist on a weekly basis;
- removing all cocaine and cocaine-using paraphernalia from her apartment, because it is more difficult to stop using if one is constantly stimulated to use by the knowledge that a supply is in the next room, or by signs that remind one of the feelings and sensations associated with being high;
- turning down invitations to parties where people would be using, or where she would see men with whom she had used;
- refusing to have sex with any men with whom she had used cocaine.

The therapist explained that it would be important for Annette to be candid with the therapist about her behavior—she explained that it would be easy enough for Annette to deceive the therapist about her use, but she would also be engaged in a process of deceiving herself, making their discussions meaningless. The therapist did not want to waste Annette's time and money in this way, and so encouraged her to be open about the results of the experiment, however it turned out. Because Annette was sure her use was not a problem, she agreed to undertake this one-month "abstinence experiment" and to follow the other recommendations as well.

For the first week, Annette was compliant with maintaining abstinence, avoiding parties and avoiding sex with cocaine-using men, perhaps because this did not involve a marked change in her previous pattern. At the third session, she reported she had used cocaine but had employed some methods to limit her use—she had unexpectedly run into friends with whom she had used, went partying and resumed use—but avoided getting together with a friend she knew was a regular user. The therapist recommended that she attend some meetings of a 12–step program (AA, NA, or CA) to explore the extent to which her drug use may have sneaked up on her and become more of a problem than she realized. She agreed to go to one AA and one CA meeting.

At the fourth session, she reported using again. She said she was offered coke by a man she had no respect for. She explained that she had been in a struggle with herself about her commitment to avoid using—had thought about what the therapist might say and had considered the stories of people at the AA and CA meetings about how hooked they had become—but she had such a strong urge to use that she went ahead and did so anyway. She also ended up having sex with the man without condoms, although she realized that she should not have.

The therapist proposed that Annette was more "addicted" than Annette had thought, as evidenced by her strong psychological dependency and tendency to put herself in situations that involved risks to her safety; and that Annette would need more extensive treatment for her addiction, perhaps even an intensive outpatient, day-treatment, or inpatient program.

Annette protested that she would try anything to avoid going to a drug treatment program. She was convinced her problem was not that serious. The worker developed a written contract with Annette that she would agree to go into a day-treatment or inpatient program if she couldn't establish one month of abstinence in the next eight weeks. (Even if she could, however, this would be no guarantee that specialized drug treatment would not be necessary at some point.) The therapist recommended that she intensify her attendance at AA, NA, or CA and look into support groups for professionals working on recovery from chemical dependency.

Questions for Class Discussion

1. What is the impact of Annette's role as a health care professional on her view of her situation?

2. Why was abstinence necessary?

3. What are the strengths and weaknesses of the treatment plan? What alternative goals/methods could have been utilized?

4. Should the therapist have been more aggressive in confronting Annette about her cocaine and alcohol use as soon as the therapist discovered it? What would be the rationale "for" and "against"?

5. What is the value of the therapist's discussing cocaine in terms of its "tendency to sneak up on people"; the fact that people often found themselves more "attached" to the drug than they had intended; and that Annette would need to "explore her relationship" with cocaine to "head off future problems"? Are there some potential problems in framing the issues in this way?

Teaching Points

1. Middle class and upper-middle class clients (and especially health professionals) who have been highly functioning for much of their lives often see themselves as less vulnerable than others to addiction. Perhaps they used some alcohol/marijuana in the past and it did not seem to get out of control. Because they often view themselves as successful with high degrees of self-determination, they may believe that they can use without becoming dependent. A good income and extensive socializing may help disguise drug dependence to a point where it seems manageable to the user. It is generally helpful for the worker to emphasize to clients their ability to build equally important life structures that encourage abstinence and recovery. Denial often takes the form of a reversal of cause and effect—that is, burnout and confusion about career direction may be viewed as the cause, rather than the effect, of drug use.

2. Given Annette's experiences, abstinence was a necessary part of the therapeutic contract. There is often resistance to giving up "soft drugs," or drugs which the client views as less harmful, such as alcohol, valium, xanax, or marijuana. The worker can be helpful in providing education regarding the mechanism of psychological dependence and the tendency of people "hooked" on one mind-altering drug to substitute another for it during struggles to remain abstinent from the original drug. Washton (1989) recommends that the therapist tell the client to just take it on "blind faith" initially that use of any mind-altering drugs will lead to the compulsive use of others.

3. Identifying cocaine cues is important because the sight of cocaine is a powerful reinforcer of the urge to resume use.

Washton (1989) recommends that workers discuss with clients how, when, and where they would most likely encounter cocaine "accidentally" and plan for this eventuality. He recommends they also ask the question: "Even if you don't actively try to find cocaine, how is it likely to find you?"

Increased attendance at therapy sessions to focus on abstinence-maintaining methods is important once there is a commitment to treatment. Attendance at meetings of 12–step programs should be recommended daily for the first three months.

Other compulsive behaviors, including sex, are often associated with heavy cocaine use. The therapist would need to see Annette co-caine-free for some substantial period of time to understand whether compulsive sex is part of her situation. Relapse to one often leads to relapse to the other.

Suggested Readings

Amodeo, M. (1995). The therapist's role in the drinking stage. In S. Brown (Ed.), *Treating alcoholism* (pp. 95-132). San Francisco: Jossey-Bass.

Amodeo, M. (1995). The therapist's role in the transitional stage. In S. Brown (Ed.), *Treating alcoholism* (pp. 133-162). San Francisco: Jossey-Bass.

Washton, A. M. (Ed.). (1995). *Psychotherapy and substance abuse: A practitioner's handbook.* New York: Guilford.

Washton, A. M. (1989). *Cocaine addiction treatment, recovery, and relapse prevention.* New York: Norton.

Tommy: Smoking Marijuana and Reading Carlos Castaneda

Workers dealing with substance abuse often face an internal conflict between respecting the client's views and requiring changes the worker knows are necessary for the client's well-being. In this case, the client believes that insight will lead to behavior change; the worker believes that behavior change will lead to insight. The therapy reflects an attempt to balance these two perspectives. Teaching points identify additional motivational approaches and recommend discussing the client's experiences growing up with an abusive, alcoholic father.

Setting: A small, private outpatient agency.

Client: A 21-year-old single white male living on his own. Tommy was referred by his mother who thought he would benefit from having someone to talk with. She was concerned about his chronic habitual pot-smoking.

Worker: A 31-year-old white, married, middle-class male.

Case Record

First Session

When Tommy first arrived, he was dressed in ragged jeans and a torn shirt. He seemed almost hostile, making frequent racist, sexist, and heterosexist remarks and denouncing social workers, therapists, and other "do-gooders." It seemed incongruent that he was interested in counseling but so disparaging of it at the same time. He was quite intelligent and astute, and used those assets to second-guess every inquiry and challenge every statement. Tommy reacted to any attempt to get background information by stating that it was irrelevant or not really my business. When questioned as to what he wanted, he stated that his reason for coming was that his mother suggested it to him, and he respected her. On further reflection, Tommy noted that he smoked pot daily, often got drunk, and that he would like to stop doing so. He was certain that stopping was a matter of reasoning and will power, and that determining *why* he smoked pot would enable him to stop.

I provided some information about drugs and usage patterns, and suggested to Tommy that although many people before had tried to stop using drugs by developing insight about why they used them, very few stopped using as a result of such insight. He expressed annoyance and predicted that next I would be recommending AA or some other such program. I complimented his foresight and proceeded to do what he expected. I suggested that he had nothing to lose by attending AA, and it might prove to be helpful. I added that the only way to find out was to try it. He sneered at me and said that I was much too predictable. He asked if I thought he was an addict. I told him that only he could decide that. What was important, I suggested, was that he find a way to achieve his goals.

I was somewhat surprised when Tommy indicated that he was interested in coming again. Throughout subsequent sessions, he was clear and consistent in his stated goal of "figuring out why I keep using it"; I sensed that if I pressed my perspective on this, he would discontinue counseling. Although I said I would discuss whatever concerned him, I also asserted that if he continued to use drugs and alcohol, I would continue to encourage him to seek out a support group. Although he reacted to this negatively, I persisted. Each time we met, I reiterated that he should talk about whatever he wanted to, but I would save five minutes at the end to discuss AA, NA, or other self-help groups. I shared with him my perception that something very interesting, almost mysterious, happened to people who got involved in AA, that they discovered a different way of being in the world, and that I couldn't really explain it. I added that although it wasn't for everyone, it might work for him. He grumbled, "Yeah, yeah," shaking his head, but always agreed to return the following week at the same time.

Six Months

I generally used a client-centered, problem-focused, short-term model of practice, seeing clients for approximately 8–12 sessions. I found myself intrigued as the relationship with Tommy continued well past that time frame. Six months later, we were still following the original contract. He would talk about whatever he wanted until the last five minutes, when I would suggest that, because his drug and alcohol behavior hadn't changed, perhaps he should try AA.

I consulted colleagues and others about alternative strategies. I tried several without success. I wondered if what I was doing was in the best interest of the client, but he kept coming, and, in my eyes, kept thwarting any attempts to change his plan.

Over the first six months, I learned a lot more about Tommy. He was the youngest of six siblings. Two of his three older brothers were alcoholics, as was one of his sisters. His father was an alcoholic with a terrible temper, and Tommy was frequently beaten until he was bloody. His father would stand him against the wall, and, holding Tommy up with one hand, swing the other massive fist back and forth, battering him, sometimes into uncon-

sciousness. Tommy expressed little emotion as he described this, indicating that he thought it was worse for his older brothers.

Tommy displayed an extraordinary knowledge of both ancient and modern philosophy, and seemed to take delight in attempts at drawing me into philosophical quandaries. He resisted suggestions that behavioral change might precede insight, and angered easily when I suggested AA. Nevertheless, over time he seemed to resign himself to the fact that each week, in the last five minutes of the session, I would talk about AA, how it might prove useful, and how he had nothing to lose.

Twelve Months

A full year went by. Sometimes, I despaired that my treatment plan was completely inappropriate because I couldn't note any measurable change. My client kept smoking pot, had not changed his perception that logic would lead to change, and still refused to try AA. I wondered if I had fallen into the role of the unwitting enabler. A couple of times, when I tried a more confrontational approach, he would get angry and not return for a few weeks. I resisted interpreting this behavior, because I thought he simply didn't like what I had to say. I continued to reserve the last five minutes of each session for recommending drug treatment, but other than that, we talked about whatever he wanted.

Eighteen Months

We continued to meet regularly, usually at two-week intervals. Tommy was beginning to develop skill at working with computers, but he derided "money-hungry business bastards." He evidenced a talent for programming, and many other skills, though he was unhappy and unmotivated for any job related to his computer abilities. He continued to read voraciously, and spent months delving into the works of Carlos Castaneda, the sociologist who studied with a Yaqui Indian sorcerer, Don Juan. The language of "Yaqui power" began to infiltrate his conversation.

Ten years earlier, I had read the writings of Castaneda and had found them to be personally meaningful. I was intrigued by Tommy's exploration of these concepts. At the same time, I was concerned and wondered if he wasn't getting further away from everyday reality. He continued to smoke pot heavily every day, and rationalized it as a mind exploration. I pointed out that in his later works, Castaneda reported that Don Juan said he had given him peyote to help Castaneda "see," because he was so narrow in vision, so slow to open his mind. Don Juan noted that with more open minds, drugs were irrelevant. Tommy did not really appreciate this observation.

As we seemed to be at an impasse, I wondered what to do. Should I terminate the therapy? Maybe breaking it off would reflect the seriousness of my concern. Then I wondered if perhaps I was making a difference in some way. Tommy had a job now, and an ongoing relationship with me. Were these enough? Maybe I was being too constricted in my view of success. Maybe pot and other substances weren't really that significant in his life. This line of reasoning never felt comfortable; I knew I was rationalizing and had to find another approach.

When asked, Tommy still expressed a desire to stop his substance abuse. He didn't like the cycle of feeling it engendered in him—the depression, isolation, and mild paranoia so common to chronic pot users. He still smoked pot daily, he drank to excess on occasion, and snorted coke when he could afford it. He was at high risk for many things, including increased drug use and legal charges. Something had to change.

Two Weeks Later

I reviewed the course of our work together. Gentle persuasion and support had not helped; neither had passive listening, education, reasoning, or confrontation. I began to feel the need to do something for myself, for my client, and for my profession. I needed to find a way in, a way that had meaning for my client and created new possibilities; perhaps something more dramatic, perhaps a strategic intervention. I read articles, consulted more colleagues, but still nothing occurred to me.

Then one day I had the insight that I had become powerless to help him. As long as I was participating in this as a power struggle, as addicts do with their relationship to substances, I was hopeless and helpless. I had to admit my powerlessness to myself and to Tommy. Finally, it hit me. In Castaneda's writings, Don Juan, the Yaqui sorcerer, plays a central role. Don Juan teaches Castaneda about the ways of power, how it is attained, and used, and how it is defeated. Power had a very special meaning in those writings.

I knew what I would say to Tommy.

The next time we met, I didn't wait until the last five minutes but started right in, suggesting to Tommy that he should go to AA since all our work together had not changed his behavior. He expressed annoyance and returned to his usual complex reasoning and philosophizing. I persevered. "You should go to AA," I said. He appeared agitated. Then I said, "I have tried everything I know to no avail. I respect your power to defeat me." Tommy stared at me, his eyes grew large, then he lashed out, "Don't you use Castaneda with me! F--- you. Don't you dare use Castaneda with me!"

"I mean it," I said. "I am utterly powerless to help you, and I have the most profound respect for your power, and your ability to defeat whatever I try. You are a powerful person."

Tommy was livid. He called me several names, and then left the session.

One Month Later

I had not heard from Tommy since our last session. I began to doubt whether I had done the right thing. What if I had harmed my client in some way? I considered calling him, but decided to wait a little longer. The next day I got a call from Tommy, who requested an appointment for the following week. I agreed.

The next week, Tommy arrived, walked over to his chair, sat down, and in a derisive, sarcastic tone, said to me: "Well, I went to AA. In fact, I've been going every day now for almost three weeks. And you know what? AA has helped me a lot more than you ever did!"

Tommy and I worked together for two more years, until I moved away. Our relationship matured as he recovered. He worked hard on many important issues, and even acknowledged that sometimes I worked hard as well.

Questions for Class Discussion

1. What is the impact of the source of referral on the engagement and evolution of the treatment?

2. What theoretical perspectives guided this work? How effective were these? Were there others that could have been employed?

3. How might the family history of alcohol abuse inform the worker's understanding of and intervention with this client?

4. What role did the client's reading of Castaneda play in his beliefs about drug use? How did the worker help the client "turn the corner" by using the client's understanding of Castaneda's readings?

5. Did the social worker enable the client to continue to use drugs in his effort to join with the client and his feelings?

Teaching Points

1. The clients' referral by his mother probably led to increased resistance by Tommy and a perception that the worker was an authority figure who would try to force behavioral change.

2. The work was based on the social work practice principle of starting where the client is, through the use of a client-centered and problem-focused approach. The use of confrontation, education, and support, particularly in the repeated return to the usefulness of AA, is based on an addictions counseling model. The last intervention, in which the worker acknowledged his own powerlessness, is derived from the recovery model of AA, which suggests that as a first step one must admit powerlessness over the use of substances. The worker might have tried additional techniques of motivational interviewing, particularly those that focus on exploring and validating ambivalence, and helping the client weigh the pros and cons of change, while avoiding argument and confrontation.

3. Children of alcoholics often have core difficulties in adjustment, including: the need to maintain control of thoughts, feelings, and behaviors; distrust of self and others; the belief that feelings are wrong, bad, and scary; a sense of over-responsibility and responsibility for others' emotions and actions; an all-or-none approach to functioning; a tendency to disassociate; a tendency to live in and create a crisis-ridden existence. Exploration of some of these difficulties as they pertained to Tommy—the need for control, distrust in the therapy, disassociation, the continued use of drugs as a source of crisis in his life—may have helped Tommy take steps to end his drug use sooner, and to acknowledge the role his father's drinking and physical abuse played in his childhood.

4. Tommy was challenged and supported when his unique personal meaning system (the writings of Castaneda, the teachings of Don Juan), was brought to bear on his dilemma. The client's own frame of reference provided a potent way to deliver the message. The worker modeled a different approach for the client by admitting his own "powerlessness" in the therapy.

5. This worker struggled with a common dilemma with clients who are actively using substances: In an attempt to join with the client and his feelings, does the worker enable the continued use of substances? While ultimately the worker did gain the client's trust, and was able to use the client's meaning system in a helpful way, there may have been ways of speeding up this process.

Suggested Readings

Amodeo, M., & Drouilhet, A. (1992). Untangling a complex web: Countertransference with substance abusing adolescents. In J. Brandell (Ed.), *Countertransference in child and adolescent psychotherapy* (pp. 285-314). NJ: Jacob Aronson, Inc.

Doweiko, H. E. (1996). Marijuana. In H. E. Doweiko, *Concepts of chemical dependency* (3rd ed., pp. 119-128). Pacific Grove, CA: Brooks/Cole.

Gravitz, H., & Bowden, J. (1985). *Guide to recovery—A book for adult children of alcoholics*. Holmes Beach, FL: Learning Publications Inc.

Kopp, R. (1995). *Metaphor therapy: Using client-generated metaphors in psychotherapy*. New York: Brunner/Mazel.

Miller, W., & Rollnick, S. (1991). *Motivational interviewing—Preparing people to change addictive behavior*. New York: Guilford.

Smith, T. E. (1984). Reviewing adolescent marijuana abuse. *Social Work, 29*(1), 17-21.

Peter: Engaging an Involuntary Client

Engaging mandated clients in treatment is always challenging and requires that workers are careful not to abuse their power. To be both an ally to the client and an agent of social control is a difficult position for a worker, necessitating an examination of personal needs for control. Successful outcomes are more likely when workers and clients share responsibility for and control over the therapeutic process. Below, this sharing of responsibility is demonstrated by the worker's flexibility about the meeting schedule, topics to be discussed, handling of reports to the court, and decisions about the client's readiness to face high-risk situations. The clinical approach includes exploring childhood trauma, identifying triggers to relapse, and helping the client prepare for "coming out" to homophobic family members.

Setting: An outpatient substance abuse and mental health clinic outside Santa Fe, NM.

Client: A 38-year-old gay white Catholic male of Irish-German descent, working as a carpenter to support his work as a sculptor.

Worker: White female social worker in her early 30s.

Presenting problem: Engaging a client who has been mandated to attend outpatient substance abuse treatment following a second DUI offense.

Case Record

Part I

Peter was referred to the Counseling Center, an outpatient mental health clinic in the suburbs of Santa Fe, to receive "aftercare" treatment for his second DUI offense. He had just completed two weeks of inpatient treatment in a program designed specifically to treat second-time offenders. The referral source was Dr. Weiss, the clinical director of the program. In a phone interview, Dr. Weiss described Peter as "a quiet man" who was "cooperative and pleasant" and "seemed to get a lot of the educational portion of the program, but didn't participate at all in the group discussions." Although the Counseling Center is listed in the yellow pages as a substance abuse treatment center, it does not specialize in this field and receives only a nominal number of mandated referrals. Such referrals tend to be given to a select number of clinicians at the agency who have a greater understanding of substance abuse and dependence and who are more comfortable sitting with coerced clients (who are often angry and resistant to treatment). I happen to be one of those clinicians, and Peter was referred to me.

Peter is a 38-year-old white male who identifies himself as "an artist unable to make a living from art." He is a sculptor and makes large, spiny, abstract sculptures in the backyard of his small home in suburban Santa Fe. To supplement his income, he works a 40-hour job as a carpenter. Peter's family of origin is of Irish and German descent and he was raised as a Catholic. Peter is the fourth of five children, all boys. His father was a lifetime Navy officer and his family moved around the country every two to three years. Peter is gay and stated, "I always knew this and am quite comfortable with it now." He has long been disillusioned with the Catholic church because he feels the church is wrong to reject him simply because of his sexual orientation.

My first session with Peter had been arranged by Dr. Weiss and took place two days after Peter completed his inpatient treatment. Peter came to the session neatly but casually dressed in a flannel shirt and blue jeans. He sat down and slumped into the chair I offered him and dropped his leather jacket in a heap on the floor next to him.

He started the interview immediately: "I can't come this time of day. I just spent two weeks out of work and my boss was pissed at that and now I had to come here in the middle of the day and take some more time off. I just can't afford that and I definitely can't afford to lose my job!"* I responded: "We can try to negotiate a better time, and if today's not good we can reschedule." Peter interrupted and in a calmer tone said, "No, I'm here; we may as well start. What do we need to do?" I said, "The best place to start is to get to know one another to see if we can work together." Peter interrupted again, "What do you want to know about me?" His questions were both plaintive and challenging and I needed to breathe slowly to keep from giving quick responses. Studying his harried face I asked, "What do you think would be important for me to know about you?" He said, "That I come from a dysfunctional family, that I have a problem with alcohol, and that I am gay." Peter studied my face.*

Part II

I nodded and asked, "Could you tell me about how each of those three things relate to you and me sitting here today?" Peter nodded and seemed to relax. He began to tell me his story. In inpatient treatment he learned more about alcoholism and had realized for the first time that his father was an alcoholic. His father drank sporadically and would give up alcohol for months or weeks on end. Peter recounted incidents where he was beaten by his father while his father was drunk on a binge. He said he relished the days when his father was off at sea. During these times of respite, he could spend time with his mother, who he said was a "saint."

Peter did not do well in academics but excelled in art and sports. In high school, he said that he fell in with "the wrong crowd" and began drinking, smoking pot, and occasionally doing acid (LSD). His grades suffered and he was dropped from the track team. His relationship with his father became more tumultuous. He said he began using alcohol and other drugs because he felt so angry that he wanted to kill his father and the drugs "numbed my pain." After barely graduating from high school, Peter said he moved to California to find himself.

At age 18, Peter went to San Francisco and found a job as a carpenter. He also found himself in a place where he could explore his sexuality and openly acknowledge his attraction to other men. He frequented bars and bathhouses and found that alcohol increased his confidence. He also began experimenting with cocaine, but could not tolerate the swing of exhilarating highs and crashing lows. He continued to drink and began experiencing blackouts. On many occasions he woke up in places with no recollection of how he got there. Peter said that he remembers feeling disappointed that he could not develop any enduring relationships with other men. He became increasingly frightened of what he termed his "aimless life style" and enrolled in art school at the age of 20. For the next six years, he worked at various odd jobs while attending school. He continued to drink alone and to frequent bars occasionally. He said that he was "too busy" with his own work to think much about having a steady relationship with another man.

When Peter graduated from college at age 26, he had a degree in sculpture, but was unable to make a living from his work. He continued to work in construction, and met his "big love," Alex, while renovating a restaurant in San Francisco. This was his "first and only meaningful relationship with another man." Alex was a chef. Peter moved in with him and they lived together for the next three years. During this time, Peter's abuse of alcohol abated as his life style changed. Alex was a "health nut" who discouraged drinking, using drugs, and smoking. Unfortunately, Alex was one of the first victims of AIDS in the early 1980s. He became seriously ill with pneumocystic pneumonia and died soon afterwards. Peter was "heartbroken" after he died, and binged on alcohol for a month. He could not contact his family for support around Alex's death; they had not even known that Alex existed. Luckily, Peter had not contracted HIV. Within several months, Peter fled from San Francisco because "there were too many bad memories." He came to Santa Fe because he wanted "to turn grief into art."*

Peter found a job in construction in Santa Fe. He continued to drink and live a reclusive life. He would work all week, drinking in the morning to get himself through the day, and binge all weekend. He drank wine and Scotch. Many mornings he woke with empty bottles around him, with no recollection of drinking their contents. He was always able to get to work but not without mishap. One day when he was hung over, he sawed off the top of his index finger. In the mid-1980s, he began going to bars again. Soon after, he was arrested for his first DUI. He marvelled that this was the first time he had been arrested, given his years of drinking and blackouts. Because it was his first offense, he went to the alcohol education courses, but said that he was "hung over and not paying attention most of the time." At that time, the lesson he learned was "to stay home and drink," because he didn't want to lose his license.

For the next six years he continued in this life style. Occasionally he would stop drinking for periods of weeks or months because his work was suffering, his backyard was littered with unfinished sculptures, and he was frightened of his lack of control while drinking.

Peter never enlisted help from others and never attended an AA meeting. Any situation could induce him to drink again: a birthday, a holiday, a bad day at work. After a period of abstinence of six months, Peter was feeling better. A skilled carpenter, he was promoted to a supervisory position by a contractor. "Celebrating," Peter went out for a drink and some "good sex." The next morning, Peter found himself in a jail cell: he had been arrested for DUI. He was devastated.

He reflected: "It was almost as if I couldn't let something good happen to me. The last time I let something good happen to me I lost it, I lost Alex, and I don't want to lose like that again." Peter's eyes filled with tears and he quickly wiped them away.* I said, "It's scary to get close to people? Or to be appreciated by others—like when you got your raise?" Peter seemed surprised at my questions and said: "No, I don't think that's it, well I don't know, I don't know how to make sense of it. I'm just exhausted from being hospitalized and from talking today. I'm not used to it." I said, "Well, that's not surprising. You've been through a lot in the past two weeks and in your lifetime. But I want to ask you, when you said you have a problem with alcohol what exactly do you mean?" Peter responded, "I know that I shouldn't drink anymore, but I don't know how to deal with the idea that I can never drink again." I asked, "Are you going to AA meetings?" He responded, "Yeah, twice a week I go and get the little piece of paper signed for my probation officer, Monique. Meetings are OK but sometimes it's hard to listen, and I feel self-conscious because I'm gay. I don't want to go to the gay meetings because I'm afraid that I'll get involved with somebody and in AA they tell you to stay out of relationships for at least a year." I asked, "Do you have a sponsor?" Peter said, "No, I lie pretty low in those meetings, but I know if I'm tempted to drink I can call AA at any time and talk to somebody."

I said, "We'll need to stop in a few minutes. If you'd like to continue working with me we'll need to talk about contracting." He responded, "Yes, I know, you'll need to call Monique and tell her that I'm coming." His anger was reminiscent of the beginning of the interview."* I said, "It's my guess that you wouldn't be sitting here across from me if it weren't for the mandate." Peter laughed, "You damned sure got that right, but so long as I'm paying for it, I might as well see what I can get out of it." I smiled and said, "I need you to sign a release of information now, so that I can call Monique and ask her for the terms of the mandate. What is your relationship like with her?" He said, "I hope I don't offend you, but Monique is a bitch," and then launched into a diatribe about the hassles that she had put him through in the two months since his sentencing.

We scheduled a time for the meeting the following week. On his way out the door Peter said, "I don't want Monique to find out that I'm gay." I said, "Of course. She doesn't have to know that." Peter smiled and we said good-bye.

In the second session, I reported back to Peter the conversation that I had with Monique. The mandate called for Peter to have 15 to 26 weeks of weekly psychotherapy. The length of treatment would be determined by Peter's progress toward his treatment goal of sobriety. I was required to write a monthly report outlining Peter's general progress toward this goal and submit it to Monique. Before each progress report was written, Peter and I would discuss its contents, and Peter would be able to review the report before it was sent. With some grumbling about Monique, Peter agreed to abide by this contract.

Part III

Peter engaged quickly in treatment. Although he continued to blame problems on the "criminal justice system" and a "f____-up society,"

he began taking more responsibility for his own actions. He was getting something from his attendance at AA meetings, and he began talking about his relationship with God. He talked about the 12 steps and how they related to his life. Peter's goal was to maintain abstinence and we approached this in the following way. We reviewed in great depth his drinking and drug history. By identifying the "triggers" that set him off to drinking, Peter could strategize about how to respond to them without taking that "first drink." We worked on a specific trigger to drinking: having unpleasant feelings. Peter began to learn that he could experience and tolerate all types of feelings. Peter's use of alcohol had prevented him from getting close to people. And it soon became apparent that Peter never allowed himself to grieve either the loss of Alex or his estrangement from his family.

Peter's issues with his family came to the fore in the eighth week of treatment; his youngest brother was getting married at the end of the month and there was to be a bachelor party and wedding. Peter wanted to go, and he regarded these upcoming events as "some kind of test sent from the universe." Peter was extremely anxious about seeing his brothers; he hadn't been back home in ten years. He felt a great deal of anxiety about being with his parents; and he wondered what it would be like for him to be with his father. He had kept in touch with his mother by phone calls and letters. He knew that his father was very sick with a heart condition and his mother devoted all her time to caring for him. The wedding would be in Fort Lauderdale where his parents lived. Peter had never told his family that he was gay, but was sure that they must have suspected. All his older siblings were married with families of their own. Peter's brothers were "very homophobic" and he always felt uncomfortable around them. They were also "hearty drinkers" and Peter was worried about experiencing pressure to drink.*

Worker's Reflections

I found the whole situation rather alarming and saw these pressures as a threat to Peter's sobriety. Yet, he seemed determined to follow through with his plan, so I helped him strategize for these events. He called Florida, and obtained a listing for the AA meetings in the Fort Lauderdale area. He identified the meetings that he could attend the mornings of the bachelor party and of the wedding. He decided that he would bring his own bottles of ginger ale in case there was nothing nonalcoholic to drink at the party and the wedding reception. He made the decision to raise his hand for a sponsor in his next AA meeting, in the hopes that this person could be available to him by phone on these difficult nights.

I was impressed by Peter's efforts, but I was worried about him. Before he left we discussed what would happen if Peter "fell off the wagon." Peter said that he would not be able to face me; that he would feel "too ashamed." He knew from AA that people "slip" and begin drinking again. He was afraid of the consequences should he slip now. We discussed the differences between his former and current attempts at abstinence: he was not trying to go it alone, he had greater insight into his own behavior, he had a working knowledge of alcohol dependence, he was planning to prevent himself from drinking. In the end, we both agreed that we did not know what was going to happen, but if he should slip, we would start again "one day at a time."

Part III continued

Peter went to Florida. When he came back he came bouncing into my office exclaiming, "I did it! But I'm telling you, it wasn't easy." Peter had followed through with his plans as we had outlined, but with an extra twist. He mustered the courage to tell his next eldest brother, Joe, that he had a problem with alcohol and was worried about all the partying that would be going on. Joe revealed that he was also a recovering alcoholic and had been sober for five years. Throughout the bachelor party and wedding, Joe kept handing Peter glasses filled with ginger ale; their common problem bonded them in a way that they had not experienced since early childhood. However, it was difficult for Peter to be with his parents. His father had become feeble and withdrawn. He no longer drank, but seemed to be very depressed. His mother seemed exhausted, and was totally absorbed with the wedding plans. Relatives and old friends teased him about being the "last one left" to marry. Peter felt the burden of having to hide the fact that he was gay. Everyone wanted to know what he was "doing all those years," and Peter found himself stammering an answer. He said that he watched people get drunk at the bachelor party and the wedding and he felt a vicarious sense of shame for them, thinking "that could be me." Peter felt "proud" that he did not drink, but knew "in reality that didn't mean a thing—I could pick up again, at any time—so it *is* one day at a time."

This was a critical incident for Peter. He had reestablished a relationship with his family and was able to tolerate the pain and confusion it brought up for him. He was beginning to see his parents for who they were: aging adults trying to cope with the world the best they knew how. Seeing his father ravaged by alcoholism, Peter saw this potential in himself and appreciated that he was on a road toward health—that he did not need to follow in his father's footsteps. His newfound relationship with Joe was a great source of solace, although he pondered how or if he should tell Joe that he was gay. In the end, he decided that he did not need to decide that now.

As treatment continued, Peter began to feel better, and with renewed energy he pursued his carpentry and sculpture. Our sessions focused on the feelings that had emerged during this week, and he grappled with trying to understand them. He was surprised how the urge to drink was receding but could be reactivated when "I think about how I haven't thought about drinking." He began to talk generally about having a relationship with a man, but knew that he needed to wait until he was "more solidly into sobriety." He also knew that he had to deal with his feelings about Alex, and that he would when he was ready.

After 20 weeks of treatment, Peter and I terminated. He had completed his contract and had found supports in the community, most notably through AA. As part of saying good-bye, we reviewed our first interview. Peter remembered how "pissed off" he was initially, but said he subsequently felt that I wasn't going to "push him around." He said, "the DUI was the best thing that could've happened to me." We parted with the agreement that Peter could recontract and resume treatment in the future if he should feel the need.

---

* Asterisks within the text have been included for the class exercise on page 139.

Questions for Class Discussion

1. Prior to meeting Peter, and based on the referral information from Dr. Weiss (i.e., mandated client, second DUI offense, just discharged from two-week inpatient treatment), what thoughts and/or concerns would you have about taking him on as a client?

2. What skills did the worker use in the first few minutes of the session that helped engage this mandated and challenging client?

3. How would you diagnose Peter's stage of alcohol dependence/addiction? What elements of his history, behavior, attitudes, and feelings support this diagnosis?

4. How do you understand the relationship, if any, between Peter's identity as a gay man and his use of alcohol? How would you address this in treatment with him?

5. What elements in this case (e.g., client's readiness, worker's approach, external circumstances and resources) might have contributed to its successful outcome?

Teaching Points

1. Mandated or coerced treatment is an oxymoron to many social work practitioners, yet they are often called upon to work with non-voluntary clients. Examining personal attitudes and values related to treating coerced clients is an important first step.

2. (The worker was careful to give him as much control and responsibility as possible; giving him the option to leave seemed to free him up to stay.) In treating court-mandated clients, the therapy is driven by the contract surrounding the court mandate. Thus, a therapist needs to be more directive than usual, but this needs to be tempered by the circumstances and concerns that are unique to each individual. When Peter asked, "What do we need to do?" the worker resisted the urge to tell him. In one statement, Peter outlined the major issues which involved the next 20 weeks of therapy: "that I come from a dysfunctional family, that I have a problem with alcohol, and that I am gay."

3. Judging from the length of Peter's relationship with alcohol (20-plus years), his frequent blackouts, his inability to quantify how much he drank, his binging, his failed attempts to stop or cut down, and the extent of the problems related to alcohol, Peter was probably in what Jellinek (1952) outlined as the middle stage of addiction. In this stage, tolerance to alcohol increases and drinking has a debilitating effect on a person's relationships with

others and with the outside world. Multiple DUI arrests are also a strong indication of a serious problem with drugs or alcohol: it is estimated that a person may drive drunk 200 to 2,000 times before being arrested for a DUI (Jones & Joscelyn, 1978). Denial and related defenses are the coping strategies that enable an alcohol-dependent client to continue drinking, despite mounting evidence of alcohol-induced difficulties. Two fundamental approaches for treating an alcohol-dependent client are:

- chip away the "walls" of denial with the "mounting evidence," and
- help him/her to replace the relationship to alcohol with supportive relationships with people. AA and NA are powerful forums where such relationships can be forged.

4. It is important to address Peter's identification as a gay man and how that impacts upon him and his use of substances. Although being gay does not, in and of itself, cause substance abuse and dependence, gays and lesbians have disproportionately higher levels of substance abuse and addiction (Ratner, 1988). This is attributed to several factors: the stress that homophobia and discrimination puts upon gays; the fact that bars are often the only safe places to congregate (although this is changing); the stress of losing loved ones to AIDS; the idea that denial is often a comfortable coping mechanism, because gays often have to deny major portions of their lives to be accepted in society; and the social and psychological isolation that can occur when one lacks a niche in society (Ratner, 1988). All these stresses and strains are resonant in Peter's life.

5. Peter also presented some significant strengths. He was relatively successful in his work, despite his drinking. He had identified that he had a "problem with alcohol" and that he wanted to stop drinking. His motivation was high, despite some ambivalence about being coerced into treatment. In the past, he had responded well to a positive relationship with Alex, and had been able to take better care of himself. Although most involuntary clients' claims of abstinence should be approached with skepticism, Peter was credible when he said he had not been drinking. Alcohol dependency numbs feelings. The powerful feelings he exhibited in this interview—anger toward his family, and sadness about losing Alex—seemed newly awakened.

6. Mandated treatment for substance abuse problems works best during the window of opportunity provided by a crisis, when the client's wall of denial has been cracked. Even if treatment is "unsuccessful"—the client drops out or ends up in jail for noncompliance—the intervention of the worker may have meaning at some later juncture.

References

Faltz, B. (1992). Counseling chemically dependent lesbians and gay men. In S. Dworkin & F. Gutierrez (Eds.), *Counseling gay men and lesbians* (pp. 245-258). Alexandria, VA: American Counseling Association.

Jellinek, E. M. (1952). Phases of alcohol addiction. *Journal of Alcohol Studies, 13*(4), 673-684.

Jones, R., & Joscelyn, K. (1978). *Alcohol and highway safety: A review of the state of the knowledge,* Technical Report DOTHS 803714. Washington, DC: National Highway Traffic Administration.

Ratner, E. (1988). A model for the treatment of lesbian and gay alcohol abusers. *Alcoholism Treatment Quarterly, 5* (1/2), 25-45.

Ziebold, T. O., & Mongeon, J. E. (Eds.). (1985). *Gay and sober: Directions for counseling and therapy.* New York: Harrington Park Press.

Class Exercise
Peter: Stepping into the Client's and Worker's Shoes

Below are instructions for using the previous case study, Peter, for a classroom exercise. This exercise facilitates learning of the skills for the beginning phase of work: respect for the client, ongoing assessment, engagement, contracting, and collaboration.

Instructions for Instructors

1. This psychodramatic teaching method has its basis in psychodrama in that it asks that students take on various roles and say what the client or worker is feeling and thinking. It asks that the students practice a verbal response by answering the question, "What do you say?" and then, "What would you say next?"

2. Explain that you will be asking students to step into the shoes of the "players." Students can "pass" if they want to, because there are times when the worker and client don't want to say anything or are at a loss for words. They are to play the part in the present, speaking in the first person. There is not one right answer. There is no wrong feeling.

3. Read the case aloud. At each * ask the students to step into the shoes of the worker and the client. What is each feeling and thinking? "As the worker, what do you say to Peter's reply about what is important information?"

4. Initially, you may want to give the students Part I in order to focus on engagement. Following the discussion, you can give out Part II, which shows what the worker actually said and what happened as a consequence. Also, Part II could stimulate a discussion about the worker's attempts to assess Peter's supports for sobriety and the worker's attention to a beginning contract. Part III could show the course of the work phase and some of the dilemmas that arise (e.g., reconnection with family, possibility of relapse, issues of self-determination).

Jose:
Working with a Recovering Heroin Addict

When clients have cultural backgrounds different from the worker's own, workers may doubt their perceptions of case dynamics and be reluctant to confront clients when they act out. The case below illustrates dilemmas faced by workers when clients are involuntary and have some level of denial about the severity of their problems. Teaching points offer ways that workers can discuss ethnic and gender differences and ways those differences might affect the therapeutic relationship. Recommendations are made for structuring the relationship, exploring motivation for change, and taking into consideration the client's developmental stage, influenced by his daily use of drugs since age 11.

Setting: Outpatient substance abuse clinic.
Client: Jose, a personable 35-year-old Puerto Rican man on pretrial status.
Worker: Female social work intern in her early 30s.

Jose had lived in the United States for six years when he was arrested and charged with conspiracy to distribute heroin. He does not know yet when he will go to trial on these charges. Jose recently completed a two-month stay in an inpatient drug treatment center. He has been drug free for those two months and for the eight weeks since completing the program. His pretrial officer hopes to help him stay clean via outpatient counseling.

Jose was assigned to me after he saw my supervisor once for a preliminary evaluation to rule out major mental illness. I am a second-year social work student with some clinical experience with addicted clients, but not a great deal. Jose has had a lot of practice in telling his story, yet he still doesn't truly connect drug use with the problems in his life. I saw my challenge as forming a trusting relationship that focused on his substance use, but also treating him as a whole person and not simply as an addiction problem.

Jose's substance use began at age 11 with marijuana. He smoked 1–4 joints every day with his friends. The amount varied with availability, but it seems he didn't try to hide his use. He viewed it as somewhat culturally acceptable. At age 17, he started sniffing heroin, and would get high whenever possible, usually 5 days out of 7. He began shooting heroin at age 27 after being diagnosed with HIV. He attributes this illness to a blood transfusion after a knee operation in Puerto Rico. At this time, he became demoralized and used drugs daily and heavily in a passively suicidal manner. He also drove cars recklessly and got into fights because "living was not important." After his arrest, he tested positive for heroin on several urine samples before entering a detoxification center.

He is in the very early stage of recovery from heroin addiction. He has shown a persistent pattern of major damage in his life from using drugs. His strongest reason for not using heroin currently is that a "dirty urine" test will result in incarceration. His other reasons are that he doesn't want to hurt his mother anymore, and that his current girlfriend is in recovery and won't take him back again unless he is abstinent.

Jose has had medical, social, family, and financial problems for years, and all of these problems can be linked to drug use, although Jose sees external circumstances as responsible for his difficulties. For instance, he attributes the breakup of his three marriages to "choosing the wrong girl," and believes that his current girlfriend is the only one who can "manage" him "because she's tough and she doesn't believe me." He says that he really likes heroin, even now, and is looking to external forces to help him stay clean, especially his girlfriend and the threat of prison.

He has been both physically and psychologically dependent on heroin. Consequences have included lack of educational/vocational development, job loss, three divorces, his flight from Puerto Rico to "start a new life," breakups with his current girlfriend, and neglect of his parental duties to his two sons. He also missed out on a possible Olympic boxing opportunity in his teens because his blood test was positive for drugs. He admitted violating his own values by stealing from his mother and his wives to support his habit, and regularly risking his life by "testing" new batches of heroin in exchange for a supply.

On the medical side, he slept for days when using, getting up only to get the next fix, and experienced severe withdrawal when he couldn't get the drug. His moods were unpredictable, ranging from euphoria to paranoia. He became impotent, a common side effect of heavy use. Most of his energy was concentrated on when and how to get his next fix.

Now Jose is awaiting a trial date. With no money and no job, he is living with his sister's family in a small apartment. He is understandably depressed and ruminates about getting back to his girlfriend and non-using friends. It has been difficult to interest him in doing anything to improve his life. He says he can't get a decent job and he can never make it to the Spanish-speaking Narcotics Anonymous meetings. Lately he has been missing every other counseling session with me. We've had a total of four sessions. He doesn't feel that counseling is necessary, and he's coming because he needs to do what he's told.

Worker's Observations

From the start, a power differential existed between us—Jose was mandated to outpatient counseling and would not have been there unless he had to be. I was another authority figure in his life, another in the long list of people who were concerned about his behavior and trying to control it. His family, his girlfriends, and his wives had all tried and failed to help him quit using drugs. He was only clean because he did not want to jeopardize his court case; in a few months he would go on trial for conspiracy to distribute heroin, and having "dirty urine" would not look good in court.

It seemed that Jose was not sure what all the fuss was about—why anyone else should care about his drug use. In trying to help him connect his drug use with the trouble and problems in his life, I often felt that he was agreeing with me because I was part of the "system." I also felt that I was assuming a role that was familiar for him and frustrating for me—a woman reminding him of other women in his life who cajoled, nagged, and wondered: "Why won't he attend NA meetings? Why doesn't he get some kind of job so that he doesn't have so much time on his hands? Why doesn't he volunteer his time to teach basketball to boys when he loves the sport and likes to work with young people?"

Jose would complain of boredom or would talk about wanting to go to the western part of the state to be with his girlfriend, but he had no plans to make these things happen. I couldn't tell if he was a fatalist, thinking that he had little power to influence his life, or if he was passive-dependent—waiting until I would offer suggestions, but still nothing would change. He never looked for a job, never went to NA, never took action. I didn't want to keep playing this game, but I didn't know how to change the rules.

Was I culturally biased, unreasonably expecting him to plumb the depths of his soul and share his insights with me when he needed something totally different from counseling? Was I wrong to want him to take more responsibility for the quality of his life? Was I biased in urging him to action? He had stated his perception of our cultural differences in a telling way when we were discussing why he liked heroin so much. He said that he liked heroin because it made him feel mellow, while "gringos" tended to choose drugs that made them feel speeded up, increasing their natural "drivenness." Sometimes he almost had me believing that he was satisfied with his life, that he accepted both the good and bad of drugs, and still would prefer to have drugs in his life no matter what the consequences.

Questions for Class Discussion

1. What methods could the worker have used to engage Jose more effectively given that he is a male, from a culture different from hers, and has a history of relationships with women who show more concern about his life than he does?

2. Should the worker discuss the involuntary nature of the client's attending therapy? What should be said about it?

3. In terms of treatment goals, what constitutes "starting where the client is"?

4. How can the clinician discern which aspects of the therapeutic difficulty are related to (a) cultural differences, (b) the cycle of addiction, (c) personality, or (d) the involuntary nature of the treatment?

5. What are the clinical implications of daily marijuana use beginning at age 11? What can we predict about Jose, in terms of his development, when we learn that by age 17, he was high on heroin five out of seven days per week?

Teaching Points

1. The therapeutic alliance, which seems fragile, would be enhanced by a discussion between worker and client about ethnic/cultural differences. An important point for the worker to make is that she hasn't worked much with Puerto Rican men and would like to hear more from Jose about his cultural background, especially his childhood and early family life, and how he thinks this differs from that of most "gringos."

2. Exploring how the client thinks the involuntary nature of the therapy influences his investment in the therapy would be essential. If he acknowledges that he is coming only to do what he's told, the worker can discuss with him her policy of only seeing people who come to "work" during sessions. She can present this as a dilemma—she has enjoyed working with him thus far and they have made some progress, but the agency requires a task focus if she is to continue. He can choose which focus to work on, but it must be "work" relevant to his situation. She can point out that he also has the option to reject therapy altogether and return to court—it is his choice to make.

3. Since Jose has had little experience of life without drugs, he has little reason to believe life would be better without them. The worker would do well to focus on the client's stated reasons for wanting abstinence:
   - his girlfriend will take him back,
   - he will not cause his mother more pain, and
   - he will not be incarcerated.
   Rather than focus on the long-term benefits of recovery, the worker can discuss the short-term avoidance of pain, e.g., the client's losing his girlfriend, further disappointing his mother, and facing the rest of his life behind bars.

4. If the worker can help Jose identify his motives for attending counseling, can bring more structure to the situation (e.g., written goals and expected time line, requirements re attendance and being drug-free during sessions), and can clarify her role as

facilitating his work, the answer to this question would become clearer.

5. When drug use begins at such a young age, it interferes with crucial components of human development such as learning how to regulate affect, acquiring problem-solving skills, and developing a future orientation. If, by age 17, Jose was high on heroin five out of seven days per week, it is likely that he has not mastered additional developmental skills related to identity and intimacy.

Suggested Readings

Comas-Diaz, L., & Jacobsen, F. M. (19--). Ethnocultural transference and countertransference in the therapeutic dyad. *American Journal of Orthopsychiatry, 61*(3), 392-402.

De La Rosa, M. (1991). Patterns and consequences of illegal drug use among Hispanics. In Sotomayor, M. (Ed.), *Empowering Hispanic families: A critical issue for the 90s* (pp. 39-57). Milwaukee, WI: Family Service Association.

Glick, R., & Moore, J. (Eds.). (1990). D*rugs in Hispanic communities*. New Brunswick and London: Rutgers University Press.

Martin, S. S., & Scarpitti, F. R. (1993). An intensive case management approach for paroled IV drug users. *Journal of Drug Issues, 23*(1), 43-59.

Platt, J. J. (1986). *Heroin addiction: Theory, research, and treatment*. Malabar, FL: Robert E. Krieger Publishing Company.

Ramos, R. (1990). Chicano intravenous drug users. In E. Y. Lambert (Ed.), *The collection and interpretation of data from hidden populations* (pp. 128-145). NIDA Research Monograph 98, U.S. Department of Health and Human Services.

Identifying Short- and Long-Term Recovery Issues

Ben:
Seeking Therapy after Eight Years of Recovery

Years after initial abstinence from alcohol and other drugs, personal and family problems may emerge that require therapeutic attention. Resentments and anger, unaddressed losses, and fear of intimacy are dynamics that may surface and threaten some clients' sense of well-being. These dynamics are more likely in individuals who experience a "spontaneous remission" from addiction—who establish abstinence without treatment and with minimal self-examination.

Ben is a 38-year-old African-American married man with four children. Ben was referred to the substance abuse treatment program by his wife, who participated in an Adult Children of Alcoholics group at our hospital. Ben seeks treatment because his angry outbursts at home led to difficulties in his relationships with his children and wife.

Throughout his life, Ben's social relationships have been mainly in the black community. He went to a segregated "black school" in Alabama and describes how painful the "busing" was. Ben has a strong sense of racial identity and finds it very important to be a part of the black community. He is an active member of an Baptist church in a Baltimore neighborhood and has responded to several opportunities to tutor and participate in athletic events with black teenagers who do not have contact with their fathers.

Ben was a substance abuser until the age of 31 when he joined the Baptist church. He abused alcohol and cocaine. He met his wife in his church. With her help and the spiritual support of the church community, he was able to become drug-free and remain so for almost 8 years.

Ben was a physically abused child from age 5 to 8. He was beaten up frequently by his grandmother because he had a "strong will." Ben felt that he was "not a good child" and deserved punishment. When he became an adult, he considered himself a "bad man." At age 12, Ben was informed by his mother that his biological father had been killed years before and that the man who had raised him was his stepfather. Ben felt totally betrayed by his mother, stunned that she had not told him sooner. Ben's stepfather was a "good man" but an alcoholic and a "questionable character." Ben had always felt isolated from his stepfather. He responded to this news by spending little time at home. He excelled in basketball in high school and developed a strong father-son relationship with his coach.

Currently, Ben repeats his grandmother's behavior by yelling at his children constantly and controlling their lives in every aspect. His relationship with his youngest son is the most conflict-ridden. The boy is the same age as Ben was at the time his grandmother abused him. Ben describes his son as a "child with a strong will" who needs to be punished to learn discipline. Ben identifies strongly with his son but takes on the role of the abuser.

Ben grew up on a small farm in Alabama with his six siblings. Because his family had to overcome economic hardship, Ben became very money-conscious early in his life. He feels continually frustrated over financial issues at home, and because his wife does the family budgeting, this is a source of conflict between them. Ben thinks he might like to take care of the finances himself but does not know how.

Currently, Ben's relationship with his wife is strained. He describes her as a "good mother and caretaker" who wants to stay home with the children. But he is discouraged about losing one weekly paycheck if she stops working. Ben is resistant to discussing issues in his marriage other than the children. He thinks that his uncomfortable anger is unacceptable. However, he feels reassured because his wife doesn't say anything about it and just takes the children and leaves him alone until he calms down.

Ben believes that he will be able to eliminate his angry outbursts and save his marriage if he makes up his mind to do so. This is how he overcame his addiction. In the case of his addiction, he found that attending church resulted in a "removal of the craving for alcohol and drugs." He was able to stop using and never resume.

Questions for Class Discussion

1. Has the client's current situation been influenced by his method of recovery?

2. What are the strengths you see in the client's situation—in him as a person, in his family, in his social environment? How can the worker build on the client's strengths?

3. Do you think the client's view of recovery from addiction is "realistic"?

4. Is there a way that the client's recovery from addiction can be used by the worker as a model for anger management and resolution of other family problems? What would you say to the client about how you think the therapeutic work should proceed?

5. Could the client benefit from a psychodynamic approach? If so, to deal with which issues? How would you carry out this work?

Teaching Points

1. Recovery from addiction is often conceptualized in stages (Usher, 1991) or through a developmental model (Brown, 1985) in which abstinence is followed by accomplishment of a variety of additional psychosocial tasks for the individual and family. The result includes the ability to engage in satisfying intimate relationships, to pursue goals that are appropriate to one's stage of life and history of addiction, and to cope with frustrations with a variety of stress-reduction and conflict-resolution methods. In her model for couples and families, Usher identifies four stages:

   • confronting the substance abuse,
   • engaging in the process of learning,
   • undergoing reorganization, and
   • consolidation.

   When clients achieve abstinence in the way that Ben apparently did (i.e., with support from his church but no specific attention to other behaviors or problems that might have emerged during his drug-taking years or precipitated his addiction), they sometimes fail to confront other painful aspects of their lives.

2. Ben's strengths:
   • strong sense of racial identity
   • membership in Baptist church—ability to utilize this group support
   • altruism as demonstrated by his tutoring black teenagers and participating in athletic events with them
   • abstinence from drugs for almost 8 years
   • emotional capacity to have a close relationship as evidenced by his strong attachment to his basketball coach
   • insight—sees his uncontrollable anger as unacceptable; aware of ambivalence about taking on family finances, although he has been critical of his wife's handling of the finances

   Family and environmental strengths:
   • wife's participation in an ACOA group
   • a commitment to the Baptist church that is shared by the couple

- wife is perceived by Ben as "good mother and caretaker" who wants to spend time raising her children; she provides safety for them if Ben is in a rage
- couple desires to improve their marriage and family life.

3. Although the client was able to achieve abstinence by experiencing a "removal of the craving for alcohol and drugs" through church attendance, a new relationship, and making up his mind to stop, not everyone is able to follow this course. Further, although these methods worked for Ben before, they may be less effective in helping with the current problems affecting the entire family system.

4. Recovery from addiction as a model for future change:
   - The same "tools" or skills can be used, such as developing alternative responses to impulsive behaviors, asking others for help, expressing feelings rather than acting on them, examining expectations of self and others to determine whether they are realistic (e.g., letting go of the need for perfection).
   - Similar sources of support could be tapped, such as the church group.
   - Because change often occurs in stages or phases, rather than all at once, the worker can explore whether this happened with Ben, have him describe the stages, and help him develop a multi-phase plan for approaching this situation. Working with the family system would need to include impulse control methods for Ben, a safety plan for his wife and children, strengthening the marital relationship, helping Ben and his wife develop appropriate methods of reinforcement, support, and setting limits for responding to the "strong-willed" son.

5. If a psychodynamic approach were used, important issues to be explored would be:
   - the effects on Ben of physical abuse by his grandmother
   - the effects of his betrayal by his mother
   - his identification with his stepfather, grandmother, and strong-willed son
   - the meaning of money, and
   - who his wife represents to him.

Suggested Readings

Brown, S. (1985). *Treating the alcoholic: A developmental model of recovery*, New York: Wiley.

Beverly, C. (1989). Treatment issues for black, alcoholic clients. *Social Casework*, 370-374.

Brisbane, F. L., & Womble (Eds.). (1985). *Treatment of Black alcoholics*. New York: Haworth.

Usher, M. L. (1991). From identification to consolidation: A treatment model for couples and families complicated by alcoholism. *Family Dynamics of Addiction Quarterly, 1*(2), 45-58.

Ziter, M. L. P. (1987). Culturally sensitive treatment of Black alcoholic families. *Social Work*, March-April, 130-135.

Clara: A Black Latina and Her Daughter in Residential Treatment

During residential treatment, a source of great concern is the effects of discharge. Workers worry about the sudden lack of supports for clients. Some clients have an idealized view of being on their own and fail to recognize the challenges. In the case below, the client has been caring for her daughter in a residential program with multiple caretakers but will soon be the sole caretaker when she leaves the program. Her own history of trauma and poor self-esteem makes her vulnerable to relapse. Teaching points recommend the "phasing in" of added parental responsibilities, trauma work, and insight therapy.

Agency: A residential facility for alcohol and drug-addicted women.

Worker: Second-year social work intern, female and bilingual.

Client: Clara is a 36-year-old black Latina born of a Spanish father and a black mother. She is a single mother of 5 children, ages 15, 12, 5, 4, and 3.

Clara describes herself as a chronic relapser. Before coming to this agency she had been in many detoxification programs, residential programs, and long- and short-term treatment programs of various kinds, but the longest time she had been sober was six months. At the time I started working with Clara she had just completed six months in the program. This was a difficult time because she was scared of relapsing again. She was mandated to substance abuse treatment by a child protective agency in order to get her children back from foster care. She had been given the ultimatum of enrolling in a long-term program or losing her children permanently.

Clara was born in Honduras. Her mother left when she was eight years old and Clara continued living with her father, who was extremely physically and emotionally abusive. During the seven years she lived with her father, her older sister sexually abused her. Clara left Honduras when she was 15, joining her mother in the U.S. Clara started drinking when she was 12. At age 20 she was introduced to marijuana. By the time she was 26, she was a very heavy drinker and regular cocaine user with two children. Because of her heavy drinking and drug use, Clara lost custody of her children on several occasions. She would get clean long enough to get them back, but would again relapse.

This is the first time that Clara has been able to stay sober for more than six months. She has obtained custody of her youngest daughter who is allowed to live at the residential treatment house with her. Clara plans to get custody of all her children and to move into an independent living situation with them.

The focus of the current therapy is helping Clara better understand her responsibilities as a sober, independent woman and mother. After she leaves the program, the focus will be on helping her through the transition to independent living, especially balancing her recovery and her responsibilities as a mother and head of a household.

Clara has experienced much trauma at the hands of significant figures in her life. She also has severe self-consciousness and self-hatred because her father rejected and ridiculed her because she was black. Clara's mother is black but she rejected Clara because she was Latina. As a result of this, Clara refused to speak Spanish until she was 13 years old. Even now in therapy, if she is discussing a painful issue, she reverts to speaking English.

Currently, Clara has been abstinent from alcohol and other drugs for almost a year.

At a Session

I asked Clara how her week had been. She talked about how good it was for her to have Cynthia, her 3-year-old daughter, living in the house with her. Wanting to explore how much Clara was in touch with the responsibilities and difficulties implied by having her child back, I asked her if her life had changed since Cynthia came to live there. Her immediate response was "no." I asked again if she was sure nothing had changed for her. Clara looked at me and started talking about how sometimes she feels that having Cynthia is overwhelming. When it is Cynthia's bedtime she gives Clara a hard time, or she wakes up around 11 p.m. asking for food. Clara explained that even though her daughter is in the house, Clara still has responsibility for chores like cleaning the house at night after dinner. I asked her if she felt it was too much for her to take care of Cynthia and still comply with all the requirements of living in the house. She said that sometimes it is a struggle to do both, especially when Cynthia takes more time than Clara expects. For example, if she goes downstairs to clean the kitchen and somebody tells her that Cynthia is crying in her room, Clara has to stop what she's doing and take care of her daughter.

Clara talked about understanding that it must be difficult for a 3-year-old girl to have to adapt to so many changes. Cynthia has been living with her mother for only three weeks. Wondering if this "new experience" as a full-time mother was overwhelming for Clara, and if she felt that she was giving up too much of her "own" recovery to take care of her daughter, I asked Clara how she felt about her daughter taking so much of her

time. She said that she was really tired of being in the residential program with so many other women, having to deal with other people's problems every day—she was looking forward to moving out and being on her own. I asked her to tell me what kind of "other people's problems" she was talking about. She explained that when she saw other women arguing among themselves or getting in trouble with staff, it was annoying to her even though it did not involve her. Clara seemed tired and overwhelmed when talking about this.

I asked her, if it were in her power, what she would like to change. After taking a deep breath, she said that she understood that was the way things had to be in this recovery home, but for her, the solution to those feelings was to move out when her time came. She kept talking about feeling "very tired" all the time and counting the days until she could move out.

I reminded Clara that it would not be easy once she moved out and Cynthia was solely her responsibility. I asked if she remembered what she used to do when she was actively using drugs and she would feel tired and overwhelmed. She answered that she would look for drugs to escape from the situation. I talked about how likely it would be for her to have those feelings again, especially when she is on her own and there is nobody else to take care of Cynthia. She acknowledged that an advantage to living in the residential treatment house was that when she felt she was "losing it" with her daughter, she could ask for and get help from staff members and other women. I asked Clara what she would do when there was no staff or other women to help. I asked her what would be different now from before that would stop her from using drugs. Clara said she hates to think of what she felt like when she was using. She said she is very determined not to do it again and is not isolated anymore, but connected with her family and friends.

Worker Observations

I have worried that this client tells me what she thinks I want to hear, but today I felt that we touched on important issues and feelings. I need to remember that this is the first time in Clara's life that she has been able to be clean and sober for an extended period. Before, she would stay clean for six months at the most and then relapse. This time she has been sober for almost a year. She is scared of her own history and is worried that she won't be able to stay sober.

Questions for Class Discussion

1. Why is the worker focusing so much on Clara's responsibilities as a mother? Might the client interpret this as a lack of confidence in her abilities to function like an adult?

2. Is it appropriate for the worker to "remind" Clara of what used to happen when she was using? What are the benefits and disadvantages of this strategy?

3. How important is it that Clara work on childhood trauma and self-esteem problems? At what point in her abstinence should this be done?

Teaching Points

1. An important part of residential treatment is helping clients plan their reentry into the community. Reentry involves Clara taking responsibility for being a mother for her young daughter. She needs to prove to herself and to the child protective agency that she can handle this responsibility, especially if she wants to get her other children back. The worker needs to keep doing reality testing related to the difficulties of raising children so that Clara can carefully consider the implications of taking responsibility for all five children in the near future. Even the second and third years of abstinence are difficult for clients, with many urges to drink and use drugs.

2. People in recovery, especially in residential facilities, tend to get isolated and "forget" what they used to do when they were active users. Because part of the treatment is to prepare them for life in the "real world" where they will get frustrated and overwhelmed with everyday problems, the worker's responsibility is (a) to review what the client used to do when her only way of coping was to get "high," and (b) to help her explore other, healthier ways to deal with those situations.

3. Because Clara is facing a crisis in terms of discharge from a supportive environment, and given her extensive relapse history, such work should probably wait until she is well-established in her new environment, has considerably more abstinence, and has more experiences of successful parenting. At that point, client and worker can consider whether this work would be of benefit, and how it might take place.

Suggested Readings

Child Welfare League of America (1990). *Crack and other addictions: Old realities and new challenges for child welfare.* Washington, DC: Author.

Daley, D. C. (1987). Relapse prevention with substance abusers: Clinical issues and myths. *Social Work*, *32*(2), 138-142.

Evans, K., & Sullivan, J. M. (1995). *Treating addicted survivors of trauma.* New York: Guilford.

Hawley, T. L., Halle, T. G., Drasin, R. E., & Thomas, N. G. (1995). Children of addicted mothers: Effects of the "crack epidemic" on the care-giving environment and development of preschoolers. *American Journal of Orthopsychiatry, 65*(3), 364-379.

Wallace, B. C. (1989). Psychological and environmental determinants of relapse in crack cocaine smokers. *Journal of Substance Abuse Treatment, 6*, 95-106.

Wallace, B. C. (1990). Treating crack cocaine dependence: The critical role of relapse prevention. *Journal of Psychoactive Drugs, 22*(2).

Richard: Examining Periodic Relapse

This case examines the relationship between relapse and developmental issues, including early losses and the threatened loss of a current primary relationship. The teaching points outline the work of early abstinence and describe how these tasks differ from those of ongoing recovery.

Setting: Private acute-care psychiatric and substance abuse treatment program.

Client: Richard is a 37-year-old white male who presented for alcohol detoxification.

Worker: The worker is a social work intern. Her role is to complete a biopsychosocial assessment and monitor the patient's progress toward treatment goals.

Presenting problem: Richard relapsed when Maureen, his partner of eight years (from whom he had been separated due to his drinking), got involved with another man.

Case Record

Richard is anxious, depressed, and guilty about this relapse. He was on a binge, drinking straight alcohol (vodka) for five to seven days prior to admission to this program. Within the past several months, he had finished a 30-day substance abuse treatment program at another facility. He states that he has disappointed people: "I'm letting a lot of people down. I help a lot of people in the AA program; they're going to be devastated." He is worried about his 3-year-old son, Mark, who Richard helps support financially, although he no longer lives with Mark's mother. He also worries that he may lose his job.

In addition to his son Mark, Richard has also helped raise Maureen's other two chil-

dren, a girl, 16, and a boy, 11. Richard dropped out of high school, but received training as an auto mechanic, which is his current vocation.

Richard has a history of alcohol dependency dating back to his teens. His alcoholic mother died of cancer after being sober for five years. Two of his brothers are alcoholics; one is now in recovery. His father died when Richard was 11, turning over the care of Richard's five younger siblings and alcoholic mother to Richard. He began drinking two years later. He says that he recognized he had a problem at age 29, when friends who drank like he did were dying.

Richard denies any abuse of substances other than alcohol. He reports good relationships overall with his ten siblings.

Richard has a history of treatment through AA and a strong identification with its principles and philosophy. His recovery has been marked by cycles of sobriety and relapse. He has a sponsor with whom he has worked on the 12 steps, and many friends in the AA program, some of whom brought him to this hospital. His longest period of sobriety was about three and one-half years, beginning with a month-long inpatient substance abuse program in 1987. After a relapse, he remained abstinent for another nine months. For the past two years he has been "bouncing in and out of recovery," attending AA regularly when sober, doing speaking commitments and sponsoring people. He recognizes a pattern in which he starts to get his life back in order (e.g., improved relationships, established routines, a sense of productivity at work), then he stops going to meetings, something happens to make him angry, and he has a couple of drinks.

He discussed specific precipitating incidents which he believes triggered his previous relapses, including betrayal by a friend at work who began the rumor that Richard was drinking when he was still abstinent, and threats to his relationship with Maureen.

Although he and Maureen were separated, he had maintained hopes for reconciliation. However, seven months ago she began dating a successful physician who is well-established professionally and who has been very involved with her children. Maureen is considering marrying this man. Richard fears he will lose her and also his fairly close relationship with her children.

Questions for Class Discussion

1. What is a relapse and what role does relapse play in an addiction?

2. Why might relapse have occurred at this point in Richard's recovery?

3. What is the significance of Richard's drinking at age 13?

4. What is the significance of Richard's mother remaining sober for five years before her death?

5. What theoretical framework would be useful for viewing this case—e.g., crisis theory, disease concept of addictions, family systems, ecological, gender-role socialization, cognitive-behavioral, psychodynamic?

6. What are the major short-term and long-term issues that should be addressed in Richard's treatment?

Teaching Points

1. A relapse is a return to drinking and/or drug use after a period of abstinence in which the individual has made a commitment to remain drug-free. (This is different from periods of non-use by someone who is experimenting with non-use but is not committed to remain drug-free.) Relapses are often experienced as great disappointments and/or personal failures to someone who has struggled to remain abstinent.

Workers can help clients deal with relapse by pointing out that learning has taken place and skills have been acquired in the process of maintaining substantial abstinence. (This may not be true if the abstinence is only for a few days.) Other gains may also have occurred in terms of building personal relationships, acquiring mastery over challenges at work, improving self-esteem, and developing stability in family life and other aspects of daily living.

Perhaps most important is the worker's role in helping the client examine the specific precipitants of the relapse so the client can identify high-risk situations and avoid them in the future. The worker can also facilitate examination of the "tools" and social supports used for maintaining abstinence, such as communicating with family members at times of stress, tightly structuring free time, attending AA meetings, calling one's AA sponsor, serving as a sponsor to other AA members, and telling friends and acquaintances that one is in recovery.

2. It seemed that Richard had been using alcohol at least in part to cope with early losses. Taking away this anesthetic left him vulnerable. A complete biopsychosocial assessment rather than an exclusive focus on alcohol and other drug issues would alert the worker to early loss. Grief work may also be indicated. When Richard lost Maureen, which probably restimulated earlier losses in Richard's life, the same "abstinence tasks" that worked in early recovery (approximately 3–12 months) were no longer effective for Richard.

3. If Richard began drinking at age 13, he may now be developmentally more similar to a 13-year-old than a 37-year-old. Excessive use of alcohol or other drugs at an early age interferes with the attainment of

developmental skills such as affect regulation and future orientation, which usually occur in adolescence, and identity formation and participation in intimate relationships, which usually occur in adulthood. The individual who becomes abstinent in adulthood may still be developmentally closer to adolescence than adulthood.

4. The fact that his mother remained sober for five years before she died may be a source of hope for Richard, if it can be highlighted by the worker. Her sobriety indicates that she realized drinking was causing problems in her life and took steps to deal with it. She may even have used some sobriety methods that, if Richard can recall them, would be helpful to him in developing methods of his own. The fact that Richard has a brother in recovery is also a hopeful sign. The worker might explore whether the two brothers have talked about their recovery and whether the recovering brother might be a source of additional support.

5. A number of theoretical frameworks could be used for various parts of the therapeutic work. The instructor can ask the class to describe how they would apply various frameworks, and discourage the need to identify only one framework as the best.

6. The possibilities of losing his job and his relationship with Maureen constitute current crises and should be addressed first. Brown (1985) is a valuable resource for working with clients in ongoing recovery. Some of the tasks outlined in Brown's work include:

- grieving losses from childhood and adolescence;
- examining how earlier behavior patterns may reemerge in adulthood upon the initiation of abstinence;
- relearning or learning for the first time how to function in an intimate relationship;
- reexamining life goals and establishing new ones appropriate to one's stage in life following the addiction; and
- establishing a sense of purpose in life which extends beyond the basics of staying free from alcohol and other drugs.

Suggested Readings

Bean, M. H., & Zinberg, N. E. (Eds.). (1981). *Dynamic approaches to the understanding and treatment of alcoholism.* New York: Free Press.

Brown, S. (1985). *Treating the alcoholic: A developmental model of recovery.* New York: Wiley.

Brownell, K., Marlatt, G., Lichtenstein, E., & Wilson, C. (1986, July). Understanding and preventing relapse. *American Psychologist*, 765-782.

Daley, D. C. (1987). Relapse prevention with substance abusers: Clinical issues and myths. *Social Work, 32*(2), 138-142

Marlatt, G. A., & Gordon, J. R. (Eds.). *Relapse prevention maintenance strategies in the treatment of addictive behaviors.* New York: Guilford.

Estella: In Residential Treatment with Other "Lazy Latinas"

When a member of a residential treatment facility is different from most other members in terms of race, culture, background, etc., she/he may feel a heightened sense of isolation. Estella, the client discussed here, expresses feelings of inferiority because she is one of few Latinas in the program and because her English skills are poor. The worker tries to explore these feelings with the client to ascertain whether they might represent concerns about being different and/or inferior in other areas.

Setting: A nonprofit agency helping women move from dependence on drugs, alcohol, and public assistance to independent, sober lives.

Client: A 28-year-old Latina referred from prison.

Worker: Second-year social work intern who is a Latina.

When I started working with Estella she had been in the residential program for six months, with six more months to go. By the time she came to the program, she had spent four years in prison. She is single and heterosexual, although she admits to having experimented with lesbian relationships while incarcerated.

Estella lived in Puerto Rico until the age of 21. She started using marijuana at age 13; by age 16 she was using marijuana and cocaine on a daily basis; at age 18 she started using crack cocaine; and by age 19 she was exchanging sex for crack cocaine and heroin. She was involved in a number of unhealthy relationships with men who abused her physically and emotionally and provided her with drugs. At age 21, she got pregnant with her daughter. Due to the severity of her substance abuse, her daughter was born prematurely and brain damaged. Trying to raise this disabled child used up what little coping ability she had left, and at one point, in a cocaine-induced rage, she tried to murder her daughter. Thus, she was sent to prison.

She has been clean and sober since she was arrested four-and-a-half years ago. She did not speak English when she entered our residential program, but is taking English as a Second Language (ESL) classes and starting to communicate in English. Language was a great barrier in her treatment because she could not understand much of what she was told. She has told me how pleased she is that I am able to work with her because I am bilingual and bicultural.

At the beginning of treatment, my focus was on helping Estella adapt to the program. She had concerns about being one of the few Latina residents, especially because she did not speak English. She was convinced that she wouldn't last because she did not feel she belonged. Estella now reports being comfortable in the program.

Once she finishes the residential program, we will continue meeting on an outpatient basis to help her maintain sobriety and anticipate difficult transitional challenges "out there in the real world" where she will be exposed to temptations to resume using drugs.

Process Recording

At 10:00 Saturday morning, Estella came in the office smiling. She seemed to be in a good mood. I said that it was nice to see her so happy.

She said that since we had arranged to have our meetings later in the morning, it was easier for her to be ready. I asked her what she meant by "be ready," not sure if she was referring to being physically or emotionally ready. She laughed and said that when I used to come earlier, she never had time to take a shower so she was kind of sloppy. She said that on Saturdays she likes to sleep later, especially given her new job and all the responsibilities she has as a member of the program. She said I had probably made the decision to come later just to "give these women clients a break."

She said, "Monica, you probably thought, 'Let me give these *vagas* (lazy in Spanish) some more time to get ready.'" I replied that the reason I asked them to meet later was because most of the time I had to wait for them. Although I preferred to meet earlier so that I could enjoy the rest of my Saturday, I didn't mind sleeping a little later either. (I was trying to address the issue of her considering herself *vaga* because she wanted to sleep longer on a weekend. I wanted to "normalize" the behavior and to show her that, like anyone else, I would enjoy some extra sleep.) I said that I considered this new schedule to be working well.

Estella said she used to be "kind of embarrassed" when she was meeting with me, wearing sweat pants, not having taken a shower, and without makeup. She said, "You know how Latinas always like to look good, be dressed, do their hair and their face. Do you think it is because we are more vain than the American women?" I responded by saying that I didn't think we could generalize, that we can find all kinds of personalities in women regardless of race, color, or ethnicity. Estella agreed, but said she notices that the Latinas in the house are more concerned about their physical appearance.

Wondering if she were talking about differences other than appearance, I asked if she felt she was "different" from most residents in other ways, and, if so, how. She said that she had a different culture, could not even speak the language, and was missing a lot of the "good things" the rest of women were receiving from the treatment. She complained of not being able to express herself in the way she wanted and complained that her Latina friends acted like they were tired of translating for her all the time. Wanting to explore if this were really the case, or if it was a distortion, I asked if Clara, Maria, or any of the other bilingual women had told her that they did not want to translate for her. She said that they did not say it but she could see it in their faces when they were forced to do it in the groups or other meetings. I stated that I found it hard to believe that her bilingual friends would refuse to help her with the language, especially because at least two of them had told me that they liked when they were asked to interpret and even felt "important." Estella finally said that maybe it was her own insecurity and that probably what makes her upset is having to depend so much on these other women—that it makes her feel inferior and more helpless.

Estella wants to improve her English because this would open a lot of doors for her. She is happy in her new job, but she knows that if she could speak better English, she would make more money. She can't believe she was able to survive for so many years in this country without speaking the language. She reflected about how deep her isolation must have been, because this is really the first time she is feeling an urge to learn English.

I find it easy to connect with this client. She has a good deal of insight about her previous life style when she was "using," and where she wants her life to go in the future. Because I find it so "easy" to conduct therapy with Estella, however, I am concerned that I must be missing something.

Questions for Class Discussion

1. In what way is it an advantage for this client that the worker is from the same ethnic background and speaks the client's first language? Are there drawbacks?

2. How effective was the worker in addressing the client's feelings about being "different"? What additional questions could the worker have asked or comments could she have made?

3. Are there additional issues related to Estella's culture and ethnicity which need attention from the program and the worker?

Teaching Points

1. Ideally, work with minority clients would involve matching the ethnicity and language of the client and therapist. However, cultural competence on the part of "mainstream" workers can go a long way to reduce clients' feelings of isolation. Possible drawbacks include the risk of

   • overidentification by the worker when the worker is similar to the client, and

   • perpetuating the idea among clients that they can only be understood or helped by people who are like them.

2. The issues of "difference" can be thought of in a number of ways, e.g., difference between Estella and the workers; Estella and other Latinas in the house; Estella and the non-Latinas in the house. Estella may have felt "different" recently or for a number of years because of:

   • being an addict;

   • having experimented with a lesbian relationship;

   • having been in prison after trying to murder her young daughter;

   • being the mother of a brain-damaged daughter;

   • having been the victim of battering by men;

   • childhood experiences in her family.

Each of these issues should be kept in mind by the worker when Estella talks of feeling inferior and helpless. It is not apparent which of these might cause Estella the greatest pain—only the client can make this clear. But the worker could suggest, through general statements, that there may have been many situations in Estella's life that have led to these feelings and the worker wonders which ones, both current and past, come to Estella's mind.

3. Often clients of color have to work on both their recovery from addiction and on experiences and feelings related to oppression, discrimination, and internalized racism. The client may not be experiencing discrimination at the treatment program, but may have experienced this in other places in the past. She has not dealt with these feelings because she was oblivious to them while actively using drugs. Such feelings often surface during recovery and may get in the way if not addressed. Clients' self-esteem and sense of trust are affected by their identity as addicts and by their identity as ethnic minorities. The therapeutic work should address both issues.

Suggested Readings

Comas-Dias, L., & Jacobsen, F. M. Ethnocultural transference and countertransference in the therapeutic dyad. *Journal of Orthopsychiatry, 61*(3).

Evans, K., & Sullivan, J. M. (1985). *Treating addicted survivors of trauma.* New York: Guilford.

Kaufman, G. (1989). *The psychology of shame.* New York: Springer Publishing Company.

McNeece, C. A., & DiNitto, D. M. (1985). Ethnicity, culture and substance abuse. In C. A. McNeece & D. M. DiNitto, *Chemical dependency: A systems approach* (pp. 240-291). Englewood Cliffs, NJ: Prentice Hall.

Pinderhughes, E. (1988). Significance of culture and power in the human behavior curriculum. In C. Jacobs & D. D. Bowles (Eds.), *Ethnicity and race: Critical concepts in social work.* Silver Spring, MD: NASW.

Teaching Tools
and Classroom Exercises

Maria Lupina:
Using the Critical Incident as a Teaching Tool

This case explores a unique teaching tool for the examination of the multidimensional impact of AODA on vulnerable populations served by social workers, and the application of a range of theoretical frameworks to a client situation. As a role-play exercise it is particularly useful in getting students to participate because it encourages students to use their own life experiences. Further, it provides a look at how an intervention can evolve over time. Although the critical incident method is applicable to many content areas, it is used here to demonstrate an integration of substance abuse material and social work skills.

This case describes a 32-year-old undocumented Latina mother of two who is threatening to leave a detox center on day four of her withdrawal from alcohol. The apparent precipitant for her decision is a distressing telephone call received from her 7-year-old son, who asks his mother to take him and his 3-year-old sister from their grandparents' home where they are being cared for during the client's detox stay. The case is presented in a role play format, using the technique of a "double" for the social worker. The double "speaks" the internal voice of the worker, who struggles with a range of dilemmas and feelings as she attempts to intervene with the client in a helpful way.

Setting: Inpatient treatment facility
Client: 32-year-old Dominican woman
Worker: MSW student
Presenting problem: Client wishes to leave facility because of concerns about her two children, who are staying with their grandparents.

Below is a brief summary of the critical incident and the social, economic, clinical, and cultural characteristics pertinent to the incident, followed by a role play depicting the worker's interventions. The questions for class discussion address four areas of the curriculum: macro practice, social policy, clinical practice with groups, and clinical practice with individuals and families.

Critical Incident

Maria Lupina, the client, has received a distressing phone call from her tearful son in which he pleaded with her to come and get him and his sister, who are staying with Maria's in-laws. Maria is an undocumented emigre who arrived in the United States two years ago. Her ex-husband, an active alcoholic, is still in the Dominican Republic; her in-laws live in her current Boston neighborhood. She expresses unhappiness with the way they are caring for her children while she is in the detox. The only other Spanish-speaking client in the detox is a Latino male who is addicted to both alcohol and crack.

Background Information on Maria

Age: 32
Marital status: Separated two years ago.
Children: A boy, 7, and a girl, 3.
Ethnicity: Dominican (but identifies as Puerto Rican).
Religion: Ex-Catholic.
Employment: Was math teacher in Dominican Republic; now provides child care in her home.
Education: College graduate/middle class.
Residence: Multicultural, multiclass community.

Role Play

Social Worker: Maria. Hi. Come on in. Have a seat.

Maria: No, uh, I . . . I don't, I don't want to sit down. Uh, I need to leave. I've got to get out of here. Tell me how to do that.

Social Worker: But Maria, you're not finished. You've only been here a couple of days. If you're feeling anxious and upset it may be that you're still in withdrawal.

Maria: No! I'm very upset. I'm very upset. Since I'm clean and sober, I don't need to be here any more.

Social Worker: I can see that you're upset, but let's sit down so you can tell me what's happened.

Maria: My kids just called me. My son is crying. My in-laws are not taking care of them right. I'm afraid I'm going to lose them. My in-laws are going to take them away because I'm in a detox center.

Social Worker: Well, Maria. We . . . we can talk about this. But you know, Maria, if you leave before your treatment is done, you're going to go back and use again.

Double: I've got to convince her to stay.

Social Worker: Maria, if you leave before we have a post-detox treatment program in place for you, you'll be in more danger of losing your kids. Why don't you have a seat and we'll talk about it?

Double: I've got to do something

Maria: I don't need this anymore. I'm clean and sober. I can do it on my own. I'll never drink again. I don't . . . I . . . I feel very strange here.

Social worker: Maria, let's discuss this. That's your disease talking. You need to stay. You need more time. Yes, you're clean and sober, but if you think that is all there is to getting better, that is your disease talking.

Maria: No, no!

Double: If I stay calm I'll convince her.

Maria: I've learned my lesson.

Social Worker: Maria, please sit down. You're in danger of relapsing. You're in danger of losing your kids. Maria, please sit down. We'll see if we can work out a plan.

Double: What would my supervisor do here?

Maria: I'm not going to sit down. I'm not going to sit down. I need to leave.

Social Worker: Maria, you can't leave. You'll go back to drinking. You'll lose your kids. You'll hit bottom.

Double: I'm really mad. I don't need this.

Social Worker: Maria, please.

Maria: I don't . . . I don't fit in here. I don't belong here.

Social Worker: What do you mean?

Maria: There are no other Latinos here. I'm not like these other people here.

Social Worker: Well, it's true that there are no other Latino women, but Pedro's here.

Maria: But he's a crack addict. He's just a crack addict. I . . .

Social Worker: But Maria, a drug is a drug. It doesn't matter. What we need to do is to work on your problem.

Double: I'm really failing here.

Maria: Look. I'm not like other people here and I need to get out of here. I'm going to lose my children.

Double: I'm so confused. Is that really true about her kids or is that the disease talking?

Social Worker: Maria, we can help you. We can help you get better. We can help you keep your children.

Double: What will my supervisor think of me?

Maria: I'm leaving. I've got to get out of here.

Double: What will my agency think of me?
Social Worker: Maria, please stay.
Maria: No!
Double: I don't know what to do here.

Questions for Class Discussion and Teaching Points

1. Clinical Practice with Individuals and Families
   Goals
   - What are the worker's goals with the client in this interaction?
   Professional values
   - Client self-determination
   - Client individuality
   Professional relationship and role
   - What are the worker's biases and filters with respect to alcohol abuse and treatment with respect to Latino clients?
   - Worker's sense of responsibility for the "success" of the treatment.
   - Worker's anger and helplessness in the face of a client who appears to be rejecting treatment.
   Helping skills
   - How might the worker have used empathic responses, listening, exploration, clarification with this client?
   - How could the worker have built more of an alliance with this client?
   Biopsychosocial assessment
   - Did client come to detox voluntarily or was she mandated?
   - What is client's history of alcohol use/abuse, and on what basis was decision made that client needed detox?
   - What is the meaning of alcohol abuse for women in Dominican culture?
   - What is the significance of the client's role as a mother?
   - What are the various factors leading the client to insist on leaving detox, e.g.,

denial, effects of withdrawal on judgment and thinking, isolation on unit, real or perceived threat of losing children, etc.?
   - How has the client functioned on the unit up to this point?
   - Is the client medically stable enough to be able to leave the program?
   - What is the client's history of treatment for alcohol abuse?
   - What supports and resources are available in the community, family, neighborhood that might make it possible for the client to engage in an ongoing treatment program?

2. Clinical Practice with Groups
   Short-term and open-ended groups
   - What goals are reasonable, given that members in a detox are likely to attend the group one or two times and that membership changes constantly?
   - What level of activity and responsibility does the worker take in such a group?
   - How might a changing and diverse composition affect the potential for identity and cohesion? How might the worker encourage acceptance of differences?
   Methodology
   - What framework/approach is appropriate for helping these group members at this stage of recovery (skill development/education, psychodynamics, etc.)?
   Engagement/coercion; support/confrontation
   - How might resistance and denial get played out in non-voluntary groups?
   - What should the worker's stance be? His/her ethical concerns (self-determination, autonomy)?
   - When a member leaves a group abruptly, how does the worker explore

the meaning, deal with his/her own feelings, involve the group?

Macro practice

- Importance of knowing community and demographic trends.
- The impact of culture on help-seeking.
- Role of alcohol in the Caribbean.
- Composition of agency (board, staff, residents).
- Role of interagency collaboration.
- Relationship of agency to community.
- Role of natural support systems.

Social welfare policy

- Centrality of alcohol to U.S. culture historically.
- Relationship of alcohol and drugs to particular groups in the population by race, class, ethnicity, age, and often gender.
- Role of the U.S. immigration policy in shaping the experience of emigres.
- Role of health policies in determining access, quality, and cost of health care.
- Lack of policies that address the needs of addicted women.
- Few treatment facilities that accept children of an addicted parent.
- Lack of facilities that offer a racially and culturally sensitive feminist treatment model for women.

Suggested Readings

Breton, M. (1985). Reaching and engaging people: Issues and practice principles. *Social Work with Groups, 8*(3), 7-21.

Delgado, M. (1995). Hispanic natural support systems and alcohol and other drug services: Challenges and rewards for practice. *Alcoholism Treatment Quarterly, 12*, 17-31.

Galinsky, M., & Schopler, J. (1985). Patterns of entry and exit in open-ended groups. *Social Work with Groups, 8*(2), 67-80.

Gitterman, A. (1989). Building mutual support in groups. *Social Work with Groups, 12*(2), 5-21.

Gordon, J. U. (Ed.). (1994). *Managing multiculturalism in substance abuse services.* Thousand Oaks, CA: Sage.

Holmes, P., & Karp, M. (1991). *Psychodrama: Inspiration and technique.* New York: Tavistock/Routledge.

Leveton, E. (1977). *Psychodrama for the timid clinician.* New York: Spring Press. (Revised as *A clinician's guide to psychodrama*, 1992.)

Matano, R., & Yalom, I. (1991). Approaches to chemical dependency: A synthesis. *International Journal of Group Psychotherapy, 41*(3), 269-293.

Moreno, J. L., & Moreno, Z. T. (1959). *Psychodrama: Vol. 2.* Beacon, NY: Beacon House.

Paulino, A. (1994). Dominicans in the United States: Implications for practice and policies in the human services. *Journal of Multicultural Social Work, 3*, 53-65.

Role–Playing Situations in Hospital Settings

Below are five role-play situations designed to illustrate for students how to bring up drinking and drug-use questions in an interview, assess the dimensions of alcohol and other drug use, and work with client denial.

These situations take place in a hospital setting and reflect a range of clients who might be seen by social workers from different departments. These situations can be adapted for use in a variety of non-hospital settings as well. Each role play situation includes a patient's role and a social worker's role. Following Situation 5 are instructions for the observer's role and group facilitator's role. These roles are to be used if several role play situations are done simultaneously, with participants working in small groups.

Situation #1
Pediatrics: Lasonia

Patient's Role

You're a 22-year-old who has just had a baby. You've been working as a waitress in a downtown restaurant. You've had a cocaine problem for at least two years, snorting cocaine almost every day for the past six months, and doing several lines each day if it's available. How much you use depends on the money you have, or whether friends will share their stash with you. You've worked a lot of double shifts and weekends to make sure you can buy coke on a regular basis.

You have been a heavy drinker as well since about age 18, getting drunk whenever you "party" and drinking during the day if you're feeling low. Recently, drinking has helped to "smooth out" the cocaine high so that you don't feel jittery and crash too quickly.

You haven't used other drugs very much—you don't like how most of them make you feel.

You live with your mother, her boyfriend, three sisters, and an aunt. They are all heavy drinkers. Once in a while, they use street drugs if they can get them cheap. Everyone in the apartment goes his/her own way—you're not very involved with any of them.

Only if the worker is supportive and gains your trust should you acknowledge snorting a few lines and having a few beers prior to the delivery of the baby, but be emphatic that it was your first and only time doing cocaine. You believe cocaine is no problem for you.

If the worker talks to you in a helpful and credible way, continue to be wary and guarded but eventually acknowledge the full extent of your cocaine and alcohol use. Make the worker ask you specific questions before you volunteer information about your drug-use history.

Make it clear that treatment is out of the question. You might consider attending an NA meeting or talking to a drug counselor if the worker convinces you that it is really necessary.

Social Worker's Role

Lasonia is a 22-year-old black woman whose baby is now a few days old. Because the delivery was very quick and somewhat early, and the baby, Naomi, has a slight respiratory problem, the medical staff decided to do a toxicology screen for drug use. The results were positive for cocaine. When Lasonia was confronted about this by the labor and delivery nurse, she denied using cocaine or any other drugs, including alcohol. Lasonia's sister, who was present at the time of the discussion, supported Lasonia by saying that Lasonia was never involved with drugs.

Your goal is to get a clearer drug history, including:

- types of drugs used
- how they were used (route of administration)
- frequency of use
- quantity of use
- duration of pattern
- behavioral, social, financial, medical effects

The following are potential approaches to try after explaining your role and attempting to develop trust and rapport.

- *Open-ended:* What does she think about the baby testing positive for cocaine? How does she explain it to herself? Does it worry her? When she's heard about other people having these tests, what does she think the results mean?

- *Put emphasis on emotional support for her and her baby:* She's beginning a new life with her baby. You know she wants to be a good mother. She may need some help with being the kind of mother she'd like to be. There may not be as much support in her life as she might wish. The baby is viewed as being at high risk based on the positive toxicology screen. Let her know that it's important for you to know what drugs/alcohol she's been using to know how to help her and the baby.

- *Put emphasis on cocaine dependence/addiction:* Emphasize that it's clear from the test results that she's using cocaine. You are confident the tests are accurate. People rarely use cocaine only during pregnancy and not prior to that. You suspect she may have been using for some time. Many people get hooked on cocaine and other drugs. The hospital has been very helpful to them. You'd like to talk about it so you can help her and the baby.

  If you can get a history, begin to address the denial by helping the patient accept some

kind of assistance (e.g., attending NA meetings) or intervention from the hospital.

Situation #2
Psychiatry: Veronica

Patient's Role

You are 22 years old and have had two previous psychiatric admissions to local facilities for depression—one at age 16, the other at age 18. You stayed in the hospital for several weeks each time, but your second admission terminated when the staff found a half-empty liquor bottle among your belongings after issuing you a weekend pass. When confronted, you left against medical advice.

You admitted yourself to the hospital this time because you've been feeling severely depressed for several weeks, sleeping excessively, losing weight, feeling anxious, and wishing you were dead. (You do not have plans to kill yourself.)

You've had little to do with your family for years. You've been on the streets since you were about 13, living with various friends and moving around. Your mother, stepfather, and younger sister are alcoholics.

Although you dropped out of school at 17, you completed a GED with the help of a social worker who did a child abuse investigation of your family some years ago. You have been doing secretarial work for a small computer firm for the past year and a half.

You have been using an assortment of drugs since you were 16—heroin, cocaine, and alcohol primarily, but you've also used PCP, amphetamines, and a number of "downers" including quaaludes, valium, demerol, and barbiturates. You have a history of severe alcohol abuse/alcoholism.

You cannot imagine life without drugs, but you tell yourself that you are not dependent upon them. You think the hospital staff will try to convince you to give them up completely if you admit to using them. The idea of quitting completely at age 22 is terrifying to you—drugs have been a major part of your life. You believe you will quit when you are 40 or 50, but now it would be impossible.

You are wary and defensive, but, depending upon how supportive and convincing the worker is, provide an accurate drinking and drug history. Do not answer questions that are not posed directly to you, but respond to direct requests for information if you really believe this worker can help you.

Social Worker's Role

Veronica is a 22-year-old woman with two previous psychiatric admissions to local facilities for depression, one at age 16, the other at age 18. She remained in the hospital for several weeks on each occasion, but her second admission terminated when the staff found a half-empty liquor bottle among her belongings after a weekend pass. She left against medical advice when confronted about it.

She was admitted to the hospital this time for depression, sleeping excessively, weight loss, free-floating anxiety, and suicidal ideation. She does not have a history of suicidal gestures or attempts. When questioned upon admission about alcohol and other drug use, Veronica contradicted herself—acknowledging that drugs may have played a role in psychiatric problems in the past, and saying that she hadn't used anything in five years, that she gets depressed now whether she's using or not, and that she wasn't using now.

She has had little to do with her family for years. Her adolescence and young adulthood were spent largely on the street. She describes her mother, stepfather, and younger sister as being alcoholics.

Although she dropped out of school at 17, she completed a GED with the help of a social worker who investigated her family some years ago for child abuse. She has been doing secre-tarial work for a small computer firm for the past year and a half.

Your goal is to get a clearer drug history including:

- types of drugs used
- how they were used (route of administration)
- frequency of use
- quantity of use
- duration of pattern
- behavioral, social, financial, medical effects

If Veronica clearly acknowledges her drug abuse, consider making clear statements to her such as:

- "I think you have a serious problem based on what you've told me." (Give examples to support this statement.)
- "You need treatment for your drug use."
- "There are many resources available."
- "I want you to talk with an expert about your drug use."
- "Many people recover if they get help."

Situation #3
Internal Medicine: Dennis

Patient's Role

You are a 39-year-old former correctional officer who was admitted to the hospital with painful cardiac symptoms. You had your first heart attack four years ago and you are fearful that this is your second one. You remain anxious as you await the results of your tests; both of your parents died of heart attacks.

You lost your job at the penitentiary because of your cocaine habit. You are currently working part-time as a hospital security guard at night. You talk about your hospital job to all the hospital staff, letting them know how important it is to you. You sell drugs during the day, and this is how you support your cocaine habit. You know you are at a higher risk of dying if you continue to use cocaine as heavily as you do, but you also feel that you can't live without it.

You are obsessively focused on your health and give a detailed history of every symptom upon admission. You are suspicious that you will not be seen as a high-priority patient by the medical staff. None of the hospital staff has asked if you take illicit drugs, but they have asked if you are on any medications.

Only if the worker is supportive and gains your trust should you acknowledge snorting cocaine during social occasions, but be emphatic that you did this very infrequently. You don't think cocaine is a problem for you.

If the worker talks to you in a helpful and credible way, continue to be wary and guarded, but eventually acknowledge the full extent of your cocaine use. Make the worker ask you specific questions before you volunteer information about your drug use history.

Social Worker's Role

Dennis is a 39-year-old former correctional officer who was admitted to the hospital with painful cardiac symptoms. He suffered his first heart attack four years ago. He has a family history of cardiac problems and both of his parents died of heart attacks.

Dennis works part-time as a hospital security guard at night. He talks about how important this job is to him; when he describes his work to you, it doesn't sound like a particularly stressful job and you begin to wonder what might have caused coronary problems in a man so young. There's nothing in Dennis' chart about alcohol or drug use, which may only have been an oversight of the medical staff in light of their efforts to address Dennis's cardiac symptoms first.

Your goal is get a history from Dennis about his possible alcohol or drug use including:

- types of drugs used
- how they were used (route of administration)
- frequency of use
- quantity of use
- duration of pattern
- behavioral, social, financial, medical effects

If you can get a history from the patient and are successful in developing trust and rapport, try the following approaches.

- Educate the patient about how cocaine use affects the heart over time; about how his cocaine use will exacerbate his predisposition to heart problems (given his family history).
- Help the patient to accept the diagnosis of cocaine dependence.
- Inform him that support is available to help him change his behavior (e.g., he might attend the NA meeting that takes place in the hospital).
- Help the patient to accept some kind of specific treatment. You might suggest, since he works at night, that he attend the intensive day treatment program at the Broadway Center, and give him information on how he can register for the program.

Situation #4
Internal Medicine: Jim

Patient's Role

You are 27 years old and have been living with various friends and relatives. You have been hospitalized for cellulitis because of your IV drug use with non-sterile needles. Prior to this hospitalization, you were healthy. You are uncomfortable because you are going through mild withdrawal and have drug cravings. You are eager to leave the hospital.

You are very open about discussing your heroin and cocaine habits. You tell the hospital staff that your drug use is not a problem; you can handle it. After various tests are performed in the hospital, you are found to be HIV-positive. Your mood alternates between depression and anger.

As your hospital stay lengthens, you become more uncomfortable and your cravings increase. You become hostile to the health care team in general, and threaten to leave the hospital against medical advice. You refuse to recognize your drug use as a problem and, in fact, make light of it.

Only if the worker is supportive and gains your trust should you acknowledge the full extent of your drug use. Make the worker ask you specific questions before you volunteer information about your drug history.

If the worker talks to you in a helpful and credible way, continue to be wary and guarded, but begin expressing second thoughts as to whether your drug use is a problem. Eventually acknowledge that you just don't know what to do about it.

Social Worker's Role

Your patient, Jim, is 27 years old and has been living with various friends and relatives. He has been hospitalized for cellulitis because of his IV drug use with non-sterile needles. Prior to this hospitalization, he was healthy. He's uncomfortable because of mild withdrawal and drug craving. He is eager to leave the hospital.

Although he was initially forthcoming about his drug use, he has become more uncooperative about discussing this issue as his hospital stay has lengthened. Jim was found to be HIV-positive. His mood alternates between depression and anger. He has been quite hostile to the health care team and threatens to leave the hospital against medical advice. This evokes negative

feelings in you.

Your goal is to get a clearer drug history from him that includes:

- types of drugs used
- how they were used (route of administration)
- frequency of use
- quantity of use
- duration of pattern
- behavioral, social, financial, medical effects

If you can get a history, and are successful in developing trust and rapport, try the following approaches.

- Attempt to connect with the patient in a supportive way and help him look at the medical consequences of his drug use.
- Focus on his behavior and help him understand that using dirty needles has led to his being hospitalized with cellulitis.
- Help him to understand the relationship between his drug use and testing HIV-positive.
- Help raise his awareness by offering basic education that focuses on the consequences of future alcohol and drug use, especially its adverse affect on his immune system.
- Inform the patient that support is available to help him change his behavior and assist in his recovery.

Situation #5

Pediatrics: Mr. and Mrs. Peterson

Patient's Role

You are parents in your 30s with a six-month-old baby delivered at the hospital to which you are now bringing the baby for treatment. You brought the baby to the emergency ward because of breathing problems. Upon examination, it was found that the baby had four fractures, some old and some new. A Care and Protection Petition has been filed. You have other children and have been involved with a child protective agency in the past because of concerns about abuse of another child.

This is the second contact the two of you are having with the social worker after visiting the baby. When questioned, you both admit to having used cocaine and alcohol heavily in the past, but strongly contend that you have been clean from all drugs for the past two years.

The two of you have returned to drinking and drug use but have sworn to tell no one about it. During the past weekends when you used cocaine, you beat the baby when she cried and fussed hour after hour. When questioned about the trauma to the baby, neither of you have a plausible explanation of what had happened.

You are very ambivalent about the drug use— you love it at the time you're using it, but hate how it can change you. Be open about your drinking/drug use of years ago, but do not acknowledge the current drug use unless the worker is supportive, shows an understanding of the predicament you're in regarding drugs, and helps you to see a way out.

Social Worker's Role

The Petersons are parents in their 30s with a six-month-old baby who was delivered at your hospital. They brought the baby to the emergency ward because of breathing problems. Upon examination, it was found that the baby had four fractures, some old and some new. A Care and Protection Petition has been filed. The couple has other children and have been involved with a child protective agency in the past because of concerns about abuse of another child.

This is the second contact during this hospitalization that you are having with the couple, who have been visiting the baby. You know that the social worker in obstetrics is familiar with this family. When questioned previously, both partners admitted to having used cocaine and alcohol heavily in the past, but strongly contend that they have been clean from all drugs for the past two years.

Because of the implausibility of the original stories the parents told about the cause of the baby's trauma, you suspect that the couple has had a relapse to drug use, but you don't want to sound accusatory. Try to assess the role of the substance use in the baby's trauma by getting a clearer picture of past and present drinking and drug use. Discuss how difficult it is for some people to admit that they relapsed once everyone believes they are drug-free. Eventually, try to raise the issue of their speaking with a substance abuse counselor, but don't rush into it unless they can acknowledge some concerns about their drug use.

Observer's Role

Following the role play, comment on:

- Worker's use of noncharged, nonjudgmental language, and a nonpunitive approach to drug-related issues.
- Worker's ability to ask specific questions about drug use including:
  - What specific drugs were used?
  - How were they used (routes of administration)?
  - In what amounts?
  - At what frequency?
  - Money spent on drugs per day/week/month?
  - What behavioral, social, financial, medical consequences?
- Worker's ability to back off or change focus if denial and defensiveness was too intense.
- Ways that denial/defensiveness manifests itself in this interview.

- Specific strategies used by the worker to respond to the denial, such as:
  - Expression of concern for patient's physical or emotional safety if drinking/drug use issues are not dealt with.
  - Confrontation (direct but gentle)—e.g., pointing out inconsistencies in information provided; illustrating possible negative consequences of refusal to deal with the issue.
  - Information/education related to alcohol use, abuse, dependency.
  - Expressions of hopefulness about the benefits of substance abuse treatment for the patient and the patient's ability to recover.
  - Other strengths in the social worker's approach, or other strategies used.
- Attitudes/feelings experienced by the observers, especially in relation to the client's denial.
- Attitudes/feelings experienced by the role players.

Group Facilitator's Role

Following the role play, comment on

- Worker's use of noncharged, nonjudgmental language, and a nonpunitive approach to drug-related issues.
- Worker's ability to ask specific questions about drug use including:

- What specific drugs were used?
- How were they used (routes of administration)?
- In what amounts?
- At what frequency?
- Money spent on drugs per day/week/month?
- What behavioral, social, financial, medical consequences?
- Worker's ability to back off or change focus if denial and defensiveness was too intense.
- Ways that denial/defensiveness manifests itself in this interview.
- Specific strategies used by the worker to respond to the denial, such as:
  - Expression of concern for patient's physical or emotional safety if drinking/drugging issues are not dealt with.
  - Confrontation (direct but gentle)—e.g., pointing out inconsistencies in information provided; illustrating possible negative consequences of refusal to deal with the issue.
  - Exploration of the patient's ambivalence about use.
  - Information/education related to alcohol use, abuse, dependency.
  - Expressions of hopefulness about the benefits of substance abuse treatment for the patient and the patient's ability to recover.
  - Other strengths in the social worker's approach, or other strategies used.
- Attitudes/feelings experienced by the observers, especially in relation to the client's denial.
- Attitudes/feelings experienced by the role players.

Use, Abuse, Dependence Exercise

The following statements form the basis for a classroom exercise designed to help students:

- understand the complexities of assessing drinking and drug use behavior and the need to elicit a full picture of the client's pattern and context of use before a diagnosis is made; and

- identify factors that influence judgments about severity, e.g., psychological dependence, tolerance, daily use, duration of pattern, negative consequences in major life spheres, age, and life circumstances of user.

Students are each given a card with one of the one- or two-sentence drinking/drug histories listed below. Without additional details, they are instructed to sort themselves into three groups (each standing in a different part of the classroom) based on these drinking/drug histories.

- Group 1: Use (no problem)
- Group 2: Abuse (some problem but not necessarily in need of immediate treatment and/or abstinence)
- Group 3: Dependence/addiction (in need of immediate abstinence and treatment)

Once students have chosen the groups they believe are appropriate, they must discuss their drinking and drug history cards with members of their own group and secure agreement that the group is appropriate for them before they are allowed to stay. There is often disagreement about where someone belongs, and certain individuals may go back and forth between groups before a group agrees to accept them. *(Approximately 15 minutes)*

The ambiguity of this exercise is an important element because it forces students to debate various aspects of the drinking/drug histories, and examine their values and attitudes.

Class discussion follows with each person reading his/her card to the class and providing reasons for choosing the groups selected. The goal is not to have the class come to total agreement, but rather to highlight the criteria that can be applied in assessing severity and to alert students to the ordinary, everyday behaviors that may illustrate dependence and/or addiction. *(Approximately 30 minutes)*

Use, Abuse, Dependence Cards

Lester: You seldom drink unless it's a holiday or special occasion.

Roy: You never have sex unless you've had quite a bit to drink.

Albert: You used to drink a lot more, but recently you only have one or two.

Fritz: You usually have a 6-pack of beer at night after work.

Arthur: You take great pride in being able to "drink everyone else under the table."

Sylvia: You go out with the gang once a month and usually get drunk.

Rosa: You generally have tremors on the days when you don't drink.

Leslie: You have cirrhosis of the liver.

Eric: You rarely drink, but when you do, it's when you're alone.

Joanne: You have a couple of glasses of wine when you go out to dinner with friends on Saturday night.

Barbara: You go for months without using cocaine, but when you start, you are surprised to find you can't stop.

Jose: You swore you'd never drink like your father, but when you drink, you find yourself doing a lot of things that he used to do.

Ralph: You often have one or two cocktails before dinner.

Alan: People have been on your case about how you act when you have a few scotches, so you've decided to switch to beer.

Greg: Your friends say that when you drink, you change from Dr. Jekyll to Mr. Hyde.

Sam: Your wife complains about the money you spend on drinking. In the last 8 months you've run up a $1,500 bar bill.

Sally: You find it only takes a few to get you drunk.

Hanh: You smoke marijuana about once a year, when you get together with certain friends who smoke.

Natasha: You've used crack four or five times in the past month.

George: You gave up using cocaine and drinking about a year ago, and you find you can manage your anxiety with a few valium a day and an occasional joint.

Lasonia: You've had a "nerve problem" for several years. When you get nervous you take more nerve pills than the doctor said to and you go across the hall and borrow some from your neighbor.

Karl: You've been smoking marijuana every day for about 20 years.

Hien: You've tried just about every drug there is. You're trying to find the right combination to get you high, but not too *wired*.

Maria: You felt very guilty after a weekend of drinking and drug using.

Shelley: Although you've limited yourself to two drinks at any one time, you really long for chances to drink—like your cousin's wedding next week where there will be an open bar.

Dennis: You went "on the wagon" for the third time this year.

Susan: You drink 2–3 glasses of wine each night after work. During the workday, you think about how good it will taste and how great it will make you feel.

Monica: You usually have a few joints beforehand to get "up" for a party.

Antonio: You're not always sure afterward just what occurred when you were drinking.

Janice: As far as drinking goes, you can take it or leave it.

Cindy: Aerobics and shopping just don't interest you anymore. You'd rather go out and drink with your friends.

Madeline: You've been arrested twice for drunk driving.

Eileen: You have no interest in going to parties where there won't be any drugs.

Henry: When you are uptight, you find that a "few drinks" relieve the tension. Your wife has commented that your "few drinks" has now become 5–6 drinks.

Saul: You want to keep on drinking after everyone else has had enough.

Serena: You cut down because your doctor said your stomach trouble was due to drinking.

Barriers to Working with Substance-Abusing Clients: A Social Worker Self-Inventory

The following social worker self-inventory is intended to help workers examine unhelpful feelings and stereotypes that may interfere with their work with substance-abusing clients. Because each question explores some aspect of the worker's possible "negative" countertransference, workers may experience this questionnaire as "confrontational." For this reason, it is recommended that instructors not collect the completed forms, but, rather, have students use them for their own self-awareness. It may also be useful to ask for volunteers who will discuss their answers in class, or break the class into small groups and ask students to share with one another only those answers they feel comfortable sharing.

After students have completed this form, instructors may also want to ask students to discuss their "positive" countertransference, which may result from:

- having friends who are in recovery from alcohol or other drug dependence;
- having successfully guided clients into recovery;
- being in recovery;
- having seen others in recovery, resulting in a reduction in moralistic feelings and an increase in a sense of optimism and hopefulness about recovery.

The purpose of this self-inventory is to stimulate self-reflection about personal and professional barriers that may interfere with effectiveness in working with clients with alcohol and other drug problems. For each question, write in the letter of the answer which most accurately conveys your response. *This is for your own use and will not be collected.*

A. Strongly agree
B. Agree
C. Neither agree nor disagree
D. Disagree
E. Strongly disagree

1. When I picture alcoholics or drug addicts, the images that come to mind probably represent stereotypes of gender, race, age, and social class. ___

2. I have trouble seeing alcoholism and drug dependence as conditions in and of themselves. I really believe they are symptoms of underlying psychological conditions. ___

3. Because I have been unsuccessful in working with alcoholic and drug-dependent clients, I feel discouraged even before I start working with a new client who has a history of alcohol/drug abuse. ___

4. My education and training has involved almost no focus on alcohol/drug issues, leaving me feeling less than competent in this area. ___

5. My own limited use of alcohol and other drugs may incline me to be judgmental of those who become addicted. ___

6. Growing up in a chemically dependent family may have resulted in patterns of "enabling" or overinvolvement on my part when faced with chemically dependent clients. ___

7. My family believed getting drunk every weekend was acceptable "social" drinking. ___

8. In my agency, workers who are known to have alcohol or other drug problems have not been confronted or referred to treatment by their supervisors. ___

9. Growing up in a chemically dependent family has made it painful for me to work with families where there is chemical dependency. ___

10. When I hear of a pregnant woman who is addicted to drugs, I feel for the baby as the victim and see the woman as the "perpetrator." I have trouble seeing that the woman is a victim as well. ___

11. My own use of alcohol and other drugs in the past may have led me to underestimate the severity of alcohol and drug problems in my clients. ___

12. I feel naive about working with clients who have alcohol and other drug problems—I don't know what questions to ask and I'm not sure I'll understand the answers once I get them. ___

13. I have trouble focusing clients on issues they don't want to talk about—I'm afraid they'll become angry. For this reason, I hesitate to ask people about their alcohol/drug use unless it's the reason they have come for services. ___

14. I do not feel hopeful that clients with alcohol and other drug problems will recover. ___

15. I have been manipulated by clients with alcohol and other drug problems in the past. ___

16. I am confused about ways to distinguish between social use, problem use, and dependence or addiction in clients using alcohol and other drugs. ___

Exploring Individual, Family, and Community Differences Regarding AODA

In the pages that follow, five classroom exercises are presented to assist instructors in teaching about alcohol and other drug abuse as it relates to culture and communities of color. The first two exercises address attitudes and beliefs and are experiential in nature. The third and fourth exercises are designed to examine the service system and challenge students to explore resources in their communities. The fifth involves mini-dramas for small groups focusing on macro and micro issues.

Classroom Exercise #1

Attitudes and Beliefs about Alcohol: A Journey of Difference

Have students identify all the reasons they can think of that people have used alcohol over the centuries. (Instructor writes responses on the board.)

Reasons for alcohol use:
   social pressure
   raise self-esteem
   peer pressure
   warming of body
   medicinal
   sophistication
   enhances taste of food
   socializing/relaxation
   good for blood/circulation
   celebration
   permission for acting out
   lowering of inhibitions
   help digestion
   peer bonding
   religious observance
   experimentation/curiosity
   reward
   antidepressant effect
   response to trauma
   antianxiety effect
   response to acculturation stress
   rite of passage into adulthood
   kill pain
   enhance masculinity
   overdose/commit suicide
   escape
   social status
   response to boredom
   get drunk/be intoxicated/be oblivious

Have students identify all the reasons they can think of that people have used other drugs over the centuries. (Instructor writes responses on the board.)

Reasons for use of other drugs:
   socializing
   deal with sleeping disorder (sedatives/
      hypnotics)
   medicinal, kills pain (e.g., opiates)
   glaucoma treatment (sedatives,
      marijuana)
   sexual stimulant (cocaine, inhalants)
   achieve alternative state of consciousness
      (hallucinogens)
   weight reduction (stimulants)
   reduce fatigue (stimulants)
   muscle building (steroids)
   religious observance (e.g., peyote,
      hallucinogens among Native
      Americans)
   lower inhibitions (marijuana,
      hallucinogens, cocaine)
   create mood swing
   come down from another drug
   relaxation: reduce tension

Ask the class, "Do you think some of these reasons/motivations are more common in some groups (age, gender, ethnic, geographic) than in others?" Ask students to pair these motivations with groups with which they are most familiar.

Reasons for alcohol use:

warming of body

medicinal

sophistication

enhances taste of food

socializing/relaxation

good for blood/circulation

celebration

permission for acting out

lowers inhibitions

helps digestion

peer bonding (Armed Services)

religious observance (Jews, Catholics)

experimentation/curiosity (adolescents)

reward

antidepressant effects (elderly)

response to trauma (sexual abuse victims)

antianxiety effect

response to acculturation stress (recent
  immigrants)

rite of passage into adulthood (college
  students)

kills pain

enhances masculinity

overdose/commit suicide

escape

response to boredom

to get drunk/be intoxicated/be oblivious
  (adolescents)

response to loneliness and loss (elderly)

Reasons for use of other drugs:

socializing

deal with sleeping disorder (sedatives/
  hypnotics)

medicinal, kills pain (e.g., opiates,
  sedatives; chronic pain sufferers)

sexual stimulant (cocaine, inhalants)

thrill-seeking

experimentation/curiosity

achieve alternative state of consciousness
  (hallucinogens)

weight reduction (stimulants; women)

reduce fatigue (stimulants; athletes)

muscle building (steroids; athletes)

religious observance (hallucinogens)

enhance self-image (women)

create mood swing

come down from another drug (addicts,
  alcoholics)

relaxation; reduce tension

lower inhibitions (marijuana, hallucinogens,
  cocaine)

Classroom Self-Reflection and Discussion Exercise

The instructor begins by saying that the reasons people use alcohol and other drugs, the way they use them, and the types of drugs used are often related to family and cultural attitudes and values, as well as factors such as social class, gender, country of origin, type of community (rural, urban, suburban,) and level of acculturation into U.S. society.

These exercises are designed to help students reflect on their personal and family experiences as a way of understanding cultural influences related to alcohol/drug use. They are designed to help students examine what they learned about alcohol/other drugs before they began to use them. Using the following format, ask students to answer these questions by taking notes on this form or just thinking about their answers as the questions are read aloud. Assure students that nothing in writing will be collected by the instructor.

*1. Attitudes and behavior regarding alcohol/
   drug use*

  • How did your parents use alcohol? How much drinking occurred in the family? How often? Under what circumstances? How did other adults in your family use alcohol?

- Were there special occasions when you saw family members intoxicated during holiday parties?
- Were family members intoxicated during weekends? Weekdays? Weeknights? Were there special circumstances which prompted this?
- What were your parents' rules for you and your siblings about drinking? Were these implicit or explicit messages? How did they get expressed?
- Did family members get high on other drugs? Did this occur in the presence of other family members or alone?
- What were your parents' rules about use of other drugs? Were these explicit or implicit messages? How did they get expressed?
- To what extent do you think these rules/messages related to your family's cultural background? Give your reasons.
- Were there individuals in your cultural group who served as positive role models in terms of their use of alcohol/drugs?
- Were there individuals in your cultural group who served as negative role models?

- Were you then or are you now aware of stereotypes related to alcohol/drug use in your culture group? What do the stereotypes involve?

2. *Individual use within the family context*
   - Under what circumstances did you begin using alcohol/other drugs?
   - Did you follow the family rules about drinking/drug use for the most part? What happened when you broke the rules?
   - Did your parents ever see you under the influence? What did they do about it?
   - Did your parents ever see you high on drugs? What did they do about it?
   - Did your use change over time? Was this related to the influence of your immediate family, extended family, peers, or none of the above?

The instructor then asks for volunteers who will talk about their answers to these questions. Students are free to participate or not participate as they wish. After several students have spoken, the instructor asks for the most striking similarities and differences among those who spoke.

Classroom Exercise #2
Spectrogram Continuum of "Core Beliefs" about Alcohol

The following exercise is designed to help students think about their "core beliefs" regarding the use of alcohol. Readily adaptable to other drugs, the exercise can be used in the following ways.

- *As an individual written exercise:* Ask students to mark where they are on each continuum; give examples; add gradations along each continuum; and identify other "core beliefs."

- *As an experiential group exercise:* Instructor draws an imaginary line on floor. For each "core belief," she/he asks students to physically place themselves on the continuum: first, as reflected in beliefs communicated in their family of origin; second, as reflected in their current personal beliefs.

- *As a self-reflection exercise:* Ask students to think about clients they are currently working with and how the worker's and client's "core beliefs" might differ, and how the differences might impact the relationship and work.

1. Quantity OK to use (may also differentiate what is OK—i.e., beer, wine, hard liquor)

none	occasional glass	1–2 weekly	1–2 daily	2–3 daily	any amount

2. When OK to use (may also differentiate if OK alone or only with others)

none	special occasions	at parties/out	after 4 p.m.	anytime

3. View of positives versus negative

always bad	occasional use OK	appropriate for socializing	useful to unwind	medicinal value	always good

4. When drinking becomes a problem

first drink	if regular	if hurts relationships	if work problems	if medical problems	if arrested for DWI	if job losses and homeless

5. How to get help with drinking problem

just stop	keep secret	wait for family pressure	wait for legal coercion/ punishment	seek outside help	accept relapse as part of recovery	become involved in ongoing "recovery work"

Classroom Exercise #3
Community "Mapping" of Substance Abuse Services

The following exercise can be used in class or as a take-home assignment, to be completed in groups or by individual students.

1. Identify the demographics of your community in terms of race, ethnicity, gender, age, and socioeconomic level.

2. Identify self-help groups and indigenous support networks in your community.

3. Identify the following formal community AODA resources and where they are located on a map of your community (assign groups of students different quadrants of the community):
   • prevention and early intervention,
   • detoxification facilities,
   • rehabilitation facilities,
   • outpatient programs,
   • community-based programs, and
   • long-term care.

4. Identify programs for the following "special populations" in your community:
   • dual-diagnosis,
   • pregnant and parenting women,
   • linguistic minorities,
   • AODA-involved criminal offenders,
   • adolescents, and
   • elderly.

5. Examine AODA resources in terms of community demographics.

6. Examine implications of the items above in terms of early intervention and treatment of AODA problems.

Classroom Exercise #4
Identifying Culture-Specific and "Mainstream" Community Resources

The purpose of this exercise is to raise social workers' awareness of community AODA resources for various cultural groups. Because resources for people of color are quite limited in many communities, the exercise may illustrate the dearth of services available. Participants in this exercise are asked to begin by identifying factors or qualities that would make an AODA program "culture-specific."

Identify culture-specific AODA services in the community.

1. Develop a set of defining variables for "culture-specific" or culturally competent AODA services in the community, e.g.,
   - language spoken,
   - bicultural workers providing services,
   - indigenous workers providing services,
   - services are provided in a form that is culturally familiar to clients and compatible with their values,
   - individuals participating in program are from same cultural group, and

   - services are aimed at both longtime and newly arrived members of the cultural group.

2. Develop a set of defining variables for "mainstream" AODA services in the community.

3. Develop a chart that displays the range of "culture-specific" versus "mainstream" AODA services for various ethnic groups in your community (see below). Identify the programs by name.

culture-specific----------------------------------mainstream

4. Examine the "balance" along the continuum in terms of number of programs of various types, sizes/capacities, and approximate budgets.

5. Examine clinical and policy implications for the answers to the instructions above.

Classroom Exercise #5

Mini–Dramas for Small Groups: Macro and Micro Issues

Below are eight role-play situations designed to raise awareness about attitudes and values concerning drinking and drug use. The role plays or mini-dramas, each requiring about an hour of class time (30 minutes small group planning, 15 minutes enactment, and 15 minutes class discussion), can be used to illustrate:

- societal ambivalence about drinking and drug use;
- a range of prevalent perspectives, depending on age, social role, and similar variables;
- reliance by many people on alcohol and drugs for relief;
- role of advertising to promote use and perhaps abuse;
- approaches to prevention with children;
- role of parents in providing consistent messages;
- symptoms of abuse and dependence; and
- methods to address co-workers who have alcohol and drug problems.

Group Task A—Teenage Gang

You are teenagers who belong to a local gang. You often hang out on the corner and drink and take drugs. Develop a mini-drama or skit that illustrates the role alcohol and other drugs play in your relationships with one another. Try to demonstrate at least five aspects of the role alcohol plays among teens.

You will be asked to act out your mini-drama for the class. It should be no more than 15 minutes in length and can be shorter if you wish. In developing it, be as true to life as possible. Be humorous if you wish, but don't ham it up. Keep your own names when possible.

Make sure someone is appointed to:

- introduce your drama to the class, state what the group task was, and explain the characters or setting if necessary;
- keep track of the time during the drama and end it at a designated time or after the major points have been made.

If your group prefers not to develop a drama, you can devise some other way to illustrate the issues that are indicated in the group task.

Group Task B—Family Drinking

You are members of the same family. Each of you should take a particular role as father, mother, child, grandparent, aunt, or uncle. Develop a mini-drama that illustrates the circumstances in which alcohol can be used in a healthy way. You can show the family in its daily activities from morning until night or just show one event in the family's life. Try to illustrate at least five examples of drinking in a safe and healthy way.

You will be asked to act out your mini-drama for the class. It should be no more than 15 minutes in length and can be shorter if you wish. In developing it, be as true to life as possible. Be humorous if you wish, but don't ham it up. Keep your own names when possible.

Make sure someone is appointed to:

- introduce your drama to the class, state what the group task was, and explain the characters or setting if necessary;
- keep track of the time during the drama and end it at a designated time or after the major points have been made.

If your group prefers not to develop a drama, you can devise some other way to illustrate the issues that are indicated in the group task.

Group Task C—Social Service Staff

You are all workers on the staff of a social service agency. You have a co-worker who has just left on vacation—many of you think he/she has a drinking or drug problem. Prepare a mini-drama in which you discuss among yourselves some of the early signs of his/her drinking or drug problem that you've noticed on the job and after work that lead you to be worried about him or her.

Discuss alternative ways the problem could be approached. Debate the pros and cons of trying each alternative. Try to come to an agreement about a plan of action that the staff will try.

You will be asked to act out your mini-drama for the class. It should be no more than 15 minutes in length and can be shorter if you wish. In developing it, be as true to life as possible. Be humorous if you wish, but don't ham it up. Keep your own names when possible.

Make sure someone is appointed to:

- introduce your drama to the class, state what the group task was, and explain the characters or setting if necessary;

- keep track of the time during the drama and end it at a designated time or after the major points have been made.

If your group prefers not to develop a drama, you can devise some other way to illustrate the issues that are indicated in the group task.

Group Task D—TV Ad

You all work in the advertising department of a company that packages and markets alcoholic beverages. After you have found an appealing name for one of your new beverages, develop and act out a TV commercial to sell it. Persuade the public of the many ways this drink will enhance their lives and make them feel good about themselves. Avoid any suggestion of possible ill effects. Try to use myths and stereotypes in your ad.

You will be asked to act out your mini-drama for the class. It should be no more than 15 minutes in length and can be shorter if you wish. In developing it, be as true to life as possible. Be humorous if you wish, but don't ham it up. Keep your own names when possible.

Make sure someone is appointed to:

- introduce your drama to the class, state what the group task was, and explain the characters or setting if necessary;

- keep track of the time during the drama and end it at a designated time or after the major points have been made.

If your group prefers not to develop a drama, you can devise some other way to illustrate the issues that are indicated in the group task.

Group Task E—House Party

You are attending a house party where a great deal of alcohol is being served. Group members should take on the following roles:

- at least two people who are heavy drinkers,

- at least two people who are moderate drinkers,

- at least two people who are not drinking at all at this party.

Together decide what roles the rest of the group should take as drinkers to accomplish the task. Demonstrate in a role-play situation the many subtle and not-so-subtle ways that nondrinkers are pressured to drink.

You will be asked to act out your mini-drama for the class. It should be no more than 15 minutes in length and can be shorter if you wish. In developing it, be as true to life as possible. Be humorous if you wish, but don't ham it up. Keep your own names when possible.

Make sure someone is appointed to:

- introduce your drama to the class, state what the group task was, and explain the characters or setting if necessary;
- keep track of the time during the drama and end it at a designated time or after the major points have been made.

If your group prefers not to develop a drama, you can devise some other way to illustrate the issues that are indicated in the group task.

Group Task F—Alternatives to Drinking and Drug Use

Present several everyday scenes showing people who experience the impulse to reach for a drink. Have each of these scenes end with the person/s discarding or getting sidetracked from the idea of drinking or drug use, and getting involved in another more constructive way of dealing with their feelings. Try to find realistic but appealing alternatives demonstrating that drinking or drug use is not the best way to deal with the stresses or boredom of everyday life.

You will be asked to act out your mini-drama for the class. It should be no more than 15 minutes in length and can be shorter if you wish. In developing it, be as true to life as possible. Be humorous if you wish, but don't ham it up. Keep your own names when possible.

Make sure someone is appointed to:

- introduce your drama to the class, state what the group task was, and explain the characters or setting if necessary;
- keep track of the time during the drama and end it at a designated time or after the major points have been made.

If your group prefers not to develop a drama, you can devise some other way to illustrate the issues that are indicated in the group task.

Group Task G—Elementary School Children

You are a grammar school class (pick a grade). A few of you are teachers, some are teachers' aides, the rest are pupils. The lesson for today is on alcohol. Through a talk (or presentation with visual aids) by the teachers and aides and a question-and-answer period, demonstrate what young children should be taught about alcohol and drinking. Be sure to present a balanced view of the positives and negatives and try to answer all of the children's questions.

You will be asked to act out your mini-drama for the class. It should be no more than 15 minutes in length and can be shorter if you wish. In developing it, be as true to life as possible. Be humorous if you wish, but don't ham it up. Keep your own names when possible.

Make sure someone is appointed to:

- introduce your drama to the class, state what the group task was, and explain the characters or setting if necessary;
- keep track of the time during the drama and end it at a designated time or after the major points have been made.

If your group prefers not to develop a drama, you can devise some other way to illustrate the issues that are indicated in the group task.

Group Task H—Parents of Teenagers

You are a group of parents at a social get-together. You know one another fairly well. Some of you are married couples. You all have teenage sons and daughters that have come home at least once either drunk or very high from drinking at a party. You've just realized in talking together that you've all had to deal with this situation in the past.

Describe the different ways that each of you dealt with your teenager around this issue. Debate with one another what the "right way" would have been, and try to come up with a plan for what could be said now to the teenager or what could be said or done if it happens again.

Don't focus simply on a debate about discipline, but consider what children should be taught by parents about drinking.

You will be asked to act out your mini-drama for the class. It should be no more than 15 minutes in length and can be shorter if you wish. In developing it, be as true to life as possible. Be humorous if you wish, but don't ham it up. Keep your own names when possible.

Make sure someone is appointed to:

*   introduce your drama to the class, state what the group task was, and explain the characters or setting if necessary;

*   keep track of the time during the drama and end it at a designated time or after the major points have been made.

If your group prefers not to develop a drama, you can devise some other way to illustrate the issues that are indicated in the group task.

Student Assignments

Substance Abuse Policy, Programs, and Treatment

The following is a student assignment used in an advanced macro course focused on substance abuse. It asks students to conduct an assessment of agency policies and practices related to substance abuse. It was designed for assessment of nonspecialized substance abuse agencies; however, sections of the assessment are useful for specialized substance abuse agencies as well.

Semester Assignment

Instructions to Students

The major assignment for the course is an in-depth analysis of your agency as it relates to the problem of alcoholism and other drug abuse. There are two parts to the assignment. Part I is an information-gathering task covering a number of aspects of agency policy and practice. Part II is a more analytic piece, requiring use of information from Part I, readings, class discussion, experience, and your own creative thought processes. *This report should not exceed 10 typewritten pages.*

For the purpose of this analysis, "problem drinking," alcoholism, or drug abuse is considered to exist when any of the following are true:

- "excessive" drinking or drug taking is not an isolated experience, but is more or less repetitive,
- job performance is materially reduced in efficiency and dependability, or actual job losses have occurred in large part because of alcohol or drugs,
- drug/alcohol use results in recognizable interference with the individual's health or personal and social relations, or

- drug/alcohol use results in involvement with the legal system, e.g., public drunkenness, drunk driving, assaults on family members or friends, sale and/or use of illicit drugs.

The following format should be used in preparing your report. However, any additional information obtained should be included in Part II, the narrative portion.

Part I: Information

Overview

1. Purpose and function of the agency.
2. Demographics of the population served (i.e., age, sex, race, ethnic group, religious group, social class, income group).
3. Number and types of professional and paraprofessional staff (if it's a large agency, list only those on your particular service).

Policy and Practice

4. Does the agency have a formal policy relative to the treatment of alcoholism and other drug use?   Yes   No
   If yes, please state that policy.
5. If the agency does have such a policy, are all members of the staff informed of that policy and by what procedure?   Yes   No
6. If the agency does not have such a policy, is there an informal policy that governs the practices of staff members in the treatment of drug abuse and alcoholism?   Yes   No
7. Does the staff of the agency regard alcoholism and drug abuse as a:
   - Disease
   - Symptom of personality or behavioral disorder
   - Other (please specify):

7a. Does the agency have any policy on alcoholism and drug abuse relative to its own staff?   Yes   No

Record Keeping

8. Are questions relative to an individual's drinking and drug history or those of family members included in the agency's intake procedure?   Yes   No

9. For purposes of reporting, is alcoholism and drug abuse viewed as a primary diagnosis or a secondary diagnosis?

10. For purposes of treatment planning, is alcoholism and drug abuse viewed as a primary diagnosis or a secondary diagnosis?

11. Is it possible under your present reporting system to identify the clients in your current case load who have an alcoholism or drug problem—either the primary client, the spouse, or the family? Yes   No

12. If the response to Question 11 is yes, indicate the number of cases handled by your agency between January 1, 19?? and January 1, 19?? where alcoholism and/or other drug abuse was a problem either for the primary client, spouse, or family.
    • Primary clients (clients with alcohol/drug problems)
      • Male age range
      • Female age range
    • Spouses (clients whose husbands or wives have alcohol/drug problems)
      • Male age range
      • Female age range
    • Family members (clients whose family members have alcohol/drug problems, but may not be receiving service)

13. If the response to Question 11 is no, estimate the number of cases handled by your agency during any given period (please indicate monthly or yearly) where alcoholism or other drug abuse was a problem either for the primary client, spouse, or family under Item 12.

14. Would there be any advantage to the establishment of a reporting system that would identify alcoholism and other drug problems among clients?   Yes   No What advantages or disadvantages might be obtained by this identification?

Treatment

15. Are clients with an alcoholism or drug abuse problem who seek services within the agency:
    • Provided services with the capability of the existing staff?
    • Referred to other services within the community that specialize in the treatment of alcoholism and drug problems?
    • Provided services with the capability of the existing staff, but coordinated with other agencies in the area that specialize in treating alcoholism and drug use?

16. How do clients with serious drinking or drug problems get to your agency?
    • Through self-referral
    • Through medical referral
    • Through court referral
    • Through AA/NA referral
    • Other (please specify)

17. If the agency accepts some clients with drinking and drug problems, but not others, what selection criteria are used?

18. Does the staff of the agency feel that other services should be developed in the area to provide services for individuals with alcoholism and drug problems? Yes   No
    If yes, please list what services might be developed and place them in order of priority.

19. In terms of treatability, does the staff of the agency feel that, contrasted to other clients provided services in the agency, individuals with drinking or other drug problems are:
    • Less difficult
    • No different

- More difficult
- Much more difficult
- Information not available

20. If individuals with alcoholism and other drug problems are provided services within your agency, which of the following treatments are used and how frequently?

	Usually	Sometimes	Never
Individual			
Group			
Marital counseling			
Family counseling			
Didactic/educational groups			
Antabuse			
AA/NA			
Al-Anon			
Other (please specify)			

21. For what percentage of primary clients with alcoholism and drug problems is your agency's treatment focused on:
    - Attaining abstinence
    - Modifying the drinking or drug behavior
    - Modifying the underlying personality or behavioral disorder other than the drinking or drug behavior

Training

22. Has the agency provided for any inservice training, staff development, etc. relative to alcoholism and other drug abuse for staff members in the past year?   Yes   No
    If yes, what was the impact of such training?

23. If the response to Item 22 is no, has the agency ever felt the need for such training? Yes   No
    Please list those resources.

Method of Data Collection

In one paragraph, please state the methodology of your agency assessment. To whom did you talk? From whom did you gather information? Please comment on this process.

Part II—Narrative

The survey is divided into four categories related to agency functioning in:

- Policies and Practices
- Record Keeping
- Treatment
- Training

Information gathered in each of these areas will be analyzed in Part II of the assignment.

For each area, comment on how the findings indicate potential positive and negative consequences for client care. For any gaps or deficiencies, make recommendations for improvement based on your critical analysis of each area. Include a summary that relates to both the quantitative information you gathered and the subjective impressions of you and your informant(s).

Analysis of the agency survey information should be integrated with content from readings, class discussions, course lectures, and experience. Reading materials and other information resources should be cited in a bibliography.

AODA and the Social Policy Task Force Model

One method of integrating material on alcohol and drugs into foundation social policy courses is through the use of the Policy Task Force Model. This five-part model encompasses the nature, scope, correlates, and theories pertinent to understanding a particular problem, and an overview of current policies addressing the problem along with policy proposals related to the problem. Although the model provides a conceptual framework that can be applied to any topic area, it has been used on numerous occasions to analyze problems related to alcohol and drug abuse such as babies born to crack-dependent mothers, HIV/AIDS, IV drug use, and fetal alcohol syndrome. Usually, a team of five students uses the model to analyze a problem, with each student taking responsibility for one of the five areas of analysis.

The basic analytical steps and some of the particular questions that should be addressed within each are presented below.

Model for Social Problem Analysis

Definition of the Problem

- Identify the range of definitions reflected in the academic and policy literature.
- What are the social values underlying the different definitions?
- Who are the individual(s) and/or groups that propose these definitions, and what ideological, theoretical, or political perspective(s) do they hold?

Scope of the Problem

- What is the prevalence of the problem? How has it changed over time?
- What is the incidence of the problem? How has it changed over time?
- What confidence should one have in the above data?

Correlates of the Problem

- What are the demographic, geographic, etc. correlates of the problem?
- What theories of causation are suggested by the correlates?

Theories of Causation

- What are currently held alternative social, psychological, economic, and political explanatory theories or perspectives on causation of the problem?

Social Policies

- What current and past social policies are directed toward ameliorating or preventing the problem on federal and state levels of government?
- What policy proposals are recommended by the profession of social work?

Laws, Programs, and Services

- What current laws, programs, and services are directed toward coping with the problem?
- At what levels of prevention are these laws, programs, and services directed?

Effectiveness of Current Provisions

- What evidence is there about the effectiveness of current or proposed programs and services?

What specific policy proposals would you recommend to the State Legislature?

- At what level of prevention are these proposals directed?
- What is the theoretical, ideological, or political basis for these proposals?
- What special role for social workers would you urge, if any?
- What are your recommendations for financing these proposals?

Planning and Program Development Assignment: Substance Abuse among Hispanic/Latino Youth

Description and Uses of Assignment

Introduction

The following assignment is designed to test students' critical thinking skills related to community-based macro practice. It requires students to examine substance abuse issues within a specific cultural context, and to assess the needs of a target population. As outlined below, the assignment is completed through a written paper. However, it can also be used as a classroom assignment. Students are divided into three groups. Each group is given one of the following student responses to critique based on the discussion questions. A follow-up assignment, not included here, requires students to develop an intervention program that addresses the current and future needs of the identified target population.

Assignment Outline

(Given to students)

You are the senior planner at the X Mental Health Center in Chelsea, Massachusetts. You have been asked to examine data on the problem of "substance abuse," particularly among Hispanic/Latino youngsters. Develop an approach for assessing the needs of drug and alcohol abusing Hispanic/Latino youngsters within the Chelsea Public Schools. In no more than five typewritten pages, discuss the following:

1. Definition(s) of need
2. Methodology used
3. Social indicators used
4. Strengths and limitations of 1-3 listed above

5. Particular needs of the population
6. Provide a budget estimate totaling $5,000 (personnel and non-personnel expenses). Do not include your salary; this is covered by the Center. Project Period: Four months in the spring.

Make sure you address the following issues in your paper:

1. What services/interventions do you believe are necessary to help Hispanic/Latino youngsters who are abusing alcohol and other drugs?
2. Why is it so difficult to assess the needs of Hispanic/Latino youth who are using/abusing alcohol?
3. What impact does ethnic background have in assessing the needs of Hispanic/Latino youth?
4. How important is it to identify the type of alcohol favored by Hispanic/Latino youth?
5. What impact does advertising and accessibility have on alcohol use?
6. How can a planner or program developer address the problem of alcohol without stigmatizing youth, families, and the community?
7. What impact does enforcement of underage drinking laws have on alcohol use?
8. What impact does ethnic tradition have on the prevention of alcohol use/abuse?
9. What is the impact, if any, of alcohol and other drug use on an individual's resident status (citizen, documented with papers, undocumented)?
10. How important is it to target services to a particular age group?

Student Responses to the Assignment

Example #1

Alcohol Use and Abuse among Latino Youth in Chelsea, MA

As the senior planner at X Mental Health Center in Chelsea, Massachusetts, I was asked by the CEO of the center to examine data on the problem of alcohol use and abuse among older Latino youngsters in the public school. The project ran from January 2nd to April 1st, and I was provided with $5,000, exclusive of my salary.

Description of Chelsea

Chelsea is a small, impoverished city north of Boston which is now under public receivership. Over 40% of the students in the public school are identified as Hispanic non-White and Hispanic White. Boston University has entered into a partnership with Chelsea to operate the public school system.

Definition of Target Population

In defining "Latino," I combined the Chelsea Public School System categories of Hispanic White and Hispanic non-White. I do not know the criteria the schools use to identify a student as Hispanic. Unfortunately, the school does not differentiate students by country of origin; I assumed that most of the target population were Puerto Rican. I defined "older" youngsters as males and females enrolled in Chelsea High School. Because some students are immigrants and non-English speaking and the school system is a poor one, the ages of Latino Chelsea High School students ranged from 14 to about 21.

Definition of Need

I used *felt need* as the most appropriate measure of need, a decision emanating as much from the limits of other measures as the strengths of this one. For instance, *expressed need* seemed inappropriate because Latinos have historically used natural support systems to address problems, making demand for service an inaccurate measure of need. The scarcity of research concerning Latino youth, and more specifically Puerto Rican youth, eliminated the possibility of using *normative need*. *Comparative need* had its shortcomings because of the differences between Chelsea and similar kinds of communities—for example, Lawrence, New Bedford, and Fall River.

Although using *felt need* as a measure can be expensive and is limited by both the phrasing of the interview questions and the client population's knowledge and willingness to talk about need, these disadvantages were far outweighed by the advantages. *Felt need* would solve the problem of lack of demand for service and lack of research on the needs of Latinos; it would help me identify problems specific to the Chelsea community; and it had the potential for increasing the legitimacy of and future referrals for X Mental Health Center among the target population.

Methodology

To begin building bridges to the community, I first set up meetings with key informants from Chelsea, including the principals of Chelsea High School and Williams Junior High School, two Latino and one non-Latino teacher from Chelsea High School, the

Chelsea Public Schools Director of Counseling Services, a Chelsea area caseworker from both the Department of Social Services and the Department of Youth Services, priests of the Latino churches, the head of a tenant's organization, Latino community activists, one Latino and one non-Latino police officer, and three Latino store owners.

From January 2 to January 23, I visited the key informants in their offices or places of business to solicit their opinions concerning alcohol use and abuse among older Latino youngsters, and to ask them to serve on an advisory committee which will work with the mental health center to assist in developing the interview schedule, analyzing the data, and developing a plan of action. The full advisory committee met during the last week in January and first week in February to devise an interview schedule.

To reach the Latino students in Chelsea High School, I asked 35 bilingual Latino "Corps Members" of a community service organization in Boston called City Year to conduct the interviews. There were four advantages to using these individuals. First, they lent institutional legitimacy to X Mental Health Center because City Year had operated in Chelsea for a number of years. Second, they were approximately the age of the Chelsea High School students, 17–22, and most were of the same country of origin—Puerto Rico. Third, they could conduct the interviews in Spanish if necessary. Fourth, because they volunteered for this project as Corps Members of City Year, X Mental Health Center did not have to pay for this important data collection phase.

Before beginning the interviews, the Corps Members attended a one-week training program sponsored by X Mental Health Center during Chelsea High School's February vacation. They then conducted interviews over the next six weeks. To avoid duplication, each interviewer was assigned a list of students. The interviews were conducted one-on-one, confidentially, and anonymously, and the gender of the interviewer matched the gender of the interviewee. To reach the students who regularly attended school, some of the interviews took place during class time.

For students who were chronically absent from school (defined as more than 20% absences), I sent the Corps Members in teams of two to each student's residence, and, if he/she was unavailable, to the local hangouts for Latino youth. Because I felt that the youth at risk of dropping out of school were probably the most important to reach for this needs assessment, I instructed the interviewers to speak with any Latino youth they encountered at these hangouts who identified themselves as enrolled in school. To avoid duplication of data, the interviewers later cross-checked with a master list.

Before I began this process, I understood that this method would be time consuming and cumbersome, and that, because of a high rate of school absenteeism, the most difficult part might be finding the approximately 300 Latino high school students necessary to complete the needs assessment. I considered generating a stratified random sample of students attending and not attending school, and actually had a plan to change to this tactic if the first few days of interviews proceeded slowly. However, I kept to the original plan to reach out to all of the students because I wanted to introduce X Mental Health Center to the students, gain institutional legitimacy, and garner referrals.

Social Indicators

The first social indicator used was the number of alcohol-related arrests among Latino youth. On the surface, this appears to be a strong indicator because the number speaks specifically to alcohol use. However, this indicator had at least four limitations. First, arrests of juveniles are confidential. Second, the arrests are not a measure of all youth who are using alcohol. Third, if the police department and the school do not use the same method of identifying race, the Latino arrest record will be skewed. Fourth, a cursory examination offers no indication of how many of those arrested are actually enrolled in school.

The second social indicator was the number of Latino high school students who are considered at risk of dropping out of school. Research shows that drug use is related to rates of absenteeism and dropout. However, because many other factors can lead to student absenteeism, the number of "at-risk students" is an inaccurate measure of the problem of alcohol use and abuse.

The third social indicator was the number of liquor stores and bars in the Latino neighborhoods of Chelsea. Although most of the youth in Chelsea High School are not of legal drinking age, a high number of liquor stores and bars in a neighborhood could indicate a high level of consumption among their parents. Parental alcohol use has been shown to be related to children's alcohol use; however, these studies are not specific to Latinos. Also, those purchasing the alcohol may not be parents of the Latino youngsters enrolled in Chelsea High School.

Needs of the Population

Although we have not completed the data-entry process and subsequent analysis of the interviews, I feel it is safe to reveal some preliminary findings. First, alcohol use and abuse is fairly high among this population. The students cite the major reason for drinking as boredom or lack of recreational activities. Not surprisingly, it appears that those students with high rates of absenteeism consume alcohol in higher amounts and more frequently than those students who regularly attend school. Many of the absentee students expressed a general dissatisfaction with the quality of education, while many of the students who attend school were being reached by the DARE program, and generally viewed the program positively.

The students described a community where alcohol is easily obtained and where many unemployed parents and older siblings consume high quantities of alcohol.

An initial analysis of the data from these interviews indicates that we may need to take a multidisciplinary approach to the problem of alcohol use and abuse among Latino high school students in Chelsea.

Budget

Refreshments for Advisory Committee Meetings	$ 100.00
Lunch for first day of Interviewers' Training Week	$ 280.00
Refreshments for Interviewers' Final Day	$ 50.00
Long Distance Telephone Calls	$ 300.00
Photocopying	$ 300.00
Travel	$ 50.00
Coding/Data Entry Personnel* (30 minutes/interview x $8/hr.)	$1200.00
Total	**$2280.00**
Surplus ($5000–$2280)	$2720.00

The expenses for coding/data entry will be eliminated if City Year agrees to lend more Corps Members to the project.

Example #2

A Needs Assessment: Alcohol Use and Abuse among Chelsea Youth

The nature of an assignment to study the problem of alcohol use and abuse among "older" Latino youngsters in Chelsea, MA, is fairly ambiguous. First, it assumes an alcohol problem, and second, it is not clear on the age range. I planned to study a wide age range of Latino youngsters to gather broad statistics and lessen the potential for bias on a small proportion of the population. Given a fairly restrictive budget of $5,000 and only three months to do the assessment, I needed to choose cost- and time-effective techniques. Other considerations were balancing the needs of the study population, the agency, and the planner implementing the assessment; gaining the cooperation of all those involved in the process; and gathering accurate data.

Selecting a Measure of Need

The first consideration in assessing the needs of the older Latino youngsters is to determine an appropriate measure. I decided to use *felt need*, although acquiring data on felt need can be time consuming, costly, and inaccurate; can increase expectations of the community; and requires careful training for the interviewers to cut down on their potential for bias. On the other hand, asking the population under study about how they view their needs is the most legitimate, democratic, and detailed way to make an assessment.

To achieve optimum results, I planned to conduct person-to-person interviews with the youth and parents, and to survey key community informants. This combination of methods was designed to solicit felt need from a variety of people with differing viewpoints, and, from a research perspective, increase the legitimacy of the investigation.

Using Interviews

First, approximately 50 Latinos, 14–18 years old, and 50 Latino parents would be interviewed by four people: two Latino youth 18–20 years of age who live in Chelsea, one Latino adult living in Chelsea, and one professional adult from outside the community.

One important strength of this method is legitimacy—involving the youngsters in the needs assessment will allow them to see the people and the process behind the assessment, which in turn will help to legitimize our intervention. A second strength of interviewing is that it empowers people. Both empowerment and legitimacy are crucial when assessing needs for a minority group. It was important in this case that the Latino youngsters and their parents perceived that they had a voice in any decisions affecting them, rather than having others provide solutions. Interviews may also help build morale: As long as stigmatizing questions are avoided, the interviewees may gain a more positive outlook from knowing that people in the community are interested in their concerns. Further, face-to-face interviews would provide a higher response rate than phone calls or questionnaires.

I anticipated several problems with this approach, however. First, interviewees may not admit that there are problems in their community. They also may not be able to identify their underlying needs because of ignorance about services or because of their limited perceptions about what they need. Regarding the interview process, it can be costly to train and supervise interviewers, especially if there is concern about biases in their approaches. The selection of interviewers was based partially on a desire to reduce costs and bias.

Using Surveys

The second approach I planned to use in addressing the needs of this population was to question key informants—people in the community who may provide insight about the relevant issues affecting the population. The developed questionnaire would be pre-tested on a sample population of the key informants. Then a revised survey would be given to 25 individuals, including youth group leaders, school administrators, Latino mental health care workers, teachers, guidance counselors, police officers, religious leaders, and juvenile court officials. Using this mixed sample would help cut down on bias and present a comprehensive picture of needs, thereby increasing the accuracy of the research findings.

Another reason to include various groups of people in the needs assessment is to gain educational and ethical legitimacy. For instance, counselors, health care workers, and police are usually educated about the issue of alcohol use, lending educational legitimacy to the study. Community and religious leaders are usually highly regarded, and their input can give the study ethical legitimacy.

Finally, sending questionnaires to key informants is inexpensive, can help ensure honesty (because of the anonymous nature of surveys), and provides data that is easy to analyze. The only major drawbacks of this approach are the need for pre-testing the questionnaire and the potential for a low response rate.

Other Measures of Need

Another conception of need that could be used in an assessment such as this is *normative need*, which means that the needs of the older Latino youngsters would be identified by an expert in light of a desirable standard. The mental health center could hire a social scientist knowledgeable in the area of alcohol use by youth who would analyze past and current data on alcohol use or abuse in this population, look at the age it begins and the school dropout rate, and identify what resources are needed within the community. He/she would also work with Latino social service agencies in Chelsea to gain legitimacy for the study as well as a political perspective on the issue—that is, to understand to what degree there is consensus or discord on the issue.

There are three main strengths of this looking at normative need. First, because the research is conducted by professionals, they have more control over the specific information being gathered, and more expertise in analyzing and interpreting the data. Second, their expertise on the issue lends legitimacy to the research. Third, past and present statistical information would be a useful perspective to include in the assessment.

On the other hand, expertise is sometimes not as useful as experience, and it usually adds value bias to the study. Furthermore, the notion of a preset standard is quite arbitrary because people have different and sometimes conflicting standards.

Comparative need refers to a comparison among groups for service demand/use. For example, in this case an investigator would look at the type and amount of social service use among populations with demographics similar to those of the Chelsea youth. If service use/availability was found to be lacking in Chelsea, this population would be considered in need. This method can be very useful in determining which services a particular population needs, but it can be difficult to find similar communities or populations to compare. Comparative needs assessment also has the potential to set a standard for the provision of services that may cause problems when the needs of the comparison populations are not really equal.

Lawrence, MA—a nearby community—is similar to Chelsea in terms of social and economic factors; therefore, a study of services in this area would be helpful. An investigator could look at service usage by the Latino population, especially teenagers. In the event that Lawrence lacks a substantial Latino community, the investigator could examine the use of services aimed at high school–aged minority youth.

Studying comparative need in Lawrence would be an attractive option because the proximity of the two communities would control the traveling and time costs incurred in many comparative studies. In addition, research on another community, when combined with input from the Latino population and an expert opinion, would provide a well-balanced study.

Social Indicators

There are various social indicators for the existence and/or degree of an alcohol problem with older Latino youngsters. Incidents of drinking and driving, alcohol-related crimes including stealing and assaults, domestic violence reported by social service agencies or the police, and the degree of alcoholism within Latino households with older youth are all factors that should be explored in the needs assessment process. Gathering this information would entail looking at police and school reports.

"Older" Latino youngsters in Chelsea would be helped by many services. First, culturally attuned social support systems, including youth organizations, group services, and family intervention and support networks, are important. Programs providing information on the consequences of alcohol use/abuse (physical, psychological, social, legal); English-as-a-second-language classes; occupational training programs for those not in school; and tutoring programs for those who are, would all be use-

ful. Also, cultural organizations intended to build self-esteem and a strong community are important for any minority group. These types of resources have the potential to greatly improve the living conditions for Latino youngsters in Chelsea.

Budget

$12/interview for two youths doing 50 interviews	$600.00
$15/interview for two adults doing 50 interviews	$750.00
$8/hr.-youth; $12/hr.-adults for 12 hrs. training	$480.00
$25/hr.-hire someone to help train and supervise (total 15 hrs.)	$750.00
Food provided during training	$ 40.00
$50/hr. to expert analyzing questionnaire data	$500.00
$10/hr. to grad. student for photocopying, mailing, implementing pre-test (total 12 hrs.)	$120.00
Postage: initial memo, 2 sets of 25 questionnaires, thank you letter	$ 30.00
Letterhead paper, envelopes	$100.00
$15–20/hr. (depending on age) to 2 groups of 5 key informants pre-testing questionnaire (total 4 hrs.) (max)	$400.00
$50/hr. to expert doing normative study (total 15 hrs.)	$750.00
Total	**$4895.00**

Additional training and supervising the interviewers and implementing the comparative study are not included above, because I will be responsible for these tasks. Remaining money will be saved for unexpected expenses.

Anytown: Community Vignette

This vignette can be used as the basis for a community analysis and intervention assignment for a course such as "Introduction to Methods."

Instructions for Students

1. Describe the community. Look at significant demographic and historical data; key economic institutions and their actual or potential impact on community residents; and important social, religious, cultural, racial, ethnic, political, and civic organizations and leaders in the area.

2. Analyze the dynamics of the community in terms of AOD issues. What are the power centers related to AOD? Are key decisions affecting life in the community made within the community or by outside forces? Are there new or ongoing tensions between various ethnic or socioeconomic factions? What are the major AOD-related problems in the community and what are the implications for the future? Particular attention should be focused on at-risk populations within the community.

3. Identify five key people in the community to be interviewed regarding AOD. Defend your choices.

4. Identify anticipated barriers to implementing an intervention plan.

5. Describe an ideal intervention plan for any community, and a realistic plan for Anytown.

Vignette: "Anytown"

Anytown has a population of about 150,000. The "old town" area in the center is where the first settlers established the city. Anytown is located in a county that is largely agricultural—the city is surrounded by small to medium-sized farms.

Anytown has several industries, mostly related to agriculture, including a large research and development division of a major chemical fertilizer company. There are a number of small businesses as well, including insurance companies, car dealerships, and heavy equipment leasing companies. Near the "old town" area is the General Hospital. There is a newspaper and two local radio/TV stations. A large veterinary school associated with a university in another county is also located in Anytown, as well as a group of private physicians, social workers, and psychologists.

Because of the national and local economy, unemployment is at an all-time high, especially among the youth and people of color in Anytown.

The population is diverse. About half are Polish, Italian, Irish, and Swedish, many of whom still farm in the surrounding area or live in areas where members of that ethnic group predominate. Many are Roman Catholic and are quite involved with church activities. More than half have an annual income less than $30,000. The rest are largely middle class.

African Americans make up about a fourth of Anytown's residents. They are merchants, teachers, ministers, and employees of the Anytown government. Others are professional chemists, biologists, and computer experts who have recently moved into Anytown to work for the chemical fertilizer factory. Still others are former migrant workers from the South who have settled in the old town area. Many African-American families are active Protestants, with the church serving as the center of their social life. Children and adults attend Bible study classes and a variety of recreational and social events.

The rest of the population of Anytown is Mexican with a small number of Latinos from Central America. Most are farm workers and laborers. A growing number of young, highly educated scientific and technical workers who are African American, Latino, and white have moved into renovated housing in old town.

Anytown has an exceptionally high number of liquor stores which do a booming business. Because of some mild community opposition in the past to their practice of offering customer discounts on large quantities of liquor, they banded together to form an Association of Liquor Outlets, which currently includes local restaurants, lounges, and billiard halls that serve alcohol.

Every summer, the Association sponsors a week of sports competitions aimed at youth. These competitions also include Special Olympics-type events for the mentally retarded. Although alcohol is not served, food, prizes, and other free gifts are distributed including backpacks and sweatshirts with the logo of the Association of Liquor Outlets prominently displayed. Although support for this annual event has been strong in the past years, community sentiment, especially among parents, seems to be shifting for the following reasons:

- Traffic accidents involving drunk drivers have increased;

- More and more teenagers seem to be getting access to alcohol, either by using false IDs, getting older kids to buy for them, or "passing" as 21 years old, the legal drinking age;

- Thrill-seeking and daredevil behavior has increased, with two teens recently disabled from motorcycle accidents in Anytown's quarry, one teen rushed to the emergency room after a drinking competition behind a pool hall, and a high school cheerleader

dead from an overdose of alcohol and sleeping pills.

Not too long ago, there was a well-publicized drug arrest in the parking lot of the town hall. Arrested were a known drug dealer, two town hall employees, and several adolescent employees of a local fast food restaurant. The trial received heavy media coverage because the City Manager was arrested and convicted for possession of crack cocaine, and there were unconfirmed allegations that employees of the hospital were also involved.

A small group of high school students have been trying to start a SADD (Students Against Drunk Driving) Chapter at the school, but broad-scale support from the students, teachers, or administrators has not emerged. The PTA recently turned down an opportunity to conduct an AODA public awareness program in the schools because of their limited budget. Anytown lacks substance abuse treatment programs open to the public. The private psychiatric hospital admits AOD abusers who have insurance benefits. Historically, Anytown has suffered from shame and secrecy surrounding family and personal problems such as unemployment, physical and mental illness, or AODA.

Teaching Points

1. Community power structure.
2. Public health model of host, agent, environment.
3. Community AODA prevention approaches. The following strategies for high-risk youth are currently used in many prevention programs:
   - *Individuals*. Some programs provide life skills training, which includes instruction in making decisions, controlling anger, solving problems, developing social skills, and building self-esteem and social competence. Other programs attempt

to build self-confidence and teamwork by providing wholesome recreational activities such as wilderness trips, dance and theater groups, and sports. Some programs offer counseling and therapy for youth with more serious problems, and several advocate the use of community and program support groups.

- *Peers.* Training peers to act as role models for younger children has been very effective in some programs. Other youth are trained to make presentations on alcohol and other drugs to youth in schools and communities, or to counsel youth on how to deal with their problems.
- *Families.* Several programs actively recruit parents to participate in program activities or to support the program's mission in the community. Parents can become involved by sharing special skills or by volunteering as chaperones for events. Also popular are parent training programs such as Parent Effectiveness Training (PET) or Systematic Training for Effective Parenting (STEP) for parents of youth and for young clients who have children of their own.
- *Schools.* One school strategy that rises above all others in importance is the development of a clear and consistent policy concerning alcohol and other drug use and its consequences. Changing teaching methods to involve youth more in the learning process has been effective in reducing some risk factors. Another strategy is to offer AOD education within the schools, but re-

search on the effectiveness of such programs alone indicates the need for a broader approach to prevention. Some school programs include tutoring and supervised homework periods. Other programs offer counselors who serve as advocates and mediators for youth.

- *Communities.* Some programs have youth group components in which participants perform civic volunteer work. Cultural enhancement components teach or reinforce a positive cultural identity by explaining history, traditions, customs, and values. In many programs, youth groups have been developed in answer to the lack of constructive community activities. These programs have been effective in reducing juvenile delinquency. Some programs recruit members from the community to serve as mentors to troubled youth. Other community activities found in various programs include sponsoring media campaigns; establishing networks with churches, schools, businesses, and other agencies; and training service providers on how to identify and help high-risk youth.

Suggested Reading

Kumpfer, K. L., Shur, G. H., Ross, J. G., Bunnell, K. K., Librett, J. J., & Millward, A. R. (1993). What to measure: Theories of causation and risk factors. *Measurements in prevention* (pp. 7-20). CSAP Technical Report 8, U.S. Dept. of Health and Human Services.

Appendices

Glossary

abstinence: not using alcohol or other drugs for days, weeks, or months.

addiction: when the body cannot function normally without daily use of alcohol or another drug; in physical addiction, the body goes through withdrawal when alcohol or other drugs are not used for 24 to 48 hours; symptoms of physical addiction include sweating, shaking, rapid heartbeat, and agitation.

alcohol or other drug abuse (AODA): a pattern of alcohol or drug use that causes serious problems; often seen are problems in family relationships, health, and occupational functioning.

alcoholism: a broad term referring to:

a) severe problems from drinking, for example, remaining intoxicated for two or more days at a time;

b) trouble functioning because of drinking, for example, frequently missing work, getting into trouble with the police due to violence, driving while drinking, partner or child abuse, or

c) physical dependence including withdrawal symptoms.

blackout: when memory is affected by drinking large quantities of alcohol; people experiencing blackouts do not remember events occurring while they appeared to others to be alert and still functioning; repeated blackouts from drinking often indicate alcoholism.

cirrhosis: a serious, often irreversible, and frequently deadly disease of the liver often caused by chronic heavy drinking.

craving: a strong or intense desire to use a mind-altering drug such as alcohol, marijuana, cocaine, or heroin.

delirium tremens: withdrawal symptoms caused by alcohol addiction, including tremors, confusion, disorientation, and sometimes hallucinations.

denial: when people are unable to let themselves know or accept a painful truth about themselves or their lives; individuals are "in denial" when the facts of a situation are apparent, but they are unable to admit the truth to themselves.

dependence: a more serious disorder than abuse; an individual with alcohol or drug dependence experiences withdrawal symptoms when the drug is not used for one or more days; feels ill from withdrawal symptoms such as shaking, sweating, rapid heartbeat, or agitation; or has a strong psychological connection to the drug.

detoxification: the process of allowing the body to rid itself of a large amount of alcohol and/or other drugs; the person going through this process, which can last for several days, feels ill and has trouble eating, sleeping, and concentrating; because this process is medically dangerous, especially when the person is detoxifying from alcohol or sleeping pills, it often occurs in a hospital or detoxification center under medical supervision.

drug: a chemical mixture, frequently from plants, that changes the way the body or mind functions; drugs can be used for health purposes or can be abused.

fetal alcohol syndrome: a disorder seen in a small number of children born to mothers who drink heavily during pregnancy; a child with fetal alcohol syndrome can have low intelligence and learning problems.

heroin: a drug from the opium family that is produced by chemically processing morphine to a more potent strength; a heroin user tends to become addicted very quickly; heroin users often inject the drug into their veins.

intoxication: a temporary physical state caused by the presence of high amounts of alcohol or another mind-altering drug that alters brain function; an intoxicated person may have difficulty talking, walking, and reacting, and often shows poor judgment.

mind-altering drug: a chemical mixture, not necessary for health, which changes the ability to think and react appropriately, and the experience of bodily sensations; examples are cocaine, alcohol, valium, LSD, and heroin.

opioids: a type of drug that has a calming, pain-relieving effect, and slows down the action of the brain; examples include heroin, morphine, percodan, codeine, and opium.

polydrug abuse: the simultaneous use and abuse of two or more drugs such as alcohol, marijuana, and cocaine.

standard drink: a standard drink equals a half-ounce of alcohol, which is about the amount in a 12-ounce can of beer, 4-ounce glass of table wine, or 1-ounce shot of 90-100 proof whiskey.

tolerance: the capacity to remain functional after ingesting drugs in large amounts; for example, an individual who has 6 drinks in 1 hour without appearing intoxicated has a high tolerance; high tolerance generally develops from high consumption and frequency of use, and puts a person at risk for developing a physical addiction.

withdrawal symptoms: definable physical changes occurring when a person stops or decreases very heavy use of drugs such as alcohol, sleeping pills, or heroin; withdrawal symptoms usually include shaking, sweating, rapid breathing, and agitation, and may include hallucinations or convulsions.

Criteria for Case Selection

The criteria listed below were used by the editors in selecting cases for this volume. They may be useful to faculty wishing to assemble cases for other teaching purposes. These characteristics can be applied to cases highlighting other client populations such as adolescents, the elderly, or families, or focusing attention on other social problems such as child abuse, homelessness, or HIV/AIDS. Nine criteria for choosing teaching cases guided our decisions:

1. *Relevance to social work practice*—extent to which the case illustrates common dilemmas faced by workers in AODA-involved client systems, and ways to approach these dilemmas.

2. *Educational applicability*—the case's usefulness across the social work curriculum; its adaptability for a range of courses and settings.

3. *Generalizability*—degree to which the case content can be applied to other client-system problems; the richness of the case study or case excerpt in offering opportunities for teaching.

4. *Vibrancy and comprehensiveness*—degree to which the case "comes to life" for the reader; the extent to which it is vivid and compelling, with enough detail that readers are able to put themselves in the worker's and/or client's shoes.

5. *Completeness*—extent to which the case offers detail and allows students to identify themes and understand worker dilemmas; in the absence of comprehensive information, the extent to which the case allows for appropriate inferences.

6. *Sensitivity to issues of diversity*—extent to which the case illustrates the need for adapting approaches to respond to special client-system characteristics.

7. *Creativity*—extent to which the case illustrates creative interventions.

8. *Intellectual challenge*—extent to which the case elements (i.e., the case study itself, the worker's observations, the questions for class discussion, the teaching points) provoke students to examine the situation from multiple theoretical perspectives.

9. *Responsiveness to contemporary practice conditions*—extent to which the case brings into focus the changing demographics of society and of those seeking social service assistance, and reflects contemporary social problems and current changes in service delivery systems.